HARPER FORUM BOOKS

Martin E. Marty, General Editor

THE THEOLOGIAN AT WORK

A Common Search for Understanding

HARPER FORUM BOOKS

Martin E . Marty, *General Editor*

Published:

IAN G. BARBOUR
SCIENCE AND RELIGION: New Perspectives on the Dialogue

A. ROY ECKARDT
THE THELOGIAN AT WORK: A Common Search for Understanding

JOHN MACQUARRIE
CONTEMPORARY RELIGIOUS THINKERS: From Idealist Metaphysicians to Existential Theologians

GIBSON WINTER
SOCIAL ETHICS: Issues in Ethics and Society

Forthcoming: Summer 1968

JAMES M. GUSTAFSON & JAMES T. LANEY
ON BEING RESPONSIBLE: Issues in Personal Ethics

EDWIN SCOTT GAUSTAD
RELIGIOUS ISSUES IN AMERICAN HISTORY

SAMUEL SANDMEL
OLD TESTAMENT ISSUES

Forthcoming: 1969

JOSEPH D. BETTIS
PHENOMENOLOGY OF RELIGION

WILLIAM DOUGLAS
THE HUMAN PERSONALITY: Religious and Non-Religious
  Views

WINTHROP HUDSON
RELIGION AND NATIONALITY: Concepts of American
  Identity and Mission

IAN RAMSEY
PHILOSOPHY OF RELIGION

OWEN C. THOMAS
ATTITUDES TOWARD OTHER RELIGIONS:
  Some Christian Interpretations

FRANKLIN YOUNG
NEW TESTAMENT ISSUES

THE
THEOLOGIAN
AT WORK

A Common Search for Understanding

edited by

A. Roy Eckardt

1817

HARPER & ROW, PUBLISHERS

NEW YORK, LONDON, AND EVANSTON

Also by A. Roy Eckardt:

CHRISTIANITY AND THE CHILDREN OF ISRAEL

THE SURGE OF PIETY IN AMERICA

ELDER AND YOUNGER BROTHERS

For two possible theologians:

PAULA AND STEVE

Harper Forum Books

Often dismissed with a shrug or accepted with thoughtless piety in the past, religion today belongs in the forum of study and discussion. In our society, this is particularly evident in both public and private colleges and universities. Scholars are exploring the claims of theology, the religious roots of culture, and the relation between beliefs and the various areas or disciplines of life. Students have not until now had a series of books which could serve as reliable resources for class or private study in a time when inquiry into religion is undertaken with new freedom and a sense of urgency. *Harper Forum Books* are intended for these purposes. Eminent scholars have selected and introduced the readings. Respectful of the spirit of religion as they are, they do not shun controversy. With these books a new generation can confront religion through exposure to significant minds in theology and related humanistic fields.

MARTIN E. MARTY, *General Editor*
The Divinity School
The University of Chicago

PREFACE

THIS sequence of readings composes a journey into theology as
it relates to personal faith. We mean to address ourselves to the
condition of today's student. In the interest of pricking him on
to his own reflection and decisions, we are concentrating upon
the business of theologians, who they are, and the persisting
questions they confront—or, better, that confront them.

I list several assumptions behind the present effort—not to
justify them but for explanation's sake and to set readers on
their guard: (1) A sensible way to discover what an enterprise
means is to look at what its practitioners do. We are apprised of
the meaning of theology when we inspect the professional
efforts of theologians. Practically speaking, the convenient procedure here is to study what they write. (2) Theology must stay
open to the longings and ponderings of new generations. It has
to come to grips with options entirely different from its own,
particularly the contentions of those many human beings for
whom theological affirmation is nonsense. (3) That the selections included here are more or less contemporary is not an
insinuation that theological attainment is somehow a twentieth-
century monopoly. The only consideration is that the closer the
materials are to the student's own milieu, the more meaningful
and relevant will be our content and our media of expression.
Nevertheless, certain classical theological questions remain the
most vital ones, as a glance at the table of contents will illus-
trate. (4) An editor is an active voice as well as a passive

reporter. His primary calling is not to make various majorities happy. He is certainly obligated to strive for measures of balance and of representativeness, and (in allegiance to learning) for a modicum of repetition. But it is he who has to choose from the vast ocean of possibilities. Functionally speaking, an editor is mostly a man who counts words. His choices are determined by his convictions of what remains important for the present and the future. To put the point another way, theology, like every living subject, means controversy.

The main criteria in assembling these writings have been vitality of style and expression, solidness of content, cogency of argument, and reasonable breadth of coverage. Certain topics, which appear on first glance to have been ignored, receive some attention under other headings. However, the volume is necessarily selective rather than encyclopedic. I have endeavored to shun both the superficial and the unintelligible. And as part of a series, this volume is not meant to overlap the content of any other.

Beginning scholars will profit from the guidance of a teacher; more advanced readers may readily work along on their own. But it is anticipated that those in both groups will be led to sit up, take notice, and want either to talk back or to applaud—with resulting further adventures in the exciting world of theology.

To two assistants, Jacqueline L. Knerr and Doris M. Wilkinson, and to my wife, Alice Lyons Eckardt, go unrestrained praise and thanks.

—THE EDITOR

CONTENTS

PART VI. BEYOND THEOLOGY

INTRODUCTION

A. Roy Eckardt

THEOLOGY means thinking about God. There are two axioms here: that God is real and that there is a theological way of reflecting upon God. Let us inspect these axioms.

I

A great difference is found between the interrogation, "Is there a God?" and the declaration, "There is a God." The difference is not absolute, because the interrogator may already have some rudimentary expectations on the subject, while the declarer may not be free of all doubts. But in principle the two quoted sentences point to the distinction between extratheological understanding and theological understanding. The theologian already assumes the reality of God. Here is the presupposition of his entire vocation. It is the religiously uncommitted man, perhaps the philosopher, who asks, "Is there a God?" To be sure, the theologian and his confreres may argue heatedly with one another over what it *means* to affirm that God is real, but with respect to the affirmation itself they will not disagree. (This is why the expression, " 'God-is-dead' theology" is hard put to avoid self-contradiction. If the words, "God is dead," are to have any intelligible and practical meaning, the most they are saying is that there once *was* a God but he is no more. From this latter point of view, all that the theological enterprise could do would be to deal with the past, with the "once upon a time" when God ostensibly lived.)

Theology is more than a bare assent to the divine reality. Any man can say, "There is a God," without the words having any decisive consequences for his life. But the theologian, at least ideally, places God at the center of his existence. He is devoted to God. He trusts God. He worships God. This is why there is inevitable affinity between the theological stance and the existentialist posture. Many existentialists are, of course, simple atheists; for them, to "trust God" is meaningless and, indeed, an affront to human dignity. But precisely here is a point of contact between the existentialist thinker and the theologian. Both parties insist that human beings do not attain true dignity until they engage in life-and-death choices, until they commit themselves in freedom to some cause or demand. Existentialism is intolerant of bystanders, of spectators. The real man is the participant, the one who stakes his life upon something or someone. In this there is an echo, or at least a parallel, of the theologian's ideal devotedness to God in heart, soul, and mind.

One other mark of the theological enterprise considered as the affirmation of God must be included. The theologian is attesting much more than *that* a divine being is real; he also ventures to ponder and to speak of *what* God is like. How the theologian can ever dare to utter certain things concerning the nature of God is a very serious and problematic question, yet this is exactly what he does. Here is the grandeur of theology—and its audacity. Almost needless to say, the theologian denies that he is left to his own resources in what he affirms of God. Jewish, Christian, and Muslim theologians emphasize that they are no more than representatives and interpreters of objectively compelling divine revelation.

A most difficult challenge has already appeared in the conversation here beginning between the reader and the contributors to this book. One odd and intriguing feature of theology is that in the very effort to ascertain what the enterprise is all about, one antecedently injects something of a particular theological outlook. I have in mind here much more than the obvious truth that the very decision to include one or another selection in such a volume as this reflects certain human judgments concerning the constitution of theology. A more fundamental problem is suggested by the seemingly innocent phrase used in the paragraph above, "Jewish, Christian, and Muslim theologians." To put the question summarily: In what sense, if any, does theology depend upon divine revelation? More exactly and unavoidably, in what sense, if any, is theology the child of a particular faith? Is it not the case that any claim or confession respecting the nature of God is inevitably tied to a given religious tradition?

The smoke of theological battle has already begun to rise. There are no finally neutral parties in the life of theology. It is possible, however, to discern with reasonable objectivity a minimum of three protagonists: (*a*) At one extreme are those who insist that there is no such thing as "theology"; there are only "theologies." The noun is meaningless until it is assigned a qualifying adjective. Thus, we may speak of Jewish theology, Christian theology, etc., but never of theology as such (except perhaps when, for the sake of convenience alone, we have temporary need for an essentially abstract or generalizing term). The only tenable theology is a *confessing* theology, a point of view that serves to explain or reason out a particular confession of faith. (*b*) At the other extreme is the proponent of "natural theology," as it is traditionally named, who claims that there is present in the minds of men (or at least in minds prepared or able to exert sufficient rational effort) a residual knowledge of God deriving from such intellectual demands as that for a Creator who has made possible the created process. (*c*) If the first extreme means little or no understanding of the theological claims that representatives of more than one faith actually share, the second extreme does not really settle the question (among many others) of whether the creator "God" is an unconscious process or a living, deciding reality. A third alternative is possible, for which the term *synoptic theology* may be suggested. A synoptic theology concentrates upon shared elements—or, more circumspectly, shared problems—within more than one faith. It is fully aware that some theologies are literally "incomparable" (for example, orthodox Buddhist "theology," which is avowedly atheistic, and orthodox Jewish theology, which affirms one, living God), but it is just as insistent that there are common or at least closely related doctrines within more than one faith (for example, the affirmation of the living God in Judaism and in Christianity). However, within two faiths that share similar doctrines, unavoidably there are conspicuous differences (for example, between the Muslim insistence that the Koran is, in effect, the sole abiding Word of Allah and the Christian insistence upon the canonical truth of the New Testament).

No sequence of readings from representatives of different traditions, and of different points of view within a single faith, either could or should approximate unity of persuasion. Yet it is only fair to apprise the reader that behind the difficult work of choosing selections for this book lies a greater sympathy for the third protagonist referred to above than for either of the others, although this is by no means to say that the contributors necessarily retain that same sympathy. (Part of the agreed ethic of theological behavior is the obligation to state openly the general point of view that helps motivate the participant.)

II

If theology has to do with faith in God, it is nevertheless not identical with religious activity as such. It is a matter of "thinking," of reflecting upon God, his being and his ways. The theologian is both a believer and an intellectual, and he is not one at the expense of the other. Within the bounds of faith, or of a faith, theology is unashamedly an effort of scholarship. It endeavors to *reason* about God. I refer now to the second of the two axioms alluded to at the outset: that there is a theological way of reflecting upon God.

It was suggested above that theology is linked to particular commitments and to particular faiths. Accordingly, when we attest to our second axiom, the last thing we imply is that there is only one universally accepted or acceptable methodology for reasoning about God. The paragraphs that follow seek to convey the understanding of only one theologian. While they are intended to be introductory to the volume as a whole, the reader will know that the different contributors to our assembly of readings would want to grapple in noticeably divergent ways with this second major assumption of theology.

The special approach I shall follow is to bring out the intellectual character of theology by comparing and contrasting it with two other ways of thinking: science and history.[1]

What is science? According to Ernest Nagel, the sciences endeavor "to discover and to formulate in general terms the conditions under which events of various sorts occur. . . . This goal can be achieved only by distinguishing or isolating certain properties in the subject matter studied and by ascertaining the repeatable patterns of dependence in which these properties stand to one another. . . . To explain, to establish some relation of dependence between propositions superficially unrelated, to exhibit systematically connections between apparently miscellaneous items of information are distinctive marks of scientific inquiry."[2]

A good example of the everyday application of scientific method is the calculating of insurance rates by an actuary. Actuarial tables provide useful statistical data. Thus, the insurance expert may use past knowledge of the relative dangers confronted by men who work on scaffolds as a basis for assigning higher premium rates to that class of persons than to, say, those who work as gardeners. Obviously, the actuary will never attempt to foretell that the more or less constant numbers of persons killed or injured in falls from scaffolds must include *this* man.

Within the present context we may say that scientific *explanation* and scientific *prediction* are simply opposite sides of the same coin. In the former instance it is noted, to continue the

---

[1] In the following paragraphs a greatly altered version is offered of an article by the present editor, "A Note on Theological Procedure," *Journal of Bible and Religion*, XXIX, 4 (October 1961), 313–16.

[2] Ernest Nagel, *The Structure of Science* (New York–Burlingame: Harcourt, Brace & World, 1961), pp. 4, 5. See also A. Roy Eckardt, "The Contribution of *Nomothesis* in the Science of Man," *American Scientist*, XLIX, 1 (March 1961), 76–87.

illustration, that per total workers involved, more persons *were* killed while at work on scaffolds than *were* killed at work in gardens, over a given period of time. In the case of prediction it is projected that per total workers involved, more persons *will be* killed while at work on scaffolds than *will be* killed while at work in gardens, over a comparable period of time. In the one instance, the explanation is given in terms of comparative working hazards that have obtained in the past; in the other instance, the prediction is made on the basis of continuing and future working hazards. It is essential to observe that the *individual case* is not the primary concern of science. Science is interested in patterns, in generalizations, in statistical expectations.[3]

What is history? Frequently, the work of the historian is distinguished from that of the scientist via the claim that the former concentrates upon events or states of affairs that are unique. In point of fact, as two analysts have recently shown,[4] the use of such a criterion must be criticized—although not, we may interject, entirely abandoned. The simple truth is that all events are unique. They only *seem* to be otherwise because human thought comes along and places different happenings under the headings of types or classes. Accordingly, we must look further for the essential distinction between science and history.

The real peculiarity of the historical enterprise is that, practically speaking, it reverses the means-end relation between fact and theory that is found in science. As we have noted, the sciences are interested in generalizing truths. Ideally, science seeks to offer universal laws governing wide ranges of phenomena. This is why we say that in the sciences particular events or facts "play an indispensable but nonetheless strictly subordinate role: the focus of interest is the general law, and the particular fact is simply a means to this end." In contrast to

---

[3] Eckardt, "The Contribution of *Nomothesis* . . . ," *op. cit.,* p. 83.
[4] Carey B. Joynt and Nicholas Rescher, "The Problem of Uniqueness in History," *History and Theory* (The Hague: Mouton & Co., 1961), I, 2, 150–62.

the scientist, "the historian's interest lies, first and foremost, in the particular facts of his domain." This does not mean that he stops with the description of particular, separated facts. Like all scholars, the historian is devoted to *understanding,* which means engaging in the interpretation, classification, and assessment of his materials. The historian is always on the watch for causal and conceptual relations among his data. Nevertheless, such generalizations as he offers are highly limited in character. And for him, "the role of generalizations is strictly instrumental: they provide aids towards understanding particular events. The scientist's means-end relation of facts to laws is thus inverted by the historian."[5]

What does all this have to do with theology? If the historian seeks to understand the past for its own sake and does not view facts in their purely instrumental role as data for laws,[6] the theologian concentrates upon certain facts of the past not only because he finds intrinsic value in them but also for instrumental purposes. In this last-mentioned respect, the theologian's intention parallels to some degree that of the scientist. However, instead of seeking to formulate general laws as such, the theologian treats his facts as, in large measure, instrumental sources and inspirations for the life of faith. The "public" to whom he relates himself is, in the first instance, his community of faith, although this does not mean that he will not himself sometimes call upon purely scientific and purely historical data.

The important preliminary suggestion here is that the theologian's procedures are in part like the historian's and in part like the scientist's, without being exactly the same as either of the other methods. The happenings to which the theologian directs his hearers are believed to represent, and even to disclose, in some positive and decisive way ultimate truth or reality. In this sense, the happenings are relied upon for the offering of *explanations* (the same concept we found to be central in science). This general stance of the theologian will become clearer and more concrete as we return now to a point made earlier: the

5 *Ibid.,* pp. 150–54, 160.
6 *Ibid.,* p. 154.

shared elements and the differences in the confessions of different faiths.

The religions of Judaism, Christianity, and Islam are at one in maintaining that certain events have occurred in human history which are decisive for the respective faiths and, indeed, in some way ultimately decisive for all humankind. But of course for each faith the event or events are different. (*a*) For Judaism, the revelatory and ultimately saving series of events is symbolized in the expression, "Exodus-Sinai." In the Jewish faith, the "center of history" is found in the liberation of the sons and daughters of Israel from their bondage in Egypt and the receiving of the Torah of God at Mount Sinai through the instrumentality of Moses. (*b*) The peculiarly Christian "explanation" is summarized in H. Richard Niebuhr's words: "The special occasion to which we appeal in the Christian church is called Jesus Christ, in whom we see the righteousness of God, his power and wisdom. But from that special occasion we also derive the concepts which make possible the elucidation of all the events in our history. *Revelation means this intelligible event which makes all other events intelligible.*"[7] (*c*) For Islam, the "center of history" is the event of Mohammed's choice as "reciter" of a "recitation" (Arabic, *qur'ān*) transmitted to him through the Angel Gabriel: the "uncreated" Koran of Allah.[8]

For the sake of our analysis, let us epitomize the varying but nonetheless related faith-claims of Jews, Christians, and Muslims by resort to the single word "Event."

The Event is, needless to say, not at all subject to identification as a "universal law." Yet, significantly, its recital does manifest one crucial resemblance to any recourse to scientific law: *it is held to be a decisive key to general understanding.* (One could argue that modern scientific explanation carries forward in this one respect the traditional role of theology and Christian philosophy within earlier Western culture.) For in and

[7] H. Richard Niebuhr, *The Meaning of Revelation* (New York: The Macmillan Co., 1941), p. 93 (my italics).

[8] James Kritzeck, *Sons of Abraham: Jews, Christians and Moslems* (Baltimore–Dublin: Helicon Press, 1965), pp. 31–33.

through the Event the meaning of the entire course of human existence is held to be in some way made manifest. Theology joins common sense in agreeing that all temporal events are unique, but it goes beyond purely historical emphases through its attestation that the Event is *uniquely* unique. That is to say, while within the sciences particular events are subordinated to a concern with general laws, within a given theology the various and sundry events of human history before and since the Event are subordinated to—i.e., they derive their ultimate significance and value from—*the* Event (Exodus-Sinai, Jesus Christ, or the transmission of the Koran). If the enterprise of history reverses, in effect, the scientific means-end relationship of fact and law, theology joins history in the latter's concentration upon particularities. However, while the historian is content with limited generalizations rooted in "transitory regularities,"[9] the theologian hazards an unlimited or eternal affirmation: that the Event is the "center of history."

As Ernest Nagel indicates, scientific explanations are defined as statements of the conditions that determine the occurrences of various sorts of happenings, while on the other hand scientific explanation means a process of abstraction amidst "repeatable patterns of dependence." It is, of course, forbidden to seek after scientific conditions for God's alleged acts of self-disclosure. However, a given theology will venture to present an "explanation," not merely of the presumed patterns of all human events, but even of the seeming chaos of these events, an "explanation" which is therefore in a sense universalistic but which nevertheless rests upon radical uniqueness. Theology is founded upon and caught up in the Event rather than being based upon a set of abstractions. From a theological standpoint, an ultimate "explanation" may be applied to pattern and patternlessness alike—"behind the dim unknown, standeth God within the shadow"—yet without having to pay the huge price that accompanies so much scientific explanation: a surrender of the individuality of things, of reality in its concreteness. Theology takes its uniquely unique Event and proceeds, with much

9 Joynt and Rescher, *op. cit.*, p. 156.

boldness, to relate it to an understanding of all events: this martyrdom and that betrayal, this sunshine and that rainfall, this success and that failure, this deed of friendship and that act of hostility. When during a recent World Series the announcer said, "The weather man has blessed us with another wonderful day," he was not giving voice to mere secularist influences. Purely secular language would simply assert, "The weather man has predicted excellent weather, and his prediction has come true." No one, religious or not, could possibly quarrel with that statement. The phrasing of the announcer fell more in the category of blasphemy; this has to be said from the point of view of theological "explanation."

The ultimate form of accounting in which theology engages must not lead us to equate faith with knowledge as such or to preempt alternative methods of understanding (including that of philosophy). Roger Hazelton is quite right in warning against "claims for theology which cannot be made good." As Hazelton points out, "there is something decidedly presumptuous in the implication that theology is a sort of master perspective by which any sort of event or meaning can be reckoned with and put in its proper intellectual place."[10] The truth is that *any* event or series of events can be subjected, in principle, to purely scientific procedures. Exactly the same is true with respect to historical procedures. And theology hardly qualifies as an intellectual *deus ex machina* that can be hurried to the aid of philosophers in difficulty. Each of the ways of thinking referred to in this introduction is internally unlimited. To hold that one of the disciplines possesses a monopoly upon a given area of human life or, contrariwise, that it must not trespass upon ground absolutely reserved by others is to misconstrue the nature of all these methodologies. Essentially, science, history, and theology consist of noticeably *different* ways of dealing with the *same* world. Accordingly, all that we need insist upon in the present context is equality of opportunity among the several disciplines. But this means that peculiarly theological "explanation" must

10 Roger Hazelton, *New Accents in Contemporary Theology* (New York: Harper & Brothers, 1960), p. 18.

not be discriminated against. From the perspective of faith, the Event is to be proclaimed as the "intelligible event which makes all other events intelligible."

Since theological thought is grounded in a uniquely unique Event, and thus represents a "scandal of particularity," there is some justification for placing theology at the opposite pole from science and for identifying theology as, in a sense, even more "historical" than the discipline we call history. Theology has found—or has been found by—an Event of incomparable price. From the point of view just stated, the relative relationships among the three methodologies may be pictured this way:

(1)   Science   History   Theology
      (generality ←————————————————————→ particularity)

However, a second continuum is equally justified. For, as already suggested, theology need not limit itself to an exclusive concentration upon the Event that inspires it. There is legitimacy in locating the enterprise of theology between the procedures of science and those of history. We have emphasized one fundamental point at which theology is closer to science than history is: the universality of the "explanation" theology proclaims. Theology does not stop with the limited generalizations proper to the discipline of history. Yet theology's concentration upon the decisiveness of happenings makes undeniable its kinship with history. A second set of relationships thus becomes:

(2)   Science   Theology   History
      (generality ←————————————————————→ particularity)

Finally, the process initiated in the change from (1) to (2) can be carried to a conclusion. *Theology takes its Event and applies it to the work of universal understanding.* Its one "explanation" is, accordingly, either out-and-out falsehood—all general "theories" are subject to this fateful eventuality—or a finally valid and objective key to the life-and-death meaning of things. If it is the latter, those who subscribe to it are in fact provided with the most rational and universal "theory" that men can achieve, a "theory" entirely qualified to "exhibit systematically connections between apparently miscellaneous items of information." The outcome is as follows:

(3)   Theology   Science   History

(generality ←——————————————→ particularity)

In its totality, theology moves about among the places allotted within the three figures above. In recent years students of theology, at least of Christian theology, have been increasingly advised to attend to their original Event and to preserve its qualitative integrity. Yet we must remember as well that whenever the ecstasy of faith is deprived of any "explanatory" function, it is made irrelevant to life.

The primary persuasion behind the foregoing remarks is that the relationship suggested by the second way of arranging our three terms ought not to be ignored. Within the continuum of generality/particularity, theology can be placed between science and history. It must be emphasized that the "betweenness" of theology in the presence of the other two disciplines is not a mere synthetic compromise. If it were, theology in its totality would simply be scientific when it was not historical and historical when it was not scientific. We have to attest, on the contrary, that the "betweenness" of theology rests ultimately upon its claim to "beyondness": historical particularity and generalizing "explanation" are wedded in the Event.

It is hoped that these reflections upon the nature of our subject in its relation to two other formidable enterprises of the human mind will have helped to underscore the intellectual quality of theology.

PART I

PORTRAIT OF A THEOLOGIAN

One who ventured. A major reason for including the biographical essay that follows is that there is no theology apart from the lives of individual theologians. No truism could be more evident than the latter point, and yet it is a truth that the personal life and commitments of theologians will tend to have a more intrinsic influence upon their vocational efforts and the intellectual position they finally espouse than is the case in, say, the vocation of chemistry as such, or that of the law.

Donald M. Baillie stood in the front rank of great Scottish theologians. His was one of the foremost minds of our century. In the pages below a scholarly man of faith is portrayed, one whose existential way exemplified that of the believer-intellectual. His intellectuality both assured a questioning mind and made possible an assenting one, while his faith enabled him to expose and accept all his doubts and then to venture beyond them. While few today will insist that ordination is a must among the qualifications of theologians, the fact that Donald Baillie was himself a clergyman points up the perennial issue of how individual commitment is to be wedded to the more impersonal and objective scholarship that is constituent to the theologian's existence. For it is equally clear that the basic tools of theology are those of painstaking study, searching analysis, reasonable dialectic. Indeed, the theologian's preeminent responsibilities, within and beyond his own community of faith, are those of an intellectual, a thinker.

This biographical account by *John Baillie*—who but a man's brother could speak so veritably?—reminds us of the bearing of a thinker's background and developing experiences upon his ultimate point of view. This is not to assert that the affirmations of theology, or of any other discipline, are "purely relative" to the exponents' life histories, and hence fail of any independent truth-value. It is simply to say that theological declaration is granted much of its form and content through the medium of the lives behind it. As a matter of fact, the link between theological attestation and human events does not pose the same difficulties for Jewish, Christian, or Muslim theology that it may compound with respect to theologies that seek after "timeless" truth. In general, Western theology presupposes and insists that historical happenings possess significance, and it is, accordingly, quite prepared to adjudge that God may act positively through human experiences.

It is not here suggested that to be a theologian, one must attain the saintliness of a Donald Baillie. However, the audacity of the subject of theology makes eminently desirable the humility and the sense of humor that Baillie manifested. Another useful criterion in judging the capability and perceptiveness of a theologian (as of any thinker) is the extent of his rapport with children.

The student may find it profitable to assay a biographical study of the background, personality, and interests of a theologian of his or her acquaintance, for possible comparisons and contrasts with Professor Baillie.

1

DONALD:
A BROTHER'S IMPRESSION*

John Baillie

THE home into which Donald Baillie was born in November
1887 was a Highland manse presided over by a Calvinist divine
of strong character and courtly bearing, and a lady of great
charm and goodness; but it was saddened by the father's too
early death when Donald, the second of three small boys, was
only three years old. A year later our mother moved from
Gairloch to Inverness, and it was with home and school life in
the Highland capital that our earliest significant memories were
associated. Our father's Calvinism had been of the most rigor-
ous and uncompromising kind and, true to the memory of a
husband with whom she had lived for only six years, our mother
was most anxious that her children's upbringing should be in the
same tradition. Her own temperament, if left to itself, might
have guided her a little differently, and time brought with it a
gradual mellowing of principle, especially after the later move
to Edinburgh and its University; until finally she felt herself
completely at home under Donald's ministry in his various
parishes, sharing all his interests and friendships and delighting
in them. Nevertheless it was a very rigid Calvinistic outlook

* Excerpts from the biographical essay by John Baillie ("Donald: A
Brother's Impression") in *The Theology of the Sacraments and Other
Papers* by Donald M. Baillie (Copyright © 1957 John Baillie) are re-
printed with the permission of Charles Scribner's Sons.

with which we were indoctrinated in our boyhood's home. The system of beliefs embodied in the Westminister standards is of a most remarkable logical self-consistency, once its premises have been allowed, and our mother was not only thoroughly conversant with its intricacies, but well able to answer any objections that might be brought against them. If her sons later developed any aptitudes of a philosophic kind, it was undoubtedly by this home training in theological dialectic that their minds were first sharpened.

The sharpening, however, would have been much less, had it not been for our growing doubts about the trustworthiness of some of the premises on which the system rested. These, as I can now see, were first generated in our minds by the considerably different climate of thought to which we were introduced by what we learned at school. None of us was indeed particularly diligent at his set tasks: Donald used to say in after life that he did no work at school. Nevertheless our minds were awakened and our imaginations stirred by what we heard there, and we were given the keys of what to us, brought up as we had been, was something of a new intellectual kingdom—even if our own independent reading and our eager discussions with some of our fellow scholars had as much to do with the actual unlocking of the doors as what our masters (several of whom were very remarkable men) had to tell us. . . .

I have often reflected that parents who dutifully bring up their children in a traditional orthodoxy which has never submitted itself to the challenge of Renaissance and *Aufklärung,* and who then send them to a school whose whole ethos is of humanist inspiration, seldom realize the extent of the spiritual stress and strain to which they are thus subjecting them. Our minds, for example, were soon set afire by the reading of Shakespeare, but there was no room at all for Shakespeare within the Puritanism of our early upbringing; no room for theatre of any kind; but especially no room for Shakespeare's large and generous and delicately discriminating appreciation of the human scene. Again, we were trained at school to develop a fastidious sense for the weighing of historical evidence, and for distinguishing fact from legend; but our training at home did not allow us to practise this skill on the Bible stories. Or once more, we were abruptly introduced to the world-view of modern science, and we could not make it square with the up-and-down, three-storey, geocentric universe of the Biblical writers and of our Catechisms, or with their assumptions about the natural history of the human race.

Donald especially was from an early age haunted with religious doubts of this general kind. Having a very sensitive conscience in the matter, he was fearful of unsettling the minds of others by any mention of them, so that it was not until our undergraduate days that I myself was aware of their existence, but I remember how he then said to me, 'If I had only known that your mind had been troubled in the same way, how great would have been the relief of sharing!' For the strain on his spirit was indeed acute. His only confidante was his mother. This may seem surprising in view of what I have already said, but actually it was not so, for the two had from the first been bound together by the closest possible ties of affection and mutual respect. Yet it says much for our mother that she was able to enter so sympathetically and so understandingly into a trouble so remote from anything she herself had ever suffered. . . .

In 1905 our mother moved to Edinburgh to see us all through the University, and Donald began his studies there in the same year. He very soon added to the circle of his friends some who were to be the intimate associates of a life-time, and the same was true of my brother Peter and myself. Our mother made them all welcome, and there were not many days during the ensuing decade when our little study, and tea-table or supper-table, was not enlivened by the presence of one or more of them. They numbered among them some of the best and ablest men it has ever been my lot to meet. Our eager discussions often continued until long after midnight and, though our 'friendly bowl' was not of the same composition as Alexander Pope's, we enjoyed no less than he 'the feast of reason and the flow of soul.'

It was in his second year of study, and in Pringle-Pattison's course of Logic and Metaphysics that Donald first came into his own as a student, winning the first place and medal in a class numbering several hundred. His earlier interest had been rather in the field of English literature, and indeed this interest never left him. . . .

One of the finest of Dr. Gilbert Murray's essays bears the title 'Literature as Revelation,' and I think that phrase very well expresses the deep concern that guided Donald in his reading of general literature. He was looking always for light upon the meaning of life and for a solution of the intellectual, and fundamentally theological, problems that continued to haunt him. . . . [However,] he very soon began to vest his hopes rather in philosophy. In this field he carried off all the academic honours under the distinguished guidance of Pringle-Pattison, his brother James Seth, R. P. Hardie and Henry Barker. After graduation he acted for some years as Seth's assistant in the department of Moral Philosophy.

Meanwhile his intellectual distress had become greater than ever, as his uncertainties extended to more fundamental issues. I remember his telling me long afterwards of how, as he sat reading a book of apologetic intent by one of the famous preachers of the day, it suddenly came to him that there was no God; and I have often thought of this incident as illustrating the grievous harm that may be done by weak and inconclusive apologetic, or by apologetic of the wrong kind, to young minds that are often keen enough to see where the argument falters, so that, as in this case, it has an effect directly contrary to what was intended. Donald was afterwards to be a valiant defender of the faith, and there are many to testify that his wise counsel was the turning-point in the solution of their own difficulties, but he himself had to pass through a long struggle from which only very slowly was he able to emerge. It brought with it nervous strain of an acute kind. He could not coerce himself to the methodical reading of the texts required for the approaching examinations, but would rather concentrate his thoughts for hours at a stretch on a single page, or even sentence, in one of them which seemed to promise some possible relief of his problem. And how often did I see him sit for a whole evening, staring at a book but not seeing it, and turning no page of it, while his mind kept reverting in spite of himself to a spiritual predicament concerning which the book had no real enlightenment to offer! He sat the final examination with half the texts unread, so that we feared for his First Class, but what he wrote was apparently enough to convince the examiners of the fine quality of his mind. . . .

After taking his degree he entered New College, Edinburgh and submitted himself to the regular four years' course of theological study in preparation for the ministry. His struggle for faith was now measurably eased, but certainly not yet a thing of the past. Indeed it was never for him completely a thing of the past. Even in his latest years he had periods of depression, in which life seemed to be emptied of its divine meaning. He was in the poorest possible health then, a martyr to a long-standing asthmatic condition, and the depression was physical as well as mental. He would put to himself and to me the question as to whether the extreme bodily lassitude was the cause or the result, or merely the accompaniment, of the darkness of soul. But one thing was always clear to him—that without God and Christ human life was without significance of any kind, devoid of all interest. He would say, 'When the darkness is on me, I walk down the street, and see people walking aimlessly about, and shops and cars and a few dogs, and it all seems to mean nothing and to matter not at all!' It was Pascal's *misère de l'homme sans Dieu*. Blessedly, such periods of depression were seldom of long duration, and certainly (whatever may be thought about cause and effect) they were always associated with the ebbings of his physical resources. Moreover, this whole side of his experience undoubtedly enabled him to enter most sympathetically and most helpfully into the like experience of a large number of students and others who sought his counsel. . . .

In 1934 he was appointed to the chair of Systematic Theology in the University of St. Andrews, which had honoured him with its doctorate in divinity a year previously, and here he was to remain for the remaining twenty years of his life. He called his house there 'The Crask,' the name of the 'brae' at the foot of which stood our father's church and manse in Gairloch, and the name likewise given by our mother to her house in Inverness. It now lacked the latter's gracious presence, but Donald was fortunate in securing a house-keeper of exceptional quality who was wholly devoted to him and remained with him to the end. Thus he was able to indulge in the open hospitality in which he delighted, being greatly aided in this by the proximity of our cousins, Professor and Mrs. W. R. Forrester and their children. He loved to surround himself with young folk, most of whom would naturally be students in the University, but he also had a constant stream of visitors to stay with him—scholars from continental universities (Karl Barth, Paul Tillich, Rudolf Bultmann, Emil Brunner, and many another), preachers in the University Chapel, Student Christian Movement secretaries and (during the war years) a number of refugees of different kinds. . . .

During his twenty years in St. Andrews my brother's hold upon his students, their eager reception of his teaching, their dependence upon his counsel, and their love of him, grew ever greater; as did also the respect and strong affection in which he was held by the University community at large and by many of the townsfolk. After the Second World War an ever-increasing number of students from abroad, and especially from the United States, found their way to St. Andrews to study under his direction. . . .

In his later years Donald frequently confessed to me that the focus of his interest had gradually moved onwards from the more general problems of what is usually called the philosophy of religion, such as had formerly occupied him, to the detail of Christian dogmatics; or at least that he now felt it was the latter field that must claim most of his attention. The wider issues were no doubt as present to his mind as they had ever been, but his increasing clarity concerning them enabled him, as it were, to pass on to, and to grapple more closely with, the more advanced doctrines of our faith. This order of going, however, and the whole intellectual and spiritual experience that lay behind it, made it inevitable that, in spite of his profound study of and veneration for the traditional theological systems, he should take nothing from them on trust, but must work out everything independently for himself. Needless to say, his ability to do this was at all times dependent on the light he received from others. There was little in contemporary theological literature, whether Protestant or Roman or Eastern Orthodox, that escaped his attention, and it was from this reading that he drew much of his nourishment. But in a sense in which it is perhaps not true of all writers on these subjects, it had all to be thought out afresh, and to undergo a process of metabolism in his own mind, before it could be assimilated by him—or served up to others. For this reason most of what he wrote is likely to be of greater service to those who have had to struggle for their religious beliefs than for those whose minds have never been thus exercised. It was his endeavor to find as it were the handle by which each facet of Christian doctrine could most easily be grasped by the contemporary mind, to discover the way of presenting it which would best reveal the genuinely and 'existentially' Christian meaning which it had been designed to express and to preserve. He was acutely conscious that traditional terminology was often a barrier to such understanding. He felt also that the historic disagreements between the various confessional divisions of the Christian Church, as well as between conflicting schools of theology, were in no small measure due to the fact that each party had pinned its colours and attached its loyalties to certain phrases and forms of expression which grew to be more and more of an offence to the other party; so that no advance could be made towards a reasonable agreement until the opposing vocabularies were considered afresh, in as great as possible a degree of detachment from the heats of ancient controversy, when perhaps the real concerns enshrined in them would turn out to be much nearer to one another than we had been in the habit of supposing. A great part of my brother's writing and teaching was irenic in this sense.

During these years he gave so much of himself to his students, and to certain other causes . . . that he felt little urge to publish; nor would he ever be stimulated in that direction by personal ambition, of which there was very little indeed in his make-up. The only book of any size which he set himself to write in this period was *God Was in Christ,* which at once received wide acclaim throughout the English-speaking world and beyond it, and still enjoys large sales both in Britain and in America. Those who know the book will perhaps recognize in it most or all of the intellectual characteristics of which I have been speaking. The clarity and even simplicity which mark every stage of its argument were distilled from a profound and exhausting labour of thought extending over many years, going back indeed to his student days. He used to say that clarity was the only grace of style for which he ever strove. . . .

. . . A concern for social justice lay very near to the core of his understanding of the Christian faith. He was zealous not only for religious but for political and especially economic freedom; zealous also for equality, not in a doctrinaire understanding of it, but in the sense of the removal of the many unjustified inequalities with which he felt our society to have traditionally been burdened. He was thus inclined rather strongly to the left in his political convictions, about which he was always outspoken, though refusing to sell out to any single system of economic doctrine and hesitating to attach any label to his views. He would say, 'I don't know whether I'm a socialist or not, but I do certainly think, etc'.

With it all, however, Donald's was a gay spirit, finding delight in simple pleasures. Children were greatly attracted to him, and many were devoted to him in no common degree. He knew just how to take them, joining most happily and naturally in their games and other ploys. He would also sparkle with fun in many a congenial adult company, sometimes amusing us with limericks, of which I may be allowed to quote a single example dating from the early days of Karl Barth's ascendancy—it was afterwards repeated to its victim, calling forth his hearty laughter:

> There was a young thinker called Barth
> Who walked by himself quite apart.
> His favourite motto
> Was Blast Rudolf Otto,
> And Ritschl was wrong from the start.

He had always been the wit of our family. From his boyhood he had had a sharp tongue, though his sallies were so wrapped in kindliness as to be robbed of caustic effect. On New Year's Day or the King's Birthday, after a brief glance at the honours list, he would fling down the newspaper in feigned disgust and say, 'Passed over once again!' When at our tea-table my mother would on occasion forget to pour him out a cup, he would announce, 'Patience Competition: First Prize—D. M. Baillie; Second Prize—Job.' Or at the dinner-table he would mildly protest against the appearance of a suet pudding (the eating of which tended to aggravate his asthma) with the rhyme:

> Eat less suet:
> Eat more fru-it.
> If you do it,
> You won't rue it.

His spare frame made him very sensitive to cold and, coming into a room that was insufficiently heated, he would exclaim, 'Now we know what the Arctic explorers had to endure.' If ever a family argument threatened to become ill-tempered, he would say, 'This correspondence is now closed—Editor.' I have heard him say frequently how grave a defect he regarded the absence from any man's make-up of a sense of humour, however worthy his other attributes. . . .

Though clear and alert in mind to the last, Donald did not suspect the extremity of his condition until the day before his death. When he then asked me and I told him, he was in no way disturbed or distressed. He asked only that I should read him the hundred and forty-fifth psalm, and this I did in what, though neither of us knew it, was to be his last conscious hour. . . .

At a meeting of the Senatus Academicus of St. Andrews

University Dr. T. M. Knox, the Principal and Vice-Chancellor, spoke as follows:

His acuteness of intellect and the range of his scholarship are enshrined in writings which won international fame for their author and made familiar to theologians in every land the name of his College and University. He was the most loyal of colleagues; and he brought to our counsels an integrity of mind and grasp of principle which commanded widespread respect. For many years he had battled against ill-health, and he was one of those who thought it his duty to labour far beyond his physical strength, whether in teaching or writing or service to his fellow men. He was no recluse; he liked good talk; he had the gift of humour and a cultivated aesthetic taste; and the dignity of our University service owed much to his liturgical sense. Many of us and many of his students knew and loved him as a friend: we have had cause to be grateful to him for sympathy in trouble, for advice in difficulty, for aid in need. But above all, he was a man of saintly character in whose presence anything mean or impure or evil seemed to shrivel away. We are all the richer for having known him and immeasurably the poorer for his loss.

The wreath placed on his grave by his University bore this inscription:

IN PIAM MEMORIAM DONALDI MACPHERSON BAILLIE .
VIRI DOCTISSIMI . COLLEGAE FIDELISSIMI .
AMICI AMANTISSIMI . ANIMAE SANCTISSIMAE .
PRINCIPALIS ATQUE COLLEGAE CURIALES ET
SENATORII

PART II

THE SUBJECT AND THE OBJECT

How is God known? What is he like? From one point of view, the question of how we may know God precedes the question of what he is like, for the simple reason that insofar as God's nature may be known, it is apprehended in various human ways. Accordingly, as we center in our next five selections upon God as the subject of theology and as the object of faith, it is appropriate that we begin with *Jacques Maritain's* successive expositions of the intuitive dimension and the intellectual dimension of the human self, move to *Martin Buber's* claim of knowing God "through a bond of mutual relationship," and come to *H. Richard Niebuhr's* concentration upon faith as itself a gift of God. Despite the differences of approach and emphasis, the beginnings of a synoptic theological outlook—as we have identified "synoptic theology" in the Introduction—can be grounded in the five contributions together. Here are to be found varying combinations of rational, experiential, and moral reflection, on the one hand, with faith (trust) in God, on the other hand. The presence of these two sides is especially apparent in the letters of *Mohammad Fadhel Jamali*. Even with Maritain, the human self is held to be aware *immediately* of Being-without-nothingness, of the eternal God. And in the case of *John B. Cobb, Jr.,* whose definition of theology excludes the word "God," there is nevertheless an insistence that the entire perspective that governs theology "is received from a community of faith." It will be clear that our theological conclusions are not ultimately separable from our judgments concerning the nature of man as a self and a social being.

For all the vigor of their several claims, none of the thinkers in the present section would allege that human beings, including men of great faith, can penetrate the very being of God. All would agree with Professor Jamali that man is constitutionally incapable of defining the divine essence, of knowing God in and

17

of himself. There is, after all, a very great difference between claiming what God *is* and attesting only to what he is *like*. Because of the emphasis within the Western theological tradition upon the need for divine aid if men are to know God, that tradition allows a certain place for skepticism and agnosticism from the human standpoint.

The question raised in both the Buber and the Cobb selections of whether theology and faith are in fact linked in any special way to sacredness or to religion receives more intensive discussion in Part V of this book. Other fundamental questions posed by the readings in the present section include the following: Is it true that, as Maritain contends, the primordial intuition of existence necessarily conveys absolute existence, or may it convey no more than nonabsolute existence? What is the meaning of "proof" in a given attempt to "prove" the existence or reality of God? Can one be a philosopher of religion and a theologian at one and the same time? Is it only theologians who are needfully involved in theological challenges and dilemmas? Are there compelling ways of knowing God and of affirming what God is like other than those proposed in the five selections below?

2

TWO WAYS TO GOD*

Jacques Maritain

1. From Plato and Aristotle to St. Anselm and St. Thomas Aquinas, to Descartes and Leibniz, philosophers have proposed proofs or demonstrations of the existence of God, or, as Thomas Aquinas more modestly puts it, *ways* through which the intellect is led to the certitude of His existence. All are highly conceptualized and rationalized proofs, specifically philosophic ways of approach. Kant rightly criticized the proof advanced by Descartes (what is called "the ontological argument"), but wrongly claimed to reduce all the ways of demonstration to this particular proof. That was a great error; for the five ways indicated by Thomas Aquinas are completely independent of the ontological argument, and stand firm in spite of all criticism.

However, it is not these highly conceptualized, rationalized and specifically philosophical ways of approach which I should like to consider at present. When St. Paul affirmed that:

that which is known of God is manifest in them. For God hath manifested it unto them. For the invisible things of Him, from the creation of the world, are clearly seen, being understood by the things that are made; His eternal power also, and divinity . . . .

* Reprinted with permission from "The Primordial Way of Approach" (pp. 1–15) and "A Sixth Way" (pp. 72–83) in *Approaches to God* by Jacques Maritain, translated from the French by Peter O'Reilly (New York: Harper & Brothers, 1954). Copyright 1954 by Jacques Maritain. Footnotes omitted.

he was thinking not only of scientifically elaborated or specifically philosophical ways of establishing the existence of God. He had in mind also and above all the natural knowledge of the existence of God to which the vision of created things leads the reason of every man, philosopher or not. It is this doubly *natural* knowledge of God I wish to take up here. It is natural not only in the sense that it belongs to the rational order rather than to the supernatural order of faith, but also in the sense that it is *prephilosophic* and proceeds by the natural or, so to speak, instinctive manner proper to the first apperceptions of the intellect prior to every philosophical or scientifically rationalized elaboration.

Before entering into the sphere of completely formed and articulated knowledge, in particular the sphere of metaphysical knowledge, the human mind is indeed capable of a prephilosophical knowledge which is *virtually metaphysical.* Therein is found the first, the primordial way of approach through which men become aware of the existence of God.

2. Here everything depends on the natural intuition of being— on the intuition of that act of existing which is the act of every act and the perfection of every perfection, in which all the intelligible structures of reality have their definitive actuation, and which overflows in activity in every being and in the intercommunication of all beings.

Let us rouse ourselves, let us stop living in dreams or in the magic of images and formulas, of words, of signs and practical symbols. Once a man has been awakened to the reality of existence and of his own existence, when he has really perceived that formidable, sometimes elating, sometimes sickening or maddening fact *I exist,* he is henceforth possessed by the intuition of being and the implications it bears with it.

Precisely speaking, this primordial intuition is both the intuition of *my* existence and of the existence *of things,* but first and foremost of the existence of things. When it takes place, I suddenly realize that a given entity—man, mountain or tree—

exists and exercises this sovereign activity *to be* in its own way, in an independence of *me* which is total, totally self-assertive and totally implacable. And at the same time I realize that *I* also exist, but as thrown back into my loneliness and frailty by this other existence by which things assert themselves and in which I have positively no part, to which I am exactly as naught. And no doubt, in face of my existence others have the same feeling of being frail and threatened. As for me, confronted with others, it is my own existence that I feel to be fragile and menaced, exposed to destruction and death. Thus the primordial intuition of being is the intuition of the solidity and inexorability of existence; and, second, of the death and nothingness to which *my* existence is liable. And third, in the same flash of intuition, which is but my becoming aware of the intelligible value of being, I realize that this solid and inexorable existence, perceived in anything whatsoever, implies—I do not yet know in what form, perhaps in the things themselves, perhaps separately from them—some absolute, irrefragable existence, completely free from nothingness and death. These three leaps—by which the intellect moves first to actual existence as asserting itself independently of me; and then from this sheer objective existence to my own threatened existence; and finally from my existence spoiled with nothingness to absolute existence—are achieved within the same unique intuition, which philosophers would explain as the intuitive perception of the essentially analogical content of the first concept, the concept of Being.

Next—this is the second stage—a prompt, spontaneous reasoning, as natural as this intuition (and as a matter of fact more or less involved in it), immediately springs forth as the necessary fruit of such a primordial apperception, and as enforced by and under its light. It is a reasoning without words, which cannot be expressed in articulate fashion without sacrificing its vital concentration and the rapidity with which it takes place. I see first that my being is liable to death; and second, that it is dependent on the totality of nature, on the universal whole of which I am a part. I see that Being-with-nothingness, such as my own being, implies, in order that it should be, Being-without-nothingness—that absolute existence which I confusedly perceived from the beginning as involved in my primordial intuition of existence. But then the universal whole of which I am a part is itself Being-with-nothingness, by the very fact that I am part of it. And from this it follows finally that since this universal whole does not exist by virtue of itself, it must be that Being-without-nothingness exists apart from it. There is another Whole—a separate one—another Being, transcendent and self-sufficient and unknown in itself and activating all beings, which is Being-without-nothingness, that is, self-subsisting Being, Being existing through itself.

Thus the internal dynamism of the intuition of existence, or of the intelligible value of Being, causes me to see that absolute existence or Being-without-nothingness transcends the totality of nature. And there I am, confronted with the existence of God.

3. This is not a new approach to God; it is human reason's eternal way of approaching God. What is new is the manner in which the modern mind has become aware of the simplicity and liberating power, of the natural and in some way intuitive character, of this eternal approach. The science of the ancients was steeped in philosophy. Their scientific imagery was a pseudo-ontological imagery. Consequently, there was a kind of continuum between their knowledge of the physical world and their knowledge of God. This latter knowledge was seen as the summit of the former, a summit which had to be scaled by the multiple paths of the causal connections at work in the sublunar world and the celestial spheres. And the sense of Being, which everywhere and always ruled their thought, was for them an atmosphere too habitual to be regarded as a surprising gift. At the same time, the natural intuition of existence was so strong in them that their proofs of God could take the form of the most conceptualized and the most rationalized scientific demonstra-

tions, and be offered as a skillful unfolding of logical necessities, without losing the inner energy of that intuition. This logical machinery was surreptitiously enlivened by the deep-seated intuition of Being.

We are in quite a different position now. In order to reach physical reality in its own enigmatic way and to conquer the world of phenomena, our science has become a kind of *Maya*— a Maya which succeeds and makes us masters of nature. But the sense of Being is absent from it. Thus when we come to experience the impact of Being upon our mind, it appears to us as a kind of intellectual revelation, and we become keenly aware both of its awakening and liberating power, and of the fact that it involves a knowledge separate from the sphere of knowledge peculiar to our science. At the same time we realize that the knowledge of God, before being developed in logical and perfectly conceptualized demonstrations, is first and foremost a natural fruit of the intuition of existence, and that it imposes itself upon our mind through the imperative force of this intuition.

In other words, we have become aware of the fact that in its primordial vitality the movement of the human reason in its approach to God is neither a pure intuition (which would be suprahuman), nor the kind of philosophical reasoning of a technical type through which it will be expressed in its achieved form, and which at each of its stages is pregnant with conflicts and with problems to clarify. In its primordial vitality the movement of the human reason in its approach to God is a *natural* reasoning, that is, intuitive-like or irresistibly maintained in, and vitalized by, the intellectual flash of the intuition of existence. In this natural reasoning it is just this intuition of existence which, seizing in some existing reality Being-with-nothingness, by the same stroke makes the mind grasp the necessity of Being-without-nothingness. And nowhere is there any problem involved, because the illumining power of this intuition takes possession of the mind and obliges it to see, in such a way that the mind proceeds naturally, within a primordial intuitive flash, from imperative certainty to imperative certainty. I believe that from Descartes to Kierkegaard the effort of modern thought—to the extent that it has not completely repudiated metaphysics and if it is cleansed of the irrationalism which has gradually corrupted it—tends to such an awareness of the specific *naturalness* of man's knowledge of God, definitely more profound than any scientifically developed logical process, and an awareness of the primordial and simple intuitiveness in which this knowledge originates.

4. I have just tried to describe the manner in which this natural prephilosophic knowledge spontaneously proceeds. It involves a reasoning, but a reasoning after the fashion of an intuitive grasp, bathed in the primordial intuition of existence. Let us say that this natural knowledge is a kind of *innocent* knowledge, a knowledge free of all dialectic. Such a knowledge is rich in certitude, a certitude that is indeed compelling, although it exists in an imperfect logical state. It has not yet crossed the threshold of *scientific* demonstration, whose certitude is critical and implies that the difficulties inherent in the question have been surmounted through a scrutiny of the rational connections and necessities involved. Such natural knowledge is still in happy ignorance of these difficulties and of all the *videtur quod non's:* because scientific certitude and the objections to be met—and the replies to the objections—all come into the world together.

It appears, therefore, that the philosophic proofs of the existence of God, let us say the five ways of Thomas Aquinas, are a development and an unfolding of this natural knowledge, raised to the level of scientific discussion and scientific certitude. And they normally presuppose this natural knowledge, not with regard to the logical structure of the demonstration, but with regard to the existential condition of the thinking subject. If the preceding observations are true, it would be necessary, before proposing the philosophic proofs, to be assured insofar as possible (by trying, where need be, to aid in such an awakening) that the minds to which one addresses oneself are alive to the primordial intuition of existence, and conscious of the natural knowledge of God involved in this intuition.

One more remark seems to be called for here. I have just used the expression "the philosophic proofs of the existence of God," and I noted above that St. Thomas Aquinas preferred to use the word *ways*. He had his reasons for this. These ways are proofs, but the words "proof" or "demonstration" may be misunderstood. To prove or to demonstrate is, in everyday usage, to render evident that which of itself was not evident. Now, on the one hand, God is not *rendered evident* by us. He does not receive from us and from our arguments an evidence which He would have lacked. For the existence of God, which is not immediately evident *for us,* is immediately evident *in itself* —more evident in itself than the principle of identity, since it is infinitely more than a predicate contained in the notion of a subject. It is the subject, the divine essence itself (but to know this from immediate evidence, it would be necessary to see God). On the other hand, what our arguments render evident for us is not God Himself, but the testimony of Him contained in His vestiges, His signs or His "mirrors" here below. Our arguments do not give us evidence of the divine existence itself or of the act of existing which is in God and which is God Himself—as if one could have the evidence of His existence without having that of His essence. They give us only evidence of the fact that the divine existence must be affirmed, or of the truth of the attribution of the predicate to the subject in the assertion "God exists."

In short, what we prove when we prove the existence of God is something which infinitely surpasses us—us and our ideas and our proofs. "To demonstrate the existence of God is not to submit Him to our grapplings, nor to define Him, nor to take possession of Him, nor to handle anything else than ideas that are feeble indeed with regard to such an object, nor to judge anything but our own radical dependence. The procedure by which reason demonstrates that God is places reason itself in an attitude of natural adoration and of intelligent admiration."

And thus the words "proof" and "demonstration," in reference to the existence of God, must be understood (and in fact are so understood spontaneously) with resonances other than in the current usage—in a sense no less strong as to their rational efficacy but more modest in that which concerns us and more reverential in that which concerns the object. On this condition it remains perfectly legitimate to use them. It is just a matter of marking well the differences in station. This being understood, we shall not hesitate to say "proof" or "demonstration" as well as "way," for all these words are synonymous in the sense we have just specified.

As to the very word *existence,* the existentialist philosophers arbitrarily corrupt its meaning when they say that to exist is "to stand outside oneself." But even in its genuine meaning—to stand "outside its causes" or "outside nothingness" (the etymological sense of the word being *"sistere ex,* that is to say, to stand or to be posited in itself, from an anterior term on which it depends")—the word existence, in order to apply to God, must lose the connotation which thus refers it to created things. It is clear that God does not stand "outside His causes"—as though He were caused; not "outside nothingness"—as though nothingness preceded God; and that He is not *sistens ex*—as if He depended on some antecedently existing source. Of itself, however, the notion of existence is in no wise restricted to such a connotation, which in fact refers to the analogue that falls first and immediately under our apprehension; from the outset it overflows all pseudo-definitions carried over from this connotation. Just as the notion of being, the notion of existence is of itself, essentially and from the first, an analogous notion, validly applicable to the uncreated as to the created. No doubt, the word being, in contrast to the word existence, does not need to be purified of accidental vestiges due to etymology. Truth to tell, however, the word existence has been spontaneously purified of them, all by itself, and in any event this does not affect at all the meaning itself of the notion. Those who think that one can say "God is," but not "God exists," maintain for being its essential analogicity but refuse it to existence—the strangest of illusions, since being itself is understood only in relation to existence. To say "God is" and "God exists" is to say exactly the same thing. One speaks the language of simple truth in speaking of the ways through which it is shown that God is, or that He *exists*. . . .

. . . .

13. The views which I propose here are based neither on a fact observed in the world of sense experience, nor on the principle "One cannot rise to the infinite in the series of causes," nor does the argument proceed with the royal simplicity of the ways of Thomas Aquinas. It may, indeed, appear too subtle, and for a long time I regarded it as belonging to the domain of research hypotheses. I have, however, come to think that it constitutes a genuine proof, a rationally valid way leading to a firmly established certitude.

Here again it is appropriate to distinguish two levels of approach—a *prephilosophic* level whereon certitude bathes in an intuitive experience, and a *scientific* or *philosophical* level whereon certitude emanates from a logically elaborated demonstration and from a rationally developed metaphysical justification.

We shall first take our stand on the prephilosophic level. Indeed it is the intuitive process that, in this case more than ever, matters first of all, although the intuition in question is of a much more peculiar sort than the primordial intuition of existing, and supposes experience of the proper life of the intellect. By feeling the impact of this intuitive experience, the mind discovers the approach to God which this experience brings along with it. Later it is led to formulate in logically conceptualized terms that which I call here a "sixth way."

The intuition of which I speak is related to the natural spirituality of intelligence. I shall try to describe it as it is in its primitive and, so to speak, "wild" state, where it first begins to sprout. I am busy thinking. Everything in me is concentrated on a certain truth which has caught me up in its wake. This truth carries me off. All the rest is forgotten. Suddenly I come back to myself; a reflection is awakened in me which seems to me quite incongruous, altogether unreasonable, but whose evidence takes possession of me, in my very perception of my act of thought: *how is it possible that I was born?*

The activity of the mind develops in two quite different orders. It develops on the one hand in the order of the life which Aristotle called "life proportioned to man." Here the activity of the mind, as it happens in our train of ordinary social or occupational pursuits, is made up of a succession of operations immersed in time and which are for the most part operations of sense and imagination sustained and illuminated by the intellect.

On the other hand it develops in the order of the life which Aristotle called "life proportioned to the intellect." Here the activity of the mind, entirely withdrawn in thought, is centered above the sense and imagination, and is concerned with intelligible objects alone. It is when a man is thus engaged in an act of purely intellectual thought (to the extent that this is possible for a rational animal) that it happens that the intuition in question takes place: how is it possible that that which is thus in the process of thinking, in the act of intelligence, which is immersed in the fire of knowing and of intellectual grasp of what is, should once have been a pure nothing, once did not exist? Where I am now in the act of intellection and of consciousness of my thought, was there once *nothing?* That is impossible; it is not possible that at a certain moment what is now thinking was not at all, was a pure nothing. How could this have been born to existence?

I am not here faced with a logical contradiction. I am facing a *lived* contradiction, an incompatibility of fact (known in *actu exercito*). It is as if I were in a room and, without my having left for an instant, someone were to say to me that I just came in—I know that what he says is impossible.

Thus, I who am now in the act of thinking have always existed. This view imposes itself on me and does not seem strange to me unless I draw myself back from it in order to consider it from without. And perhaps I express it in a deficient way; we shall see about that later. For the moment I speak as I can, and I cannot speak otherwise.

Yet I know quite well that I was born. True, I know it by hearsay, but I do know it with an absolute certainty, and besides, I remember my childhood. The certitude of having been born, common to all men, represses in us the blossoming forth—when the natural spirituality of intelligence is activated in us—of another certitude, that of the impossibility that our existence as thinking minds ever began or followed upon the nothingness of itself, and it prevents that other certitude from reaching our consciousness.

So here I am, in the grasp of two contrary certitudes. There is only one solution: I, who am thinking, have always existed, but not in myself or within the limits of my own personality—and not by an impersonal existence or life either (for without personality there is no thought, and there must have been thought there, since it is now in me); therefore I have always existed by a suprapersonal existence or life. Where then? It must have been in a Being of transcendent personality, in whom all that there is of perfection in my thought and in all thought existed In a supereminent manner, and who was, in His own infinite Self, before I was, and is, now while I am, more I than I myself, who is eternal, and from whom I, the self which is thinking now, proceeded one day into temporal existence. I had (but without being able to say "I") an eternal existence in God before receiving a temporal existence in my own nature and my own personality

14. What shall we say now if we transport ourselves onto the level of rational demonstration? Is it possible to justify philosophically the intuitive experience which we have just tried to describe?

What is important to consider first is that the intellect is above time, *intellectus supra tempus:* because the intellect is spiritual, and time, the perseverance of movement in being, or the continuity of perpetually vanishing existence proper to movement, is the proper duration of matter.

The operations of the human intellect are in time, and, indeed, subject to time, but in an extrinsic manner and only by reason of the materiality of the senses and the imagination to whose exercise they are bound. In themselves they are not subject to the flux of impermanence. They emerge above time. They exist in a duration which is a deficient imitation of eternity, a succession of fragments of eternity, for it is the perseverance in being of spiritual acts of intellection or of contemplative gaze. Thus this duration is composed of instants superior to time, each of which may correspond to a lapse of time more or less long, but is in itself without flow or movement or succession—a flash of permanent or nonsuccessive existence. Such is the proper duration of thought. Thought as such is not in time. The distinction between the *spiritual* and the *temporal* appears here in its primary sense. That which is spiritual is not subject to time. The proper place of the spiritual is above temporal existence.

We find a noteworthy indication of this in the fact that spiritual events are "metahistorical" events. Insofar as they are occurrences, they take place in history, but their content belongs in a region superior to history. This is why it is normal for history not to mention them. The word event itself is therefore ambiguous. "What happens," in the case of spiritual events, comes on the scene for an instant in temporal existence, but comes forever in the existence of souls and of thought.

But actions or operations emanate from a subject or from a person—*actiones sunt suppositorum.* And no operation is more personal than thought. Thought is exercised by a certain subject, a certain *self,* made of flesh and spirit.

This self exists in time and was born in time. But inasmuch as it exercises the spiritual operation of thought, inasmuch as it is the center of spiritual activity and capable of living or existing by the immaterial superexistence of the act of intellection, it is also superior to time, as is thought itself. It escapes the grasp of time.

This self began in time. But nothing begins absolutely. Everything which begins existed before itself in a certain way, to wit, in its causes. Insofar as it is material, the thinking self existed before itself in time, namely, in the ancestral cells, the physio-chemical materials and energies utilized by life all along the line from which the self has sprung. Whatever of it existed before it pre-existed in time.

But as spiritual, as exercising the spiritual operations of thought, as thinking, it could not have existed before itself in time, because mind can come only from a mind, thought can come only from a thought, and therefore from an existence superior to time.

Moreover, since thought is essentially personal, when it arises in time as the operation of such and such a subject born one day into temporal existence, it cannot come from an existence superior to time unless the self which exercises it now pre-existed in a certain way beyond time.

The self is born in time. But insofar as it is thinking it is not born of time. Its birth is supratemporal. It existed before itself in a first existence distinct from every temporal existence. It did not exist there in its proper nature (since it began to exist in its proper nature by being born in time), but everything that there is in it of being and of thought and of personality existed there better than in itself.

This, however, would not be possible unless everything that exists in temporal existence were a participation of the first existence in question. The latter then must contain all things in itself in an eminent mode and be itself—in an absolutely transcendent way—being, thought and personality. This implies that that first existence is the infinite plenitude of being, sepa-rate by essence from all the diversity of existents. This means that it is not the act of existing itself, subsisting through itself. Thus we are necessarily led to the principle which no concept can circumscribe—Being in pure act, from which comes every being; Thought in pure act from which comes every thought; Self in pure act from which comes every self.

It is thus that the "sixth way" leads us to the existence of God. But it would remain incompletely elucidated if, after recognizing the existence of God, we should not ask ourselves how things exist in Him before being caused by Him in their own *esse*.

Things pre-exist in God not in their proper natures but according as they are known to God, and, therefore, by that which renders them present to the divine intellect, that is to say by the divine essence itself, of which they are participations or likenesses, and which is itself the proper object of the divine intellect. In God they are the divine essence as revealing its participability. They live there, but without existing in themselves, by a life infinitely more perfect than the existence which they have in their proper natures. They live, in God who knows them, by the very life of God. They exist in the divine thought by the very existence of God which is His act of intellection.

This is true of thinking subjects, of *selves* endowed with intelligence, as it is of all other creatures. Before existing in themselves they exist eternally in God by the very existence of God, as participations or likenesses of the divine essence eternally known in that Essence. Therefore I can say that I, who am now in the act of thinking, always existed—I always existed in God. Care must be taken, however, to understand this proposition correctly. It does not mean that in God the human self has always exercised the act of thinking, or that in God it collaborates eternally in the act of divine thought. That makes no sense. In God the unique Self who thinks is the divine Self. The statement signifies rather that the creature which is now I, and which thinks, existed before itself eternally in God—not as exercising in Him the act of thinking, but as thought by Him. It bathed there in the light of God; it lived there by a suprapersonal (suprapersonal in relation to every created personality) and divinely personal life, by that life which is the eternal act of intellection of the divine Self itself, thinking itself.

Thinking subjects, *selves* capable of acting beyond time, which thus pre-exist in God, as do all those other participations of the Divine Essence which are created things—infinitely deficient in relation to their principle—are the most elevated of all things in the whole order of nature, because they are either purely spiritual creatures or creatures composed of matter and spirit, which, once they exist in their proper nature, resemble the divine Self in that they think and can be called, because of this, "images of God."

The reflections we have proposed in this chapter, as well as the intuitive experience which they presuppose, are entirely independent of any contact with Indian thought. It seems to us nevertheless that they can help to clarify in some way the meaning and the origin of the Hindu notion of the Self (Atman), and throw into relief at once the metaphysical truths to which this notion is related and the confusion which it has not succeeded in avoiding between the divine Self and the human self.

On the other hand the importance accorded to the expression *not-born* in many Hindu texts seems to us to suggest a quite remarkable affinity with the intuition of which we have treated here, and to indicate that an intuition of the same type plays a characteristic role in the philosophic thought and the natural mysticism of India.

3

THE DIALOGUE WITH GOD*

Martin Buber

IF IT IS true that the whole world, all the world process, the whole time of the world, unsubtracted, stands in the dialogical situation; if it is true that the history of the world is a real dialogue between God and his creature—then the triad [of time: creation, revelation, redemption], as which that history is perceived, becomes not a man-made device for his own orientation, but actual reality itself. What comes to us out of the abyss of origin and into the sphere of our uncomprehending grasp and our stammering narrative, is God's cry of creation into the void. Silence still lies brooding before him, but soon things begin to rise and give answer—their very coming into existence is answer. When God blesses his creatures and gives them their appointed work, revelation has begun; for revelation is nothing else than the relation between giving and receiving, which means that it is also the relation between desiring to give and failing to receive. Revelation lasts until the turning creature answers and his answer is accepted by God's redeeming grace. Then the unity emeregs, formed out of the very elements of contrariety, to establish amidst all the undiminished multiplicity and manifoldness the communication of creatures in the name of God and before his face.

* Reprinted with the permission of Schocken Books, Inc. from *Israel and the World,* by Martin Buber, pp. 26–27, 29–39, 53–54. Copyright © 1948, 1963 by Schocken Books, Inc.

Just as God's cry of creation does not call to the soul, but to the wholeness of things, as revelation does not empower and require the soul, but all of the human being—so it is not the soul, but the whole of the world, which is meant to be redeemed in the redemption. Man stands created, a whole body, ensouled by his relation to the created, enspirited by his relation to the Creator. It is to the whole man, in this unity of body, soul, and spirit, that the Lord of Revelation comes and upon whom he lays his message. So it is not only with his thought and his feelings, but with the sole of his foot and the tip of his finger as well, that he may receive the sign-language of the reality taking place. The redemption must take place in the whole corporeal life. God the Creator wills to consummate nothing less than the whole of his creation; God the Revealer wills to actualize nothing less than the whole of his revelation; God the Redeemer wills to draw into his arms nothing less than the all in need of redemption. . . .

The fealty of the Jew is the substance of his soul. The living God to whom he has pledged himself appears in infinite manifestations in the infinite variety of things and events; and this acts both as an incentive and as a steadying influence upon those who owe him allegiance. In the abundance of his manifestations they can ever and again recognize the One to whom they have entrusted themselves and pledged their faith. The crucial word which God himself spoke of this rediscovery of his presence was spoken to Moses from the midst of the burning bush: "I shall be there as I there shall be" (Exod. 3.14). He is ever present to his creature, but always in the form peculiar to that moment, so that the spirit of man cannot foretell in the garment of what existence and what situation God will manifest himself. It is for man to recognize him in each of his garments. I cannot straightaway call any man a pagan; I know only of the pagan in man. But insofar as there is any paganism, it does not consist in not discerning God, but in not recognizing him as ever the same; the Jewish in man, on the contrary, seems to me to be the ever renewed rediscernment of God.

I shall therefore speak to you about the Jewish soul by making a few references to its fundamental attitude; I shall regard it as being the concretion of this human element in a national form, and consider it as the nation-shaped instrument of such a fealty and discernment.

I see the soul of Judaism as elliptically turning round two centers.

One center of the Jewish soul is the primeval experience that God is wholly raised above man, that he is beyond the grasp of man, and yet that he is present in an immediate relationship with these human beings who are absolutely incommensurable with him, and that he faces them. To know both these things at the same time, so that they cannot be separated, constitutes the living core of every believing Jewish soul; to know both, "God in heaven," that is, in complete hiddenness, and man "on earth," that is, in the fragmentation of the world of his senses and his understanding; God in the perfection and incomprehensibility of his being, and man in the abysmal contradiction of this strange existence from birth to death—and between both, immediacy!

The pious Jews of pre-Christian times called their God "Father"; and when the naïvely pious Jew in Eastern Europe uses that name today, he does not repeat something which he has learned, but he expresses a realization which he has come upon himself of the fatherhood of God and the sonship of man. It is not as though these men did not know that God is also utterly distant; it is rather that they know at the same time that however far away God is, he is never unrelated to them, and that even the man who is farthest away from God cannot cut himself off from the mutual relationship. In spite of the complete distance between God and man, they know that when God created man he set the mark of his image upon man's brow, and embedded it in man's nature, and that however faint God's mark may become, it can never be entirely wiped out.

According to hasidic legend, when the Baal Shem conjured up the demon Sammael, he showed him this mark on the forehead of his disciples, and when the master bade the conquered demon begone, the latter prayed, "Sons of the living

God, permit me to remain a little while to look at the mark of
the image of God on your faces." God's real commandment to
men is to realize this image.

"Fear of God," accordingly, never means to the Jews that
they ought to be afraid of God, but that, trembling, they ought
to be aware of his incomprehensibility. The fear of God is the
creaturely knowledge of the darkness to which none of our
spiritual powers can reach, and out of which God reveals
himself. Therefore, "the fear of God" is rightly called "the
beginning of knowledge" (Ps. 111:10). It is the dark gate
through which man must pass if he is to enter into the love of
God. He who wishes to avoid passing through this gate, he who
begins to provide himself with a comprehensible God, con-
structed thus and not otherwise, runs the risk of having to
despair of God in view of the actualities of history and life, or
of falling into inner falsehood. Only through the fear of God
does man enter so deep into the love of God that he cannot
again be cast out of it.

But fear of God is just a gate; it is not a house in which one
can comfortably settle down—he who should want to live in it
in adoration would neglect the performance of the essential
commandment. God is incomprehensible, but he can be known
through a bond of mutual relationship. God cannot be fathomed
by knowledge, but he can be imitated. The life of man who is
unlike God can yet be an *imitatio Dei*. "The likeness" is not
closed to the "unlike." This is exactly what is meant when the
Scripture instructs man to walk in God's way and in his
footsteps. Man cannot by his own strength complete any way or
any piece of the way, but he can enter on the path, he can take
that first step, and again and again that first step. Man cannot
"be like unto God," but with all the inadequacy of each of his
days, he can follow God at all times, using the capacity he has
on that particular day—and if he has used the capacity of that
day to the full, he has done enough. This is not a mere act of
faith; it is an entering into the life that has to be lived on that
day with all the active fulness of a created person. This activity
is within man's capacity: uncurtailed and not to be curtailed, the

capacity is present through all the generations. God concedes the might to abridge this central property of decision to no primordial "Fall," however far-reaching in its effects, for the intention of God the Creator is mightier than the sin of man. The Jew knows from his knowledge of creation and of creatureliness that there may be burdens inherited from prehistoric and historic times, but that there is no overpowering original sin which could prevent the late-comer from deciding as freely as did Adam; as freely as Adam let God's hand go the late-comer can clasp it. We are dependent on grace; but we do not do God's will when we take it upon ourselves to begin with grace instead of beginning with ourselves. Only our beginning, our having begun, poor as it is, leads us to grace. God made no tools for himself, he needs none; he created for himself a partner in the dialogue of time and one who is capable of holding converse.

In this dialogue God speaks to every man through the life which he gives him again and again. Therefore man can only answer God with the whole of life—with the way in which he lives this given life. The Jewish teaching of the wholeness of life is the other side of the Jewish teaching of the unity of God. Because God bestows not only spirit on man, but the whole of his existence, from its "lowest" to its "highest" levels as well, man can fulfil the obligations of his partnership with God by no spiritual attitude, by no worship, on no sacred upper story; the whole of life is required, every one of its areas and every one of its circumstances. There is no true human share of holiness without the hallowing of the everyday. Whilst Judaism unfolds itself through that history, it holds out against that "religion" which is an attempt to assign a circumscribed part to God, in order to satisfy him who bespeaks and lays claim to the whole. But this unfolding of Judaism is really an unfolding, and not a metamorphosis.

To clarify our meaning we take the sacrificial cultus as an example. One of the two fundamental elements in biblical animal sacrifice is the sacralization of the natural life; he who slaughters an animal consecrates a part of it to God, and so doing hallows his eating out of it. The second fundamental element is the sacramentalization of the complete surrender of life; to this element belong those types of sacrifice in which the person who offers the sacrifice puts his hands on the head of the animal in order to identify himself with it; in doing so he gives physical expression to the thought that he is bringing himself to be sacrificed in the person of the animal. He who performs these sacrifices without having this intention in his soul makes the cult meaningless, yes, absurd; it was against him that the prophets directed their fight against the sacrificial service which had been emptied of its core. In the Judaism of the Diaspora prayer takes the place of sacrifice; but prayer is also offered for the reinstatement of the cult, that is for the return of the holy unity of body and spirit. And in that consummation of Diaspora Judaism which we call hasidic piety, both fundamental elements unite into a new conception which fulfils the original meaning of the cult. When the purified and sanctified man in purity and holiness takes food into himself, eating becomes a sacrifice, the table an altar, and man consecrates himself to the Deity. At that point there is no longer a gulf between the natural and the sacral; at that point there is no longer the need for a substitute; at that point the natural event itself becomes a sacrament.

The Holy strives to include within itself the whole of life. The Law differentiates between the holy and the profane, but the Law desires to lead the way toward the messianic removal of the differentiation, to the all-sanctification. Hasidic piety no longer recognizes anything as simply and irreparably profane; "the profane" is for hasidism only a designation for the not yet sanctified, for that which is to be sanctified. Everything physical, all drives and urges and desires, everything creaturely, is material for sanctification. From the very same passionate powers which, undirected, give rise to evil, when they are turned toward God, the good arises. One does not serve God with the spirit only, but with the whole of his nature, without any subtractions. There is not one realm of the spirit and another of nature; there is only the growing realm of God. God is not spirit, but what we call spirit and what we call nature hail equally from the God who is beyond and equally conditioned by both, and whose kingdom reaches its fulness in the complete unity of spirit and nature.

The second focus of the Jewish soul is the basic consciousness that God's redeeming power is at work everywhere and at all times, but that a state of redemption exists nowhere and never. The Jew experiences as a person what every openhearted human being experiences as a person: the experience, in the hour when he is most utterly forsaken, of a breath from above, the nearness, the touch, the mysterious intimacy of light out of darkness; and the Jew, as part of the world, experiences, perhaps more intensely than any other part, the world's lack of redemption. He feels this lack of redemption against his skin, he tastes it on his tongue, the burden of the unredeemed world lies on him. Because of this almost physical knowledge of his, he *cannot* concede that the redemption has taken place; he knows that it has not. It is true that he can discover prefigurations of redemption in past history, but he always discovers only that mysterious intimacy of light out of darkness which is at work everywhere and at all times; no redemption which is different in kind, none which by its nature would be unique, which would be conclusive for future ages, and which had but to be consummated. Most of all, only through a denial of his own meaning and his own mission would it be possible for him to acknowledge that in a world which still remains unredeemed an anticipation of the redemption had been effected by which the human soul—or rather merely the souls of men who in a specific sense are believers—had been redeemed.

With a strength which original grace has given him, and which none of his historic trials has ever wrested from him, the Jew resists the radical division of soul and world which forms the basis of this conception; he resists the conception of a divine splitting of existence; he resists most passionately the awful notion of a *massa perditionis*. The God in whom he believes has not created the totality in order to let it split apart into one blessed and one damned half. God's eternity is not to be conceived by man; but—and this we Jews know until the moment of our death—there can be no eternity in which *everything* will not be accepted into God's atonement, when God has drawn time back into eternity. Should there however be a stage in the redemption of the world in which redemption is first fulfilled in one *part* of the world, we would derive no claim to redemption from our faith, much less from any other source. "If You do not yet wish to redeem Israel, at any rate redeem the goyim," the rabbi of Koznitz used to pray. . . .

The Book of Jonah is a clear example of what is meant by prophecy. After Jonah has tried in vain to flee from the task God has given him, he is sent to Nineveh to prophesy its downfall. But Nineveh turns—and God changes its destiny. Jonah is vexed that the word for whose sake the Lord had broken his resistance had been rendered void; if one is forced to prophesy, one's prophecy must stand. But God is of a different opinion; he will employ no soothsayers, but messengers to the souls of men—the souls that are able to decide which way to go and whose decision is allowed to contribute to the forging of the world's fate. Those who turn co-operate in the redemption of the world.

Man's partnership in the great dialogue finds its highest form of reality at this point. It is not as though any definite act of man could draw grace down from heaven; yet grace answers deed in unpredictable ways, grace unattainable, yet not self-withholding. It is not as though man has to do this or that "to hasten" the redemption of the world—"he that believeth shall not make haste" (Isa. 28:16); yet those who turn co-operate in the redemption of the world. The extent and nature of the participation assigned to the creature remains secret. "Does that mean that God cannot redeem his world without the help of his creatures?" "It means that God does not will to be able to do it." "Has God need of man for his work?" "He wills to have need of man." . . .

Though robbed of their real names, these two foci of the Jewish soul continue to exist for the "secularized" Jew too, insofar as he has not lost his soul. They are, first, the immediate relationship to the Existent One, and second, the power of atonement at work in an unatoned world. In other words, first, the *non-incarnation* of God who reveals himself to the "flesh" and is present to it in a mutual relationship, and second, the unbroken continuity of human history, which turns toward fulfilment and decision. . . .

In those scribbled lines which seem to cry from his very soul, which Pascal wrote after two ecstatic hours, and which he carried about with him until his death, sewn into the lining of his doublet, we find under the heading *Fire* the note: "God of Abraham, God of Isaac, God of Jacob—not of the philosophers and scholars."

These words represent Pascal's change of heart. He turned, not from a state of being where there is no God to one where there is a God, but from the God of the philosophers to the God of Abraham. Overwhelmed by faith, he no longer knew what to do with the God of the philosophers; that is, with the God who occupies a definite position in a definite system of thought. The God of Abraham, the God in whom Abraham had believed and whom Abraham had loved ("The entire religion of the Jews," remarks Pascal, "consisted only of the love of God"), is not susceptible of introduction into a system of thought precisely because he is God. He is beyond each and every one of those systems, absolutely and by virtue of his nature. What the philosophers describe by the name of God cannot be more than an idea. But God, "the God of Abraham," is not an idea; all ideas are absorbed in him. Nor is that all. If I think even of a state of being in which all ideas are absorbed, and think some philosophic thought about it as an idea—then I am no longer referring to the God of Abraham. The "passion" peculiar to philosophers is, according to a hint dropped by Pascal, pride. They offer humanity their own system in place of God.

"What!" cries Pascal, "the philosophers recognized God and desired not merely that men should love him, but that they should reach their level and then stop!" It is precisely because the philosophers replace him by the image of images, the idea, that they remove themselves and remove the rest of us furthest from him. There is no alternative. One must choose. Pascal chose, during one of those revolutionary moments, when his sickbed prayer was answered: "To be apart from the world, divested of all things, lonely in your Presence, in order to respond to your justice with all the motions of my heart."

Pascal himself, to be sure, was not a philosopher but a mathematician, and it is easier for a mathematician to turn his back on the God of the philosophers than for a philosopher. For the philosopher, if he were really to wish to turn his back on that God, would be compelled to renounce the attempt to include God in his system in any conceptual form. Instead of including God, as one theme among others, that is, as the highest theme of all, his philosophy both wholly and in part would be compelled to point toward God, without actually dealing with him. This means that the philosopher would be compelled to recognize and admit the fact that his idea of the Absolute was dissolving at the point where the Absolute *lives;* that it was dissolving at the point where the Absolute is loved; because at that point the Absolute is no longer the "Absolute" about which one may philosophize, but God.

4

FAITH IN GODS AND IN GOD*

H. Richard Niebuhr

THERE is nothing distinctive or peculiar about a Protestant's
interest in the ultimate theological problem. We are concerned
with the questions of God's nature and existence not as Protestants or Catholics, Christians or Jews, theologians or philosophers, laymen or clergy, but simply as human beings. Yet each
of us raises these problems in a specific form, each asks his
question in that special way which he has not only learned from
his tradition, but which has been made necessary by his own
personal wrestling with the question of life's meaning. Hence we
often quarrel about the answers we get to our questions without
realizing that they are answers to different questions. And sometimes we quarrel about our questions, maintaining that our way
of asking is the only significant way; that our problem is the
only meaningful one. So the philosopher of religion may begin
with a certain definition of the term "God" and then ask, "Does
a being having this nature exist?" This is a perfectly legitimate
question. But it is wrong to think of it as the only proper way of
raising the problem. Many different definitions of the nature of
God may be framed, and hence many problems of existence
may be raised; and the contention about the answers may
simply be contention about the social meaning of a word, a

* From *Radical Monotheism and Western Culture,* by H. Richard
Niebuhr, © 1960 H. Richard Niebuhr (pp. 114–26), reprinted with the
permission of Harper & Row, Publishers.

matter on which we ought to be able to come to an agreement easily were it not for the emotional and sentimental attachment we have to certain words. The question about God may be raised in a wholly different way, in the manner of the metaphysician who asks, "What is the ultimate nature of reality, or what is the first cause, what the final end, what the nature of the primal energy, what are the attributes of substance?" Here we have a different series of questions, and the relation of the answers given to them to the answers given to the question whether "God" exists is not immediately apparent. If the term "God" is used in this latter, metaphysical type of inquiry, it is not to be taken for granted that the word has the same reference, the same meaning, which it has in the former type.

It is important, first of all, to recognize that each of us raises the question about "God" in a specific way, that it is necessary for us to phrase our question as sharply as we can, to seek an answer to that particular question and to avoid the defensiveness which makes us regard our question, just because it is ours, as more important than anyone else's. We need also, of course, to avoid the feeling that our question is unimportant because others have other questions. As a Protestant theologian or as a man who seeks to understand what he believes with the aid of Protestant theology, I do not raise the question of God in the way the philosopher of religion or the metaphysician does; while I cannot maintain that my way of asking is superior to theirs, neither can I be easily convinced that my question is illegitimate, that it is not a true, human, and important question.

It appears that the different methods we employ in religious inquiry are not wholly unlike the different methods used in science. Though all scientists are interested in truth they do not raise the question about truth in the abstract, but ask specific questions, such as those which psychologists on the one hand, physicists on the other, natural scientists on the one hand, social scientists on the other, raise and attempt to answer. Each scientist, doubtless, tends to think that his question and mode of inquiry is the most important, yet he learns eventually to live in a certain democracy of science, wherein he maintains his right to seek truth in a specific way without requiring all others to abandon their specific inquiries and to join him in his search. In some such fashion I conceive Protestant theology at work. It is well aware of other inquirers in the same general field and it profits greatly by counsel and debate with them. Yet it seeks to remain true to its own particular problem and to its own method of inquiry.

How, then, does Protestantism raise the question of God and how does it seek and find its answers to its problems? How does the problem of God present itself to us who work in this living tradition? It comes to us as an eminently practical problem, a problem of human existence and destiny, of the meaning of human life in general and of the life of self and its community in particular. It does not arise for us in the speculative form of such questions as "Does God exist?" or "What is the first cause, what the ultimate substance?" Our first question is *"How is faith in God possible?"* In other words, the problem of God arises for us in its subjective rather than objective, or, better, in personal rather than impersonal form. (That we are exposed to certain great dangers in consequence—to solipsism, for instance—is evident but every inquiry involves particular dangers and the possibility of particular errors.) This seems to be the way in which the great Protestant thinkers—Luther, Calvin, Edwards, Schleiermacher, Kierkegaard—and that philosopher who is most Protestant of all philosophers, Kant—raised the question about God primarily. It is also the way in which Protestantism as a religious movement has approached the religious problem of the ordinary man. It has not sought to convince a speculative, detached mind of the existence of God, but has begun with actual moral and religious experience, with the practical reasoning of the existing person rather than with the speculative interests of a detached mind.

1. WHAT IS FAITH?

The point at which such Protestants begin their analysis of the problem of God is that of practical human faith in deity.

Such faith may be described in various ways, but it is never correctly described when it is initially defined in terms of intellectual belief. The belief that something exists is an experience of a wholly different order from the experience of reliance on it. The faith we speak of in Protestantism and of which, it seems to us, the classic book of Christianity, the Bible, speaks, is not intellectual assent to the truth of certain propositions, but a personal, practical trusting in, reliance on, counting upon something. So we have faith in democracy not insofar as we believe that democracy exists, but insofar as we rely upon the democratic idea or spirit to maintain itself and to influence the lives of people continuously. We have faith in the people not insofar as we believe in the existence of such a reality as "the people" but insofar as we count upon the character of what we call the people to manifest itself steadfastly in the maintenance of certain values. Faith, in other words, always refers primarily to character and power rather than to existence. Existence is implied and necessarily implied; but there is no direct road from assent to the intellectual proposition that something exists to the act of confidence and reliance upon it. Faith is an active thing, a committing of self to something, an anticipation. It is directed toward something that is also active, that has power or is power. It is distinguished from belief both on its subjective side and with respect to that to which it refers. For belief as assent to the truth of propositions does not necessarily involve reliance in action on that which is believed, and it refers to propositions rather than, as faith does, to agencies and powers.

Now it is evident, when we inquire into ourselves and into our common life, that without such active faith or such reliance and confidence on power we do not and cannot live. Not only the just but also the unjust, insofar as they live, live by faith. We live by knowledge also, it is true, but not by knowledge without faith. In order to know we must always rely on something we do not know; in order to walk by sight we need to rely on what we do not see. The most evident example of that truth is to be found in science, which conducts its massive campaign against obscurity and error on the basis of a great faith in the intelligibility of things; when it does not know and finds hindrances in the path of knowledge, it asserts with stubborn faith that knowledge nevertheless is possible, that there is pattern and intelligibility in the things which are not yet intelligible. Such faith is validated in practice, yet it evermore outruns practice. Our social life, also, proceeds from moment to moment on the ground of a confidence we have in each other which is distinct from our belief in each other's existence and distinct also from our knowledge of each other's character, though such belief and such knowledge do form the background and the foreground of our faith. How much we live by faith in this area becomes apparent to us when we are deceived or betrayed by those on whom we have relied. When treaties are broken, when bankers embezzle, when marriage partners become disloyal, when friends betray, then doubt of all things invades our minds and we understand how much we have lived by reliance on our fellow men. But we also discover that without some confidence which goes beyond our knowledge we cannot exist at all since we are social persons who cannot live in isolation, and that we are ignorant persons who must in all their living go far beyond their knowledge of each other if they would live at all.

When we inquire into this element of faith or confidence in our life as human beings we become aware of one aspect of it which may above all else be called religious, because it is related to our existence as worshiping beings, even as our faith in the intelligibility of nature is related to our existence as knowing beings and our confidence in each other is related to our moral life. This is the faith that life is worth living, or better, the reliance on certain centers of value as able to bestow significance and worth on our existence. It is a curious and inescapable fact about our lives, of which I think we all become aware at some time or another, that we cannot live without a cause, without some object of devotion, some center of worth, something on which we rely for our meaning. In this sense all men have faith because they are men and cannot help themselves, just as they must and do have some knowledge of their world, though their knowledge be erroneous.

The universality of such religious faith is obscured for us. For one thing, we tend in highly institutionalized societies, such as our own, to confuse the reality of human processes with their institutional organization and expression. So we have a tendency to think of schools, laboratories, books, and teachers when we speak of education. Doubtless this institutional education is very important but we need again and again to be made aware of the fact that the actual process of conditioning human minds, of equipping them with the instruments of words and ideas, of giving them an orientation in the world, of transmitting a tradition and developing latent possibilities, goes far beyond the schools and can go on even without the aid of official education. The political process, also, whereby men are governed and govern each other, whereby power is balanced against power, goes on in our community even when the official agencies of politics, the institutionalized forms, are not present. It is so with religion and religious faith and worship. We tend to confuse these with the official organizations and habits, with observance of special rites, with the functioning of a special leadership, and with the expression of a specific faith. But religion is a much more various thing. And it is inescapable as institutions of religion are not. As the faith that life is worth living, as the reference of life to a source of meaning and value, as the practice of adoration and worship, it is common to all men. For no man lives without living for some purpose, for the glorification of some god, for the advancement of some cause. If we do not wish to call this faith religion, there is no need to contend about the word. Let us say then that our problem is the problem of faith rather than of religion.

Now to have faith and to have a god is one and the same thing, as it is one and the same thing to have knowledge and an object of knowledge. When we believe that life is worth living by the same act we refer to some being which makes our life worth living. We never merely believe that life is worth living, but always think of it as made worth living by something on which we rely. And this being, whatever it be, is properly termed our god.

2. WHO IS GOD?

We arrive, then, at the problem of deity by setting out from the universal human experience of faith, of reliance or trust in something. Luther expressed this idea long ago when he asked, "What does it mean to have a god, or what is God?" and answered his question by saying, "Trust and faith of the heart alone make both God and idol. . . . For the two, faith and God, hold close together. Whatever then thy heart clings to . . . and relies upon, that is properly thy God."

Now if this be true, that the word "god" means the object of human faith in life's worthwhileness, it is evident that men have many gods, that our natural religion is polytheistic. (It is also evident that there can be no such thing as an actual atheist though there may be many who profess atheism.) Whatever be our relation to the official monotheism of our religious institutions, the private faith by which we live is likely to be a multifarious thing with many objects of devotion and worship. The most common object of devotion on which we depend for our meaning and value is the self. We tend in human life to a kind of religious Narcissism whereby we make ourselves the most admired of all beings and seek to interpret the meaning of all experiences by reference to their meaning for the central self. The self becomes the center of value and at the same time the being which is to guarantee its own life against meaninglessness, worthlessness, and the threat of frustration.

But this self is never an adequate god for a self. We are forced to recognize that many things bring satisfaction into our lives from the outside, as it were, and we are so interdependent on all the beings about us that we inevitably admire, adore, and look to others as sources of value and meaning to ourselves. Hence we live not only for our own sakes but for the sake of other persons. It is not a figure of speech but a truth that mothers make gods out of their sons and daughters, that the home is the god of all men to a certain extent, since they live for the sake of that home, labor for it and adore it in many an hour of private devotion. One of the most powerful gods of all times, of primitive as of civilized periods, is sex which is represented by many symbols, for the sake of which, and for the enjoyment of which men live. Beyond the dark powers, the Chthonian deities of the physical life of man, there are our Olympian gods—our country, our ideologies, our democracies, civilizations, churches, our art which we practice for art's sake, our truth which we pursue for truth's sake, our moral values, our ideas and the social forces which we personalize, adore, and on which we depend for deliverance from sheer nothingness and the utter inconsequence of existence.

One does not need to draw too sharp a line between personal and institutional religion at this point, as though personal religion were by and large polytheistic while institutional religion is monotheistic. It would be difficult to make out a strong case for the actual monotheism of institutional faith. For instance, one of the beings on which institutionalized faith relies for deliverance from meaninglessness is religion itself.

We note that these centers of value, these objects of adoration, have many different forms of existence. Some are visible and tangible objects of whose reality our senses give us assurance. Some are essences, ideas, concepts, or images which are accessible only to abstract thought, but which exercise a certain compulsion over the mind. Some are movements known only by a kind of empathy or by an intuition that outruns sense; some have the peculiar and hard-to-define reality of selves or persons. But in some sense they all exist.

Yet this is true—and this constitutes the tragedy of our religious life—that none of these values or centers of value exists universally, or can be object of a universal faith. None of them can guarantee meaning to our life in the world save for a time. They are all finite in time as in space and make finite claims upon us. Hence we become aware of two characteristics of our faith and its gods: that we are divided within ourselves and socially by our religion, and that our gods are unable to save us from the ultimate frustration of meaningless existence.

Sometimes we speak of our internal division as though it were caused by the incompleteness of reason's domination over the more primitive desires which are rooted in our physical constitution. But then we realize that we do not desire as primitives or as animals do, but with a passion that indicates how great an investment we have made in the objects of desire. We note also that the life of reason is not without its desire and devotion. We become aware of the truth that our internal divisions are due to a diversity of religious attachments. We look to the objects of the mind for meaning, but we cannot make our physical existence meaningful by our attention and devotion to truth. Our inner conflicts seem due to the fact that we have many sources of value, and that these cannot all be served. Our social conflicts also always have religious character. We cannot and do not fight our wars simply for the sake of maintaining our physical existence. We always appeal to values for the sake of which we live and without which we think that life would not be worth living. We battle for America and England and Germany, which give worth to our lives, and not simply for ourselves. We fight for liberty or solidarity, for equality or for order, for fraternity in a large or in a narrow sense. But none of these gods is universal, and therefore devotion to one always implies exclusion of another. So the gods are divisive socially as well as within the person.

In this situation we dream of integration, of a great pantheon in which all the gods will be duly served, each in its proper sphere. So we speak sometimes of establishing a new synthesis of civilization, of the integration of personality, of the recognition of a great hierarchy of values. But the synthesis is never achieved, the integration never worked out. For each god in turn requires a certain absolute devotion and the denial of the claims of the other gods. So long as country seems an absolute source of value to us, so long devotion to one country will make us deny the claims of every other. So long as we pursue art for art's sake, so long art will be the enemy of morality and of truth. The best we can achieve in this realm is a sort of compromise among many absolute claims. We remain beings, therefore, with many faiths held in succession. We practice a kind of successive polygamy, being married now to this and now to that object of devotion.

The tragedy of our religious life is not only that it divides us within ourselves and from each other. There is a greater tragedy —the twilight of the gods. None of these beings on which we rely to give content and meaning to our lives is able to supply continuous meaning and value. The causes for which we live all die. The great social movements pass and are supplanted by others. The ideals we fashion are revealed by time to be relative. The empires and cities to which we are devoted all decay. At the end nothing is left to defend us against the void of meaninglessness. We try to evade this knowledge, but it is ever in the background of our minds. The apocalyptic vision of the end of all things assails us, whether we see that end as the prophets of the pre-Christian era did or as the pessimists of our time do. We know that "on us and all our race the slow, sure doom falls pitiless and dark." All our causes, all our ideas, all the beings on which we relied to save us from worthlessness are doomed to pass.

3. GOD

What is it that is responsible for this passing, that dooms our human faith to frustration? We may call it the nature of things, we may call it fate, we may call it reality. But by whatever name we call it, this law of things, this reality, this way things are, is something with which we all must reckon. We may not be able to give a name to it, calling it only the "void" out of which everything comes and to which everything returns, though that is also a name. But it is there—the last shadowy and vague reality, the secret of existence by virtue of which things come into being, are what they are, and pass away. Against it there is no defense. This reality, this nature of things, abides when all else passes. It is the source of all things and the end of all. It surrounds our life as the great abyss into which all things plunge and as the great source whence they all come. What it is we do not know save that it is and that it is the supreme reality with which we must reckon.

Now a strange thing has happened in our history and in our personal life; our faith has been attached to that great void, to that enemy of all our causes, to that opponent of all our gods. The strange thing has happened that we have been enabled to say of this reality, this last power in which we live and move and have our being, "Though it slay us yet will we trust it." We have been allowed to attach our confidence to it, and put our reliance in it which is the one reality beyond all the many, which is the last power, the infinite source of all particular beings as well as their end. And insofar as our faith, our reliance for meaning and worth, has been attached to this source and enemy of all gods, we have been enabled to call this reality God.

Let us raise three questions about this fact that faith has become attached to the void and to the enemy which surrounds our life. The first one is, What does it mean to attach faith to this power? The second, How does such faith come about? And the third, What are the consequences of such faith?

First, to have faith in this reality means that, having been driven away from our reliance on all the lesser causes, we have learned to conceive of and to rely upon this last power, this nature of things, as itself the greatest of all causes, the undefeatable cause. We have learned to say, "For this cause was I born and therefore I came into the world that I might make glorious the name and exhibit the power of this last cause." And we have been enabled to say it with satisfaction, with love and hope and confidence; for to have faith in something as able to give value to our lives is to love it. Without such love there is no faith. And to have faith is also to live in hope, in constant anticipation of new unfoldings of worth and meaning.

To attach faith, hope, and love to this last being, this source of all things and this slayer of all, is to have confidence which is not subject to time, for this is the eternal reality, this is the last power. It is to have a love for that which is not exclusive but inclusive, since this reality, this great X, is the source of all things and the end of all. It is, therefore, to be put into the position of those who can love all things in him or in it, and who deny all things in it. "It is a consoling idea," wrote Kierkegaard, "that before God we are always in the wrong." All the relative judgments of worth are equalized in the presence of this One who loves all and hates all, but whose love like whose hatred is without emotion, without favoritism. To have hope of this One is to have hope that is eternal. This being cannot pass away. And to hope for the manifestations of his judgments and his love is to hope to eternity.

When we conceive faith in this one, our foundations have indeed been laid in despair, not in the grandiloquent despair of *A Free Man's Worship*, but in the sober despair which has faced the reality of the death of all things and the endlessness of the creative process.

Another way of describing this faith is one which I have learned from Professor Whitehead's little book on religion. Religion, he says, "is transition from God the void to God the enemy, and from God the enemy to God the companion." When we say that we conceive faith in the great void and the great enemy we mean that we have learned to count on it as friend. We have learned to rely on it as a cause to which we may devote our lives, as that which will make all our lives and the lives of all things valuable even though it bring them to death.

Second, how is such a faith possible? How does it happen that this void, this enemy, is recognized as friend, that faith attaches itself to the last power, to the great hidden mystery, and calls it God, that man can lose himself in adoration of this being, saying with the Psalmist, "Whom have I in heaven but thee? and there is none upon earth that I desire beside thee?" or with Job, "Though he slay me, yet will I trust in him"?

It has happened in our human history and it does happen in personal histories. Men may dispute endlessly about the worth of that happening, though when they do they always do so on the basis of another faith than faith in this God. But there can be no doubt of the fact that it has happened and that it does happen.

How does it happen to the individual? It does not happen without the struggle of his reason. For by reason he discovers the inadequacy of all his gods and is driven to despair in life's meaning. It does not happen without experience, without the experience of frustration, of noting the death of all things, the experience of the internal division in which his various worship involves him, the experience of the great social catastrophes which show the weakness of the great causes and beings in which he trusted as saviors of life. It does not happen without the operation of something we must call spiritual, something which is like the intuition of the thinker, like the creative insight of the artist, like the flash of recognition of truth. All these elements are involved. Furthermore, this transfer of faith to the ultimate being does not take place without moral struggle, without recognition of the unworthiness both of our transgressions and our obediences to our moral laws.

But for most men another element is involved—the concrete meeting with other men who have received this faith, and the concrete meeting with Jesus Christ. There may be other ways, but this is the usual way for us, that we confront in the event of Jesus Christ the presence of that last power which brings to apparent nothingness the life of the most loyal man. Here we confront the slayer, and here we become aware that this slayer is the life-giver. He does not put to shame those who trust in him. In the presence of Jesus Christ we most often conceive, or are given that faith. We may try to understand how we might have received the faith without Jesus Christ; but the fact remains that when this faith was given Jesus Christ was there.

So it is in history. This faith in the One has had its occasional manifestations elsewhere. But it has happened in history that it has been conceived and received where a people who regarded themselves as chosen suffered the most cruel fate, and where a Son of man who was obedient to death actually suffered death. Here the great reconciliation with the divine enemy has occurred. And since it has occurred, there is no way of getting rid of it. It is in our human history.

We do not say that this faith in the last power is something men ought to have. We say only this, that it is the end of the road of faith, that it is unassailable, and that when men receive it they receive a great gift. We say that it is given, that it has been given, that it is being given, and that when it is received very profound consequences follow.

Third, the consequences of faith in the one, final, and only God are not automatic, for faith involves the whole person, and the gift of faith is not a possession which we can hold in our power. It is something that lives in man and by which man lives. It is not a possession which can be held fast in the form of a creed. It is a basis for all thinking, but though it may be expressed in the form of a thought, it is not itself a thought; it is the reliance of a person on a person. Beginning with that faith life is involved intellectually and morally in a continuous revolution.

This faith opens the way to knowledge. It removes the taboos which surround our intellectual life, making some subjects too holy to be inquired into and some too dangerous for us to venture into. Yet it grants reverence to the mind for which now no being is too low to be worthy of a loving curiosity. All knowledge becomes reverent and all being is open to inquiry. So long as we try to maintain faith in the gods, we fear to examine them too closely lest their relativity in goodness and in power become evident, as when Bible worshipers fear Biblical criticism, or democracy worshipers fear objective examination of democracy. But when man's faith is attached to the One, all relative beings may be received at his hands for nurture and for understanding. Understanding is not automatically given with faith; faith makes possible and demands the labor of the intellect that it may understand.

The moral consequences of this faith is that it makes relative all those values which polytheism makes absolute, and so puts an end to the strife of the gods. But it does not relativize them as self-love does. A new sacredness attaches to the relative goods. Whatever is, is now known to be good, to have value, though its value be still hidden to us. The moral consequences of faith in God is the universal love of all being in him. It is not an automatic consequence. Faith is never so complete that it is not accompanied by self-defensiveness. But this is its requirement: that all beings, not only our friends but also our enemies, not only men but also animals and the inanimate, be met with reverence, for all are friends in the friendship of the one to whom we are reconciled in faith.

So faith in God involves us in a permanent revolution of the mind and of the heart, a continuous life which opens out infinitely into ever new possibilities. It does not, therefore, afford grounds for boasting but only for simple thankfulness. It is a gift of God.

5

FAITH IN ALLAH*

Mohammad Fadhel Jamali

In the name of Allah the Most High

INTRODUCTION

When the Revolution of 14 July 1958 broke out in Iraq I was
one of those who were arrested and tried by the Special High
Military Tribunal presided over by Colonel Fadhel Abbas al-
Mahdawi. I was condemned to death, and to 55 years of
imprisonment, and to pay an indemnity of over ID 100,000.
(£ sterling 100,000; or about 300,000 American dollars.)

I remained for nearly a year and a half under sentence of
death, waiting for execution or relief. I was informed that the
Communists strongly demanded that I should be executed. I
heard, on the other hand, that several highly honoured international personalities took part, intervening with the Leader
Abdul Karim Qassim on my behalf for the death sentence to be
commuted. It was the will of Allah the Sublime that I should
remain alive and not be hanged, for my sentence of death was
commuted after a year and a half, and my freedom was restored
after I had been three years in prison.

Having escaped death I now feel as if I had travelled to

* Reprinted with permission from *Letters on Islam: Written by a Father
in Prison to His Son,* translated from the Arabic by the author (London:
Oxford University Press, 1965), pp. vii–ix, 27–35.

another world and returned anew to the world of the living. That is why I consider it my duty to inform my brethren (all living human beings) about what I felt while close to the gallows for a year and a half.

There is no doubt that the awe of death dominates every living man when he is exposed to peril, for man, like any living organism, strives by nature to survive. But, in my case, besides the feeling of awe for death, I had another feeling, that of comfort and inner peace resulting from the following factors:

1. A deep faith (which became deeper after the Revolution of 1958) in Allah the Sublime, and confidence that His Will will prevail over everything.

No man or group of men can change what Allah has destined. If my time had come to die, then death would have been inevitable. While under sentence of death I felt that the blessing of faith and the spiritual peace which goes with it is the most precious treasure in this life. Poor is the individual who is devoid of faith, for he is no more than a bankrupt man devoid of the greatest blessing which ennobles humanity; for faith gives man the assurance of spiritual survival so that he will not fear death or worry about trivial matters in life.

2. Peace of conscience which, after faith, is a second blessing in this life.

He who is faithful and performs the good, motivated by the love of good, is not afraid of death, and he is happy in this world and the next. No matter how much I examined myself and was thorough in my examination I used to feel that I had a peaceful conscience. I have done no harm intentionally to anybody, and I always intended to do the good. I dedicated my whole life to the service of my country, my nation, and humanity, as circumstances permitted and to the best of my ability. I do not claim that my judgment has always been sound, for perfection belongs to Allah alone, but, whatever I did was motivated by my conscientious convictions. Clear conscience, then, emanating from both the love and fear of Allah, is the second treasure which every man should seek if he desires to have peace and happiness in this life and the next.

3. Friends.

The sympathy and kindness which was conveyed to me from friends and acquaintances made me feel that the judgment of Mahdawi was no more than a sweeping revolutionary judgment not based on right or sound logic. I could have been hanged cruelly and unfairly as many martyrs were hanged or shot to death, but many noble men in the world appreciated my loyalty and innocence and appealed to the Leader for clemency. The truth is that the sympathy of brothers and friends in Iraq and the Arab world and the world at large was the greatest human consolation for me in the dark moments through which I passed. The possession of friends, then, is the third blessing which was mine.

Faith in Allah, clear conscience, and loyal friends, are three blessings which give life meaning and value and provide one with peace and comfort in time of tragedies and calamities. These three blessings make up the message which I carry from the vicinity of the gallows to those who seek a free and happy life, a life which does not terminate with physical death but is renewed hereafter. . . .

.   .   ,   .   .   .   , ...

Baghdad, April 7, 1961

DEAR ABBAS,

After presenting you my good greetings, I pray for your safety, success and guidance.

I forgot to thank you for your feast gift to me in your letter dated March 20. Your recognition of the practical utility of my faith is a good step. As for your freedom to pursue the truth, you are free to do so provided your freedom is associated with purity and sincerity, and these I ask Allah to provide you with.

I have told you that Islam actually is made up of beliefs, worship, social system, and morality. As for the beliefs, they consist of the belief in Allah, the Day of Judgment, the angels, the Book (the Koran), and the prophets. The foundation and the goal is faith in Allah. When that is established, other aspects of faith follow.

A study of faith in Allah requires the answering of two important questions:

1. Does the universe have an Allah?
2. What are his qualities?

I shall attempt to answer the first question very simply:

a. If you see a grand, beautiful house with a flourishing garden you will no doubt reach the conclusion that this house was planned by someone, was built by someone, and is being run by someone. You reach this conclusion without seeing the architect, or the mason, or the owner of the house.

What about this grand universe and what it contains in terms of heavens and earths and what they possess of wonderful creatures with all the precision, order, integration, and harmony between the parts? I do not doubt that this universe has a great architect, a manager, and a mover. He is the Great Creator, the Lord of the Worlds.

b. Astronomy, with all the mathematical laws on which it is built, and all its accurate measurements for the movements of the heavenly bodies, and what the radio-telescope of today is discovering of a continued evolution of the universe of space distances measured in hundreds of millions of light years, and the radiation that is going on in these worlds today and which science is studying, all these make me believe that the universe has an Allah, and that it was not born by chance.

c. The sciences of physics and chemistry and what they achieved in discovering the structure of the atom, the great energy contained in the atom, the composition of the chemical elements and their interaction, electricity and heat harnessed in the service of man, magnetism, the radiation of radium and X-rays and similar phenomena, the mechanical powers of sound and light with their make-up and speed, all these make me believe that these natural phenomena and their laws have a Creator and Designer.

d. Life and its emergence on this earth, its evolution and variations in plants and animals numbering tens of thousands of species, their ways of multiplication and propagation and adaptation to environment prove that there is a design in the universe which makes the parts inter-related and inter-active. A seed falls on the earth, is fed by the rain, it germinates, winds and insects fertilize the flowers. Male and female attract each other and copulate to preserve the species and contribute to their variation. All this has its universal plan and has a Designer.

e. Instincts in animals, from insects, to fish, to birds, give me the strongest proof of the existence of the Great Creator. Who taught the bee to make its cell and fabricate honey and who guided them to the flowers? Who made the ants perform hard labour and who taught them the system of saving? Who taught the spider to weave its web, the eel to travel thousands of miles from southern seas to northern seas to lay its eggs and return to the southern seas. When the eggs hatch who informs the young eels the whereabouts of its species and leads them thereto? Who taught the birds to travel from north to south in winter and vice versa in summer? Who taught the birds to fly and provided them with suitable organs of flight? A small bird enters the mouth of the crocodile and cleans the teeth of the larger animal. The bird is fed and the crocodile is relieved. Who brought about this relationship?

f. Genetics and its study of the chromosomes and the genes which the chromosomes contain and which represent individual heredity traits is certainly a discovery of one of the great secrets of nature. How can I resist belief in Him who puts the secrets of life in the chromosomes?

g. The body of man with its wonderful structure, the brain and its complicated wiring system which presides over the nervous system, the heart and its pulsating muscles which regulate the circulatory system, the digestive system which assimilates food into the body, the muscles and their activity, all make me think of the Great Creator.

h. Human mind and all that it contains in terms of ability to think, invent and originate, its ability to will and design, the noble sentiments it expresses like maternal love and love of country, and love and appreciation of beauty of nature, beauty of melody, beauty of expression, beauty of painting and form, all are made by the Grand Creator.

i. The development of the individual in the womb of his mother who carries him, gives birth to him, provides tenderness and care for him in his infancy, then the individual's youth, old age and death, all are subject to a designed plan. The evolution of man socially and the formation of nations and languages and what man has made in terms of civilizations, inventions, theories, social philosophies and creeds, the disintegration of these civilizations and their replacement by others, all are subject to universal designs. Man is still endeavouring to understand these designs.

j. The universe has a source of goodness, mercy, truth, love and beauty. There is an incentive for man to walk in the path of perfection.

The universe also has a refuge for man in times of difficulties and perplexities, in times of disease, in times of celestial or earthly calamities and tragedies. This refuge provides peace to the hearts of the faithful and supplies hope.

These are some of the proofs which make me believe in the existence of a cosmic purpose and cosmic plan set by the Great Creator of the Universes. He is the Creator of all the universes and he is their Mover, Allah the Lord of the Universes.

I consider faith as the greatest blessing to man. Neither materialism, nor agnosticism, nor scepticism can keep the light of faith shut from my heart, Allah willing.

My advice to you and young Moslems like you is to study more sciences—especially natural sciences. Study them with sincerity and depth for they bring man closer to Allah and acquaint him with the secrets of his greatness.

At last I say, '. . . All praise is due to Allah who guided us to this, and we should not have found the way had it not been that Allah had guided us. . . .' (*The Heights, Al-A'raf,* VII:42.)

My greetings to whoever inquires about me from friends and professors.

Keep safe for your father.

—FADHEL

.   .   .   .

Baghdad, April 14, 1961

DEAR ABBAS,

After presenting you my good greetings, I pray for your safety, success and guidance.

I was delighted to receive your letter dated April 6. Your remark that many in Beirut know me from my student days or later, has some truth in it, for I used to like meeting people and getting acquainted with them, especially during my vacations. As for my love of music, it is old, although my attachment to classical western music started seriously in 1939. I used to listen to it before that, but without serious attention. Congratulations on your swimming and your attendance at dramatic plays, but I hope that your first attention will be directed to your studies.

Concerning your response to my views, I am not writing you expecting an answer to what I write, but merely to acquaint you with my point of view so that you can think for yourself and seek the path of guidance. I'll be delighted to receive the results of your mature ripe thinking, not with the intention of entering polemics with you, but with the intention of profiting from your thoughts. If, however, you wish to comment on my views, I wish you'd postpone that until I have finished presenting them to you.

I mentioned in my last letter very briefly why I believed, in a genuine and pure manner, with Allah's help, in the existence of Allah the Creator.

As for the second question which concerns my belief in Allah the Great, namely, What is his nature, and what are his qualities? I must acknowledge here, with all awe and humility, that I am completely incompetent to deal with this subject adequately, but I will touch on it briefly and simply.

Philosophers and scientists belonging to the various religions have dealt with this subject and attributed to Allah the Great qualities commensurate with their philosophical or religious creeds. The most truthful philosophers, in my view, were those who acknowledged their inability to conceive the nature of Allah, and who were satisfied to say that He is unknowable, like

Herbert Spencer and George Santayana. The human mind can, with the guidance of Allah, believe in the existence of Allah the Great, but it is incapable of defining his essence. The human language falls short in this field and is incapable of providing a definition. However, the Islamic creed, in my view, is the acme of human attainment in its spiritual development. It corrects and modifies the creeds which preceded it, and it interacted in Baghdad and Spain with the last achievements of Greek philosophy.

I shall attempt herewith to present you very briefly with some of my conclusions from my religious upbringing, study and thoughts on Allah the Most High.

1. His existence, glory to Him, is essential.

He exists by himself with nobody having brought him into existence. It is He who brought the universe into existence, and no one brought Him into existence; for, if there were someone who brought Allah into existence, that one himself needed someone before him to bring him into existence and that one needed another one before him, ad infinitum. That is why Allah the Great is the First Creator, and he is designated by the scholars of *Al-Kalam* (*Theology*) as 'whose existence is essential.'

'That is Allah, your Lord, there is no god but He; the Creator of all things, therefore worship Him, and He has charge of all things.' (*The Cattle,* VI: 103.)

2. He is, glory to Him, eternal.

This means that He was ever existing before creation came into being and that He will exist for eternity after creation has disappeared.

'He is the First and the Last, the Evident and the Immanent, and He is cognizant of all things.' (*The Iron,* LVII: 3.)

3. He is, glory to Him, infinite.

He is not bound by time or space. He does not penetrate into things and things do not penetrate Him. No place contains Him and no place is without Him. He is everywhere.

'. . . and He is with you wherever you are. . . .' (*The Iron,* LVII: 4.)

And, in relation to man, He is 'nearer to him than his life-vein.' (*Qaf*, L:16.)

4. He is, glory to Him, One and Sole.

He has no partner and no peer. He did not adopt any she-companion, nor beget a son, for, if there were more than one Allah, they each would be limited, and, if each were limited, each would be contingent, which means that each would have to be created instead of being a Creator. If Allahs were numerous, then either one would have to be above the rest, or they would be equal to each other. Then there would be confusion in the affairs of heavens and earths.

'If there had been in them any gods except Allah, they would both have certainly been in a state of disorder. . . .' (*The Prophets*, XXI:22.)

'Say: He, Allah is One.

Allah, the eternally Besought of all!

He begets not, nor is He begotten:

And none is like Him.' (*The Unity*, CXII:1–4.)

Unity is the most important feature of the Islamic creed, for unity of the Creator is most essential for realizing the unity and interrelation of the natural laws of the universe and the social laws leading to the unity and brotherhood amongst human beings.

5. He has, glory to Him, no like unto Him.

He is not a matter, or a substance. He is not an essence. He is not contingent. He is not composite. He is not divisible. He takes no imaginable shape, for whatever is imagined by man is limited and created by the mind of man, and Allah, glory to Him, is above that. That is why it is said, 'Whatever comes to your mind (about Him), He is purer than that.' (Arabic saying.)

And the Holy Koran says: '. . . there is nothing whatever like unto Him. . .' (*The Counsel*, XLII:11.)

Some of the qualities mentioned in the Koran with regard to Allah may sound materialistic or anthropomorphic, but they are merely in the rhetorical form of simile and metaphor. When we read, 'Allah is the light of the heavens and the earth. . . .'

(*The Light,* XXIV:35) what is meant is not the material light which we know. When we read, 'The Beneficent One is firmly established on the throne. . .' (*Ta Ha,* XX:5), what is meant is not a material throne on which Allah, glory to Him, would sit; for all existence is His throne, and 'sit' here means 'dominate.' And when we read, '. . . the hand of Allah is above their hands. . .' (*Victory,* XLVIII:10), that does not mean that Allah the Great has a physical hand; it means that His power is greater than their power. In short, man is incapable of conceiving with his mind the nature of Allah; blessed is he who sees Him with his heart.

6. He is, glory to Him, Alive, Ever-awake, a Doer of what He wills, capable of doing everything. He is not subject to change, to sickness, to sleep, or to death.

'Allah is He besides whom there is no god, the Ever-living, the Self-subsisting by whom all subsist; slumber does not overtake Him nor sleep. . .' (*The Cow,* II:255.)

'And rely on the Ever-living Who dies not, and celebrate His praise. . .' (*The Distinction,* XXV:58.)

'His is the kingdom of the heavens and the earth; He gives life and causes death; and He has power over all things.' (*The Iron,* LVII:2.)

7. He is, glory to Him, omniscient, aware, and wise.

'He knows what is in the heavens and the earth, and He knows what you hide and what you manifest; and Allah is cognizant of what is in the hearts.' (*Mutual Loss and Gain, At-Taghabun,* LXIV:4.)

Allah, glory to Him, with His knowledge, will and power, created the heavens and earth in accordance with natural laws which he set, and He created in man the ability to strive to discover these laws and to strive to discover their fruits.

8. He is, glory to Him, merciful, forgiving, kind and just.

'. . . and Thou art the most merciful of the merciful ones.' (*The Heights, Al-A'raf,* VII:151.)

'He said: I will ask for you forgiveness from my Lord; surely He is the Forgiving, the Merciful.' (*Joseph,* XII:98.)

'. . . surely Allah is the Ever-benign, the Ever-aware.' (*The Pilgrimage,* XXII:63.)

'So he who has done an atom's weight of good shall see it. And he who has done an atom's weight of evil shall see it.' (*The Earthquake,* XCIX:7,8.)

9. He is, glory to Him, All-knowing, All-seeing.

'. . . surely Allah is Ever-hearing, Ever-seeing.' (*Luqman,* XXXI:28.)

'Vision comprehends Him not, and He comprehends (all) vision; and He is the Ever-benign, the Ever-aware.' (*The Cattle,* VI:103.)

'And it was said that the sound of the creeping of the black ant in a dark night on a smooth rock would not evade His hearing.' (Philosophical Arabic saying.)

10. He is, glory to Him, the Truth.

'This is because Allah is the Truth, and that which they call upon besides Him is the falsehood, and that Allah is the High, the Great.' (*Luqman,* XXXI:30.)

These are some of the qualities of Allah the Great. They should not be understood in their human, natural, limited sense. These traits are not contingent on the nature of Allah the Great, but they are His nature, Praise to Allah, the lord of the Universes.

My greetings to whoever asks about me, and keep safe for your father.

—FADHEL

P.S.—This letter may reach you around your birthday. May you be well, happy and successful throughout the year!

6

TOWARD A CHRISTIAN NATURAL THEOLOGY*

John B. Cobb, Jr.

BY THEOLOGY in the broadest sense I mean any coherent statement about matters of ultimate concern that recognizes that the perspective by which it is governed is received from a community of faith. . . .

Most theological formulations take as their starting point statements that have been sanctioned by the community in which the theologian's perspective has been nurtured, statements such as creeds, confessions, scriptures, or the fully articulated systems of past theologians. But according to my definition of theology, this starting point in earlier verbal formulations is not required. One's work is theology even if one ignores all earlier statements and begins only with the way things appear to him from that perspective which he acknowledges as given to him in some community of shared life and conviction.

Definitions are not true and false but more or less useful. Hence, I shall try to justify this way of defining theology as being helpful in understanding what actually goes on under the name of theology. First, it distinguishes theology from the attempt to study religion objectively—from the point of view of

* Reprinted with permission from *A Christian Natural Theology*, by John B. Cobb, Jr., pp. 252–63. The Westminster Press. Copyright © 1965 W. L. Jenkins. Footnotes omitted.

70

some philosophy, some branch of science such as psychology or sociology, or simply as a historical phenomenon. There are those who wish to erase this distinction and to identify theology with, or as inclusive of, all study of religion. However, the normal use of the term points away from this extension. The psychologist who studies religious experience, perhaps quite unsympathetically, does not think of himself as a theologian. Those who do think of themselves as theologians, on the other hand, do not concern themselves primarily with discussing religion. For the most part they talk about God, man, history, nature, culture, origins, morality, and destiny. The beliefs of the community that has nurtured them may be called religious beliefs, but for the most part they are not beliefs *about* religion. religion.

Second, my definition suggests that theology cannot be distinguished by its subject matter from all other ways of thinking. It is so distinguished from many of them because it limits itself to questions of importance for man's meaningful existence, but it can claim no monopoly on such topics. Philosophers also discuss them as do psychologists and artists. The line of distinction here is very vague, for theology may extend itself into questions of less and less obviously critical importance for man's existence. This may be the result of more or less idle curiosity on the part of the theologian, of the conviction that his authorities are also normative with regard to such matters, or of the belief that all truth is so inter-connected that he must concern himself with everything. However, almost everyone agrees that a classification of plants is less "theological" than a discussion of man's true end, even if the plant classification is based more directly on Biblical texts than is the discussion of human destiny. Furthermore, the work of the theologian can be distinguished from that of some philosophers only to the degree that the theologian acknowledges, and the philosopher resists, dependence on any particular community of ultimate concern for his perspective. Since the theologian may, in fact, be quite independent and original, and since the philosopher may in fact recognize that some of his ideas arose from a culture deeply influenced by a particular community of faith, no sharp demarcation is possible. We can only speak in some instances of the more or less theological or philosophical character of some man's thought. But this may not be a fault of the definition, since it seems to correspond to common practice and to help clarify that practice. Philosophical theology, as theology that makes extensive and explicit use of philosophical categories, merges by imperceptible degrees into a philosophy that denies dependence upon any community of faith as the source of its insights.

Third, my definition makes no reference to God. This is terminologically strange, since "theology" means reasoning about God. But we must be cautious about understanding words in terms of their roots. "Theology" as doctrine of God still exists as a branch of philosophy with this original meaning, such that one may quite properly speak of Aristotle's "theology." Likewise "theology" as doctrine of God exists as a branch of theology as I have defined it. As long as the two meanings are clearly distinguished, the term can and should be used in both senses. The branches of thought and inquiry they designate are overlapping. There can be, and is, extensive discussion of the question as to whether or not God exists that is not theological in the sense of my definition, and there is a great deal of theological work in the sense of my definition that does not treat of God.

One important advantage of defining theology as I have done, rather than as reasoning about God, is that it makes possible the recognition of the close parallel between the efforts to articulate Christian faith and similar efforts in such movements as Buddhism. In some forms of Buddhism there is with respect to God only the doctrine of his non-existence. Thought in the Buddhist community focuses upon man and his possibilities for salvation or illumination. According to my definition, there need be no hesitancy in speaking of Buddhist theology as the thought arising out of the Buddhist community.

A more questionable feature of my definition is that it makes no reference to the holy or sacred. The communities out of which has arisen what we normally call theology are communities in which the power of the sacred is alive. This is just as true of Buddhist atheism as of Christian theism. The reason for omitting all reference to this element is that many leading Christian thinkers today deny that Christianity essentially has anything to do with the sacred. Christianity, they tell us, is not a religion. The correlation of God's act in Christ with Christian faith is absolutely unique and not to be compared with religious experience. Some of these theologians, and others as well, believe that Christian theology is most relevantly compared with doctrines about the meaning of life that are usually called secular, such as communism, fascism, romantic naturalism, and rationalistic humanism. Christianity is held to be worthy of adherence because of its superior illumination of the questions also treated by these movements, which do not think of themselves as religious or as having to do with the sacred. To define theology as having to do with the sacred, or as expressive of a perspective formed in a community that has apprehended the sacred, would be to rule out much of the work being done by men today who regard themselves, and are generally regarded, as theologians.

The price paid for this breadth of definition is that the term "theology" must then be extended beyond the limits of its most common application. This extension is already widely occurring for just this reason, so such extension is not an eccentricity; nevertheless, it reflects only the recent history of the use of the term. According to this definition we must speak also of communist, fascist, naturalist, and humanist theologies. However, a major qualification is preserved in this respect. If the Communist insists that his doctrine is purely scientific, that his view of history is a function of purely objective rational inquiry unaffected by the community of which he is a part, then his work is not theology but bad science. Others who are not persuaded that the Communist thinker in question is really so free from the influence of his community may of course insist that his thought is covertly theological. But I have defined theology in terms of the *recognition* of indebtedness to a community of faith, and this element may be lacking. Other Communists, more honest than this, may recognize their work as theological in the sense of the definition. Naturalists and humanists, on the other hand, may find that the community that mediates and supports their perspective is extremely diffuse. They may claim, more reasonably than most Communists, that they have come to their convictions relatively independently and have only then found some support in a wider community. To whatever extent this is the case, their thought is less theological by my definition. Again, we must recognize that we are dealing with a question of degree and not with a clear either/or.

A final feature of the definition is that it excludes from theology the work of the originator of a community. Of course, it may be his theological reflection as a member of an earlier community that has led to the new insight or religious experience. But insofar as there is real discontinuity, insofar as the apprehension of the holy is direct and not mediated by the community, or insofar as the understanding of the human situation is the result of radically independent reflection, we have to do with a prophet, a seer, or a philosopher, rather than with a theologian. Again, the distinction may be a matter of degree. Many of the originators of communities have understood themselves as recovering authentic traditions from the past rather than as initiating something new. To that degree their thinking is theological. But the *radically* originative element is not. The greatest religious geniuses have *not* been theologians!

Once again let me emphasize that other definitions are perfectly legitimate. They will draw the lines of inclusion and exclusion differently. One may approve or disapprove theology in any one of its meanings. It is better not to begin with an assumption either that theology is good or that it is bad, and then to arrange a definition that supports this contention. One may identify theology with dogmatism in the sense of blind appeal to authority and refusal to be honest about the facts. In such a case he may and should despise it. But then he should also be willing to learn that most of the men who have been thought of as theologians have not done the kind of work implied in his definition. He must be willing to try to find some other term by which he will refer to those whom others call theologians. Or one may identify theology as speaking in obedience to the Word of God. But then he must recognize that only those who believe that there is a "Word of God" can believe that there is a theology. To those on the outside, the great majority of the human race, what he calls theology will appear at best the confession of the faith of one community among others. He will also require some other term to describe what is done in other communities where the "Word of God" is not obeyed.

The definition of theology here employed is relatively neutral on the question of its virtue or evil. Those who believe that the only fruitful thinking is that which attempts strenuously to clear the slate of all received opinion and to attain to methods that can be approved and accepted by men of all cultures, will disapprove of the continuance of a mode of thought that recognizes its dependence upon the particularities of one community. On the other hand, those who believe that there are questions of greatest importance for human existence that are not amenable to the kind of inquiry we associate with the natural sciences, will be more sympathetic toward theology.

My own view is that theology as here defined has peculiar possibilities for combining importance and honesty. Practitioners of disciplines that pride themselves on their objectivity and neutrality sometimes make pronouncements on matters of ultimate human concern, but when they do so they invariably introduce assumptions not warranted by their purely empirical or purely rational methods. Usually there is a lack of reflective awareness of these assumptions and their sources. The theologian, on the other hand, confesses the special character of the perspective he shares and is therefore more likely to be critically reflective about his assumptions and about the kind of justification he can claim for them. If in the effort to avoid all unprovable assumptions one limits his sphere of reflection to narrower and narrower areas, one fails to deal relevantly with the issues of greatest importance for mankind, leaving them to be settled by appeals to the emotions. The theologian insists that critical reflection must be brought to bear in these areas as well as in the rigorously factual ones.

In the light of my definition of theology, we can now consider what *natural* theology may be. Some definitions of natural theology put it altogether outside the scope of theology as I have defined it. This would be highly confusing, since I intend my definition of theology to be inclusive. However, we should consider such a definition briefly. Natural theology is often identified with that of theological importance which can be known independently of all that is special to a particular community. In other words, natural theology, from this point of view, is all that can be known relative to matters of ultimate human concern by reason alone, conceiving reason in this case as a universal human power. This definition is, of course, possible, and it has substantial continuity with traditional usage. It is largely in this sense that Protestant theologians have rejected natural theology. A consideration of the reasons for this rejection will be instructive.

In principle, natural theology has been rejected on the ground that it is arrogant and self-deceptive. It is argued that reason alone is not able to arrive at any truth about such ultimate questions. When it pretends to do so it covertly introduces elements that are by no means a part of man's universal rational equipment. Every conviction on matters of ultimate concern is determined by factors peculiar to an historically-formed community or to the private experience of some individual. Since no doctrine of theological importance can claim the sanction of universal, neutral, objective, impartial reason, what is called natural theology can only be the expression of one faith or another. If Christian thinkers accept the authority of a natural theology, they are accepting something alien and necessarily opposed to their own truth, which is given them in the Christian community.

The last point leads to a consideration of the substantive or material reason for the rejection of natural theology. The philosophical doctrines traditionally accepted by the church on the basis of the authority of philosophical reason have, in fact, been in serious tension with the ways of thinking about God that grew out of the Old and New Testaments and the liturgy of the church. The philosophers' God was impassible and immutable whereas the Biblical God was deeply involved with his creation and even with its suffering. Brilliant attempts at synthesis have been made, but the tensions remain.

My view is that it is unfortunate that natural theology has been identified substantively with particular philosophic doctrines. There is no principle inherent in reason that demands that philosophy will always conclude that God is impassible and immutable and hence, unaffected by and uninvolved in the affairs of human history. Philosophers may reach quite different conclusions, some of which do not introduce these particular tensions into the relation between philosophy and Christian theology. The modern theological discussion of natural theology has been seriously clouded by the failure to distinguish the formal question from the substantive one.

On the formal question, however, I agree with the rejection of natural theology as defined above. The individual philosopher may certainly attempt to set aside the influence of his community and his own special experiences and to think with total objectivity in obedience to the evidence available to all men. This is a legitimate and worthy endeavor. But the student of the history of philosophy cannot regard it as a successful one. It is notorious that the ineradicable ideas left in Descartes' mind after he had doubted everything were products of the philosophical and theological work, or more broadly of the cultural matrix, that had formed his mind. There is nothing shameful in this. Descartes' work was exceedingly fruitful. Nevertheless, no one today can regard it as the product of a perfectly neutral and universal human rationality. If one should agree with him, he should recognize that he does so decisively because his fundamental experience corresponds to that of Descartes. He cannot reasonably hope that all equally reflective men will come to Descartes' conclusions.

To put the matter in another way, it is generally recognized today that philosophy has a history. For many centuries each philosopher was able to suppose that his own work climaxed philosophy and reached final indubitable truth. But such an attitude today would appear naïve if the great questions of traditional philosophy are being discussed. Insofar as philosophers now attempt to reach final conclusions, they characteristically abandon the traditional questions of philosophy and limit themselves to much more specialized ones. In phenomenology, symbolic logic, and the analysis of the meaning of language, attempts are still being made to reach determinate conclusions not subject to further revision. These attempts are highly problematic, and in any case questions of ultimate concern cannot be treated in this way. If natural theology means the product of an unhistorical reason, we must reply that there is no such thing.

However, responsible thinking about questions of ultimate human importance continues to go on outside the community of faith. Furthermore, many of the members of the community of faith who engage in such thinking consciously or unconsciously turn away from the convictions nurtured in them by the community while they pursue this thinking. It is extremely unfortunate that the partly legitimate rejection of natural theology has led much of Protestant theology to fail to come effectively to grips with this kind of responsible thinking. Some theologians have idealized a purity of theological work that would make it unaffected by this general human reflection on the human situation. They have attempted so to define theology that nothing that can be known outside the community is relevant to its truth or falsehood, adequacy or inadequacy. I am convinced that this approach has failed.

In almost all cases, the theologian continues to make assumptions or affirmations that are legitimately subject to investigation from other points of view. For example, he assumes that history and nature can be clearly distinguished, or that men can meaningfully be spoken of as free. He may insist that he knows these things on the basis of revelation, but he must then recognize that he is claiming, on the basis of revelation, the right to make affirmations that can be disputed by responsibly reflective persons. If he denies that science can speak on these matters, he thereby involves himself in a particular understanding of science that, in its turn, is subject to discussion in contexts other than theology. He must either become more and more unreasonably dogmatic, affirming that on all these questions he has answers given him by his tradition that are not subject to further adjudication, or else he must finally acknowledge that his theological work does rest upon presuppositions that are subject to evaluation in the context of general reflection. In the latter case he must acknowledge the role of something like natural theology in his work. I believe that this is indispensable if integrity is to be maintained and esotericism is to be avoided.

The problem, then, is how the theologian should reach his conclusions on those broader questions of general reflection presupposed in his work. The hostility toward natural theology has led to a widespread refusal to take this question with full seriousness. Theologians are likely to accept rather uncritically some idea or principle that appears to them established in the secular world. For example, a theologian may assume that modern knowledge leads us to conceive the universe as a nexus of cause and effect such that total determinism prevails in nature. Conversely, he may seize the scientific principle of indeterminacy as justifying the doctrine of human freedom. Or he may point to the dominant mood of contemporary philosophy as justifying a complete disregard of traditional philosophy. My contention is that most of this is highly irresponsible. What the theologian thus chooses functions for him as a natural theology, but it is rarely subjected to the close scrutiny that such a theology should receive. It suffers from all the evils of the natural theologies of the past and lacks most of their virtues. It is just as much a product of a special point of view, but it is less thoroughly criticized. In many cases it is profoundly alien to the historic Christian faith, and yet it is accepted as unexceptionably authoritative.

If there were a consensus of responsible reflection, then the adoption of that consensus as the vehicle for expression of Christian faith might be necessary. But there is no such consensus that can be taken over and adopted by the Christian theologian. Hence, if natural theology is necessary, the theologian has two choices. He may create his own, or he may adopt and adapt some existing philosophy.

PART III

THE POWERS
THAT MAY CONFLICT

By whose authority? The question of where authority ought to lie extends into all human life: the home, the school, the business world, the political domain. As H. Richard Niebuhr suggests in an earlier selection, many a man labors hard to establish himself as final authority for his life. To be sure, any and every authority can always be questioned. But such questioning necessarily presupposes another authority as the basis of judgment. That human beings have no way to live without authority in some form reveals as untenable the notion that the opposite of authority is the freedom to act totally without constraint.

To affirm that one's final authority is God does not really settle anything. The issue remains of *how* and *where* divine authority is manifest. In the greater part of the materials contained in this section the question of biblical authority is at the fore, not because that question is the only way of coming to grips with the matter of theological authority but simply because of the dominant persuasion in Western theology that Scripture is a peculiar instrument, or at least a primary record, of divine revelation. (In the Christian church the canon of Scripture is comprised of a minimum of sixty-six books; in Judaism, the Bible—the "Old Testament" in Christian terminology—is customarily spoken of as the Tanak.)

Inevitably, a man's community of faith and his theological convictions will influence the way he interprets a sacred canon. *Bernhard W. Anderson* contends below that God's speaking "to us by a Son" strikes "the keynote of the Bible," and he discerns within this conviction the ground for the assigning by the Christian church of the "status of sacred scripture" to the "Old Testament" as well as the "New Testament." Such "finding" of Jesus Christ in the so-called Old Testament is of course rejected by spokesmen for Judaism (and even by some Christian scholars).

Agreements and disagreements within Judaism concerning the role of Torah—the "traditionalist" view versus the "modernist" view, as explained by *Milton Steinberg*—have parallels in Protestant Christianity, as is made evident in the sharply divergent expositions by *Harold Lindsell* and Anderson. This sort of controversy has not been as prevalent in other major branches of Christianity, largely because the issue of scriptural authority is approached there from within a general perspective of ecclesiastical-institutional authority and the authority of "tradition." This broader frame of reference is exemplified in the analysis by *Thomas Corbishley* of the Roman Catholic point of view and the one by *Timothy Ware* of the Orthodox Christian position.

Here are some salient questions: If God is Lord of all creation and time, how is it possible to adjudge that some happenings but not others represent authoritative, divine revelation? Are there independent ways of knowing when God is remaining hidden and when he is revealing himself or his will? What does it mean to assert that God "speaks" to men? Does not the assertion seem to impair the divine dignity? Or may it be instead a tribute to the divine power and magnanimity? Even if one agrees that man's "supernaturalization" (Corbishley) requires institutional mediation, must he also agree that there is only one institution which has been divinely ordained to implement this function? Is it coherent to speak, as Lindsell does, of "the Word of God incarnate, Jesus Christ, and the Word of God written, the Holy Scriptures"? Can these two "Words" coexist as ultimate authorities? What additional sources and norms of divine authority may be contended for, beyond those advocated in the present section?

7

TORAH*

Milton Steinberg

JUDAISM is a *book* religion, deriving from, centering about, and making explicit the contents of a sacred document.

THE BOOK AS BOOK

. . . In form the Torah is a narrative, an account of events from the creation of the world to the death of Moses. Between these limits it describes the origins of the nations of the earth and, with especial attention, the beginnings of the people of Israel, the lives of the Patriarchs, the enslavement of the Jews in Egypt, their deliverance and the revelations of God's will which came to them in the wilderness of Sinai.

But the Torah is much more than a narrative.

Among other things it sets forth, if not systematically at least most vividly, a doctrine concerning a one and universal God: the Creator of all things, the Lawgiver, Liberator, and Redeemer of men.

It outlines an ethic of justice and loving-kindness. Sometimes these moral principles flare into white incandescence as in the Decalogue or the Holiness Code of Leviticus XIX. More generally they are assumed and implied. In one guise or another, not a line in the text is devoid of them.

* From *Basic Judaism*, pp. 19–30, copyright © 1947 by Milton Steinberg. Reprinted with the permission of Harcourt, Brace & Co.

It prescribes rituals, holy days, and festive seasons, together with pertinent forms of worship and observance.

It promulgates a code of law, ecclesiastical, civil, and criminal.

It ordains institutions, religious, domestic, social, philanthropic, and political.

It propounds a conception of the Jewish people as a "kingdom of priests and a holy nation," through whom all the families of the earth are to be blessed.

Beyond all these, it constitutes a monumental literary achievement. It was a superb stylist who wrote the thundering first chapter of Genesis. An uncannily expert story-teller unwound the poignant, haunting story of Joseph. And no mere talented rhetorician composed the farewell orations of Moses or conjured up the picture of the dying prophet seeing the promised land from afar.

Such is the Torah-Book.

To different people it means different things.

To the perceptive unbeliever it represents at the least a literary masterpiece and the earliest clear formulation of the ethic of justice and compassion.

To the religious man of any Western communion, this is the book of the generations of his beliefs, the seed from which have sprung the theological and moral premises by which he lives.

But to the professing Jew, the Torah-Book is all these and infinitely more. It is not only a source of what he is as a Jew and religious person, it is much of the substance as well.

THE TORAH-TRADITION

Torah as a specific book is Torah only in its most restricted sense.

There are broader connotations to the concept, and other significances still more comprehensive than these. In their aggregate and latitude they constitute a whole world of ideas and values.

Into this universe of discourse, the quickest entrance is by way of a bit of etymology, that of the word "Torah" itself.

Torah is a Hebrew noun derived from the verb which means "to guide" or "to teach." Quite simply and literally therefore it stands for "guidance" or "teaching" or, to use a word of Latin origin, "doctrine."

Once Torah is so rendered, its broader connotations virtually spell themselves out. Obviously the Teaching did not cease with Moses or the books ascribed to him. The prophets carried it on, and so did the poets and sages who composed Psalms, Proverbs, and Job. Hence, the latter books of Scripture, while not Torah in letter, are very much Torah in spirit.

But so, too, are the writings of the classical rabbinic age (from the third century before the Common Era to the fifth century after). In these works, commonly described as Talmudic, the teaching was consolidated, expounded, and advanced.

But commentators on the Bible and rabbinic literature, the moralists and philosophers of all times down to our own—they have unfolded the Teaching still further.

So in the end, under this wide envisagement, Torah becomes everything which has its roots in the Torah-Book, which is consistent with its outlook, which draws forth its implications, and which realizes its potentialities.

Torah in sum is all the vastness and variety of the Jewish Tradition.

To Jews throughout history, Torah, both the Book and the Tradition, has been incalculably precious and of spiritual import beyond all comparison.

Now, obviously, the incalculable cannot be calculated, nor the incomparable compared. Any effort then at describing the full meaning of Torah for committed Jews is foredoomed to failure. Yet the attempt must be ventured. For without at least some notion of the dynamic centrality of this concept among Jewish beliefs and values one does not so much as begin to comprehend them.

Let the great men of Torah then speak concerning it, those who, being closest to it and knowing it best, can be most articulate about it. And from their words we shall be able to form some estimates of its impact on the individual and the group.

To the Book of Deuteronomy Torah is the life and good which is set before man as an alternative to death and evil; at the same time it is Israel's wisdom and understanding in the eyes of the nations.

To the Prophet it is the water for which all men thirst, the bread for which they starve—which is yet dispensed without silver or price.

To the Psalmist it is the light in which he sees light, or alternatively the spiritual sustenance whose taste is sweeter than honey and the drippings of the honeycomb.

To a Rabbi of ancient days it is something to be delved into further and further, since all things are in it; something over which a man may grow gray and old, never stirring from its contemplation, knowing that he can have no better pursuit or rule.

To medieval Jews in their Ghettos it is, by the testimony of a folk-song, a treasure better than all worldly goods.

To the modern Hebrew poet, Bialik, it is a great flame kindled on high altars in olden days.

And to all generations of Jews from Isaiah on it is the word of the Lord destined in the end to regenerate man and society.

TORAH—TRADITIONALIST VIEW

Torah, the bond uniting religious Jews, is also the theme of their most fundamental disagreement, the continental divide, as it were, at which traditionalist and modernist begin their divergence.

The basic distinction between the two viewpoints is this: Traditionalists believe the whole Torah to be God-revealed, therefore unimpeachably true and good throughout.

Modernists hold that truth and goodness are to be found in the Torah, and that to the extent of their presence it is God-inspired.

To traditionalists the entire Torah-Book, every word, every letter, was imparted by God either directly to the whole people of Israel at Mount Sinai or indirectly through Moses. The fact of revelation is decisive. It is a guarantee of absolute validity, intellectual and moral.

But revelation, according to the traditionalists, does not exhaust itself in the Torah-Book. It suffuses the writings of the prophets after Moses, overflows into the rest of Scripture, thence into classical Talmudic literature; thence again, though in diminishing degree, into later rabbinic writings. In other words, the mainstream of the Tradition everywhere possesses something of the authority of the Torah-Book—much in the same fashion as inferences in logic, carry over, if only they be drawn accurately, the authority and certainty of the premises from which they are drawn. Or to put the point as does the Talmud itself: "Whatsoever any earnest scholar will innovate in the future, lo this was already spoken at Sinai."

From this postulate, that the Torah-Tradition like the Torah-Book is of divine inspiration (though not so absolutely), significant conclusions follow.

One is that Judaism cannot be susceptible to consequential change.

After all, God is not man. When he speaks it is fully and finally, in freedom from the human necessity of correcting Himself, editing an utterance, or pinning on afterthoughts. Judaism was complete and perfect at Sinai.

As for the historical growth through which the Tradition seems to have passed, this is basically illusion. The prophets, sages, and rabbis neither modified it in essence nor added aught to its substance. All they did was to recapitulate it in fresh idioms or to give it timely applications. A truth, however, is not altered—and certainly not enlarged—by being couched in one phraseology rather than another, just as a distance is neither extended nor contracted when it is translated from feet into inches. So, under all the restatements, Judaism has persisted as one and the same from Moses to our day.

Of divine authorship, Judaism cannot be subject to amendment by man. What mortal mind dare venture improvements on what God wrought at Sinai? What new truth or novel circumstance can possibly arise, unforeseen by Providence, to necessitate putting patches on revelation.

Does this mean that by traditionalist lights Judaism is altogether unbending and eternally immutable? Not quite. Some measure of flexibility inheres in it. It is always susceptible to reinterpretation; it may even be suspended in some of its provisions should a crisis arise to require so drastic a step. Both powers, to construe and to take emergency measures, belong to that "earnest scholar," concerning whom we have just quoted the Talmud. What is more, they are his and his colleagues' not by supererogation but by explicit statement of the Torah, which ordains: "If there arise a matter too hard for thee in judgment . . . thou shalt come unto the priests the Levites and unto the judge that shall be in those days . . . and thou shalt observe to do according to all that they shall teach thee."

Besides, at least some portion of doctrine and practice commonly accepted in Judaism represents no more than current but disputable interpretation of Torah, or established custom, or even private preference.

Judaism then is neither altogether rigid nor eternally unchanging. But the free play allowed by reinterpretation is not overly extensive and the right to issue emergency decrees has always been used sparingly. Constancy, then, despite changing times and circumstances, is a major characteristic of Torah in the view of the traditionalist and under his hands.

Last of all, to traditionalism the Torah is the first, last, and always reliable test of the goodness or truth of anything. Any proposition which contravenes the Tradition must be false, no matter how impressive the argument marshaled in its support. Any moral principle that is out of harmony with the Teaching must be of an imperfect rule, though it give every appearance of being wise and expedient.

This is not to say that reason and experience are worthless, or that philosophy, science, and naturalistic morality discharge no useful functions. On the contrary they occupy a large place in man's scheme and God's.

They are indispensable first of all in that they help to illuminate the dark places of Torah, to resolve its occasional seeming self-contradictions. Too, they supply the technical skills necessary for its practical application. Finally they equip men with a wide variety of insights and values which are fully legitimate and desirable, for all that they are (strictly speaking) irrelevant to Torah.

The traditionalist then bids philosophers and scientists a sincere *Godspeed* as they set forth to their business. Yet he is confident of the conclusions at which they will arrive if only they think long enough and hard enough, at least those of their conclusions which bear on virtue asd happiness. Are not those conclusions written out for him in the Torah?

His, then, is the assurance of one who knows the answer to a riddle while others are struggling to work it out; who has read the last act of a drama and is therefore assured, even in its tensest moments, of a happy ending.

The ancient rabbis were wont to speak of some persons as "acquiring eternity in one instant." So they characterized those who vindicate their entire lives in one heroic decision. Intellectually speaking, the Jewish traditionalist is in such a case.

He makes a single but tremendous act of faith; he posits a lone but gigantic postulate. He affirms that the Tradition is divinely inspired throughout. Thereafter only one truth is possible for him; only one way is open on which he can walk.

TORAH—MODERNIST VIEW

The modernist approaches Torah from diametrically the opposite direction.

To him the first criterion of the truth of a proposition or of the validity of a principle is not its conformity with the Tradition but its consonance with reason and experience. Far from judging all things by the standard of Torah, he tests Torah against the standards by which he judges everything else. And only in so far as Torah passes muster does he accept it as authoritative.

This momentous distinction between modernist and traditionalist stems from an even more basic difference: over the susceptibility of Judaism to fundamental change.

The modernist has been persuaded by the biological and social sciences that the law of change is universal and that Judaism is no exception to it; that it is no fixed and constant entity as the traditionalist holds but the end product of a long and still continuing growth.

Even the Torah-Book, according to the modernist, did not come into being all at one time, as the work of the single hand of Moses. To the contrary it achieved its familiar shape and dimensions only as the result of an evolutionary process. The typical modernist in other words follows higher criticism in the conclusion that the Torah text as we now have it is a composite of several documents done by diverse authors and sewn into unity by some unknown editor or editors.

These documents furthermore are not equally mature. Some, generally the earliest, are heavily weighted with the folk-lore of the ancient Jews, their rudimentary science and sometimes naïve notions of God and morality. Others are consistently on the highest plane.

To be sure, even the most rudimentary passages often set forth or imply spiritual verities of the first magnitude. The universe may not have been created in six days as is asserted by the Torah, but in the eyes of religious people it remains the work of Spirit. Man may not have come into being after the fashion portrayed in Genesis, but that he is God's handiwork abides a point of faith. Perhaps there never was a universal flood, at least not in man's time or beyond the flat-lands of Mesopotamia, but who in the twentieth century will deny that by their collective sins men can precipitate catastrophes from which only righteousness can deliver them?

What is important then about the Torah-Book is not that it is all factual but that even where it is not it is still meaningful. What is even more important is that though it contains much of the primitive, it contains also the full-ripened insights which grew from these beginnings.

The modernist therefore is an eclectic about the Torah, regarding some passages with greater reverence than others and proving all alike on the double touchstone of reason and experience.

What goes for the Torah-Book applies even more closely to the rest of Scripture and to the Tradition in its later phases. The modernist accepts these not because he assumes in advance that they are beyond the peradventure of doubt and criticism; but because, striving so steadily after truth and goodness, they achieve them so often and in such extraordinary degree.

This is the Tradition as the modernist sees it: the creation not of a miraculous and supernatural event but of a natural unfolding, the record left by a particular people of its pilgrimage out of darkness to clarity and compassion.

But if the Tradition be not self-validating, if it must be approved by reason and experience, what is its authority for the modernist? Why does he not take recourse to reason and experience directly?

Part of the answer is undoubtedly the reverence for the Tradition inculcated in childhood, ancestral pieties, sentiment, habit, group loyalties. The core of it, however, is another, deeper consideration.

To the modernist the Tradition has authority not because it obviates an appeal to naturalistic sources but because it gives so full a report of what men found out when they made just such an appeal, when they applied their heads and hearts to the deepest questions of human existence. The Tradition preserves the speculations of multitudes of rationalists, the accounts of countless mystics, the conclusions of innumerable persons plumbing their own souls, the balance sheets of lives beyond calculation, and a protracted experience with the ideas of faith as to their long-range tenability and their power to humanize the heart. Not something different from reason and experience but a titanic compendium of their findings, this is the Tradition.

"But where," one may ask, "is God in this concept?"

"Where," the modernist responds, "is He not? Is not God the power behind all human aspiration and attainment, the impulse driving men toward the good, the true, and the beautiful? Who other than He stirred the remotest generations of Israel with a nameless discontent? Who impelled all the fumbling achievements of this people through the centuries? Who possessed the souls of its prophets? Who made judicious the hearts of its sages? Who rendered intransigent the spirits of its martyrs? Who, save One?"

Torah remains a revelation in the eyes of the modernist; but in general, not in detail, in its high climax rather than its lower reaches, in its directions though not necessarily in each step.

Manifestly, an abyss separates the modernist from the traditionalist in their respective views of Torah.

But an abyss, no matter how broad and deep, is a cleft in the earth's surface. The walls to either side will be of similar composition; they will be joined by a common ground below and may be even further united by a bridge from above.

So, though the traditionalist and the modernist differ over Torah, both revere it, each after his own understanding and fashion; both look to it for guidance and inspiration.

And both stand on the same ground, are made of the same stuff, and surmount their disagreements in arches of shared purpose.

8

THE FUNCTION OF
THE ROMAN CATHOLIC CHURCH*

Thomas Corbishley, S.J.

THE Roman Catholic Church exists to teach men a way of life which is only incidentally related to the social or political condition of this or that epoch, and to provide men with the means to achieve a fulfilment which cannot effectively be realised in any historical situation. In other words her chief concern is with the transcendental, supernatural aspect of human experience. To understand this claim, it will be necessary to appreciate a little more exactly the meaning of the term 'supernatural.' In ordinary language, it is often used vaguely for extraordinary phenomena, psychic manifestations and the like. In Catholic theological language it has a precise technical sense, being used to specify those characteristics or activities which are not essentially related to human nature in itself. Man, as man, possesses certain 'natural' characteristics—physical, psychological, rational. He fits into the order of Nature about him. Physically, he is subject to the activities of natural forces, the law of gravity, the effects of temperature, chemical action. The sciences of biology and psychology can study and predict his reactions to appropriate stimuli. Even the activities of intellect

* Reprinted with permission from *Roman Catholicism*, by Thomas Corbishley, S.J. (London: Hutchinson's University Library, 1950), pp. 11–17.

and will fall within the sphere of philosophical analysis and explanation. Yet, inexhaustible as that study is, so that not all the findings of scientist, psychologist, poet and metaphysician succeed in stating the whole truth about "the glory, jest and riddle of the world," the Catholic believes that there is a whole world of reality to which man has been introduced, which is beyond discovery by human thought and human imagination— because it is 'super-natural'. . . .

When we turn to discuss the meaning of the term 'super-natural,' we have to try to see it in the same sort of way. The Catholic holds that there is a higher kind of vital principle, a transcendent entelechy, which renders the complicated being we call man capable of activities which are beyond his merely human capacities. As sensation and emotion are beyond the capacity of the daisy, as mathematics and musical composition, moral judgment and free choice, are outside the ken of the elephant, so is super-natural living beyond the unaided capacity of mankind. Briefly, the Catholic holds that God has chosen to elevate man to some sort of share in His own experience. And the Church claims that it is through her that God chooses to propagate this divine life.

The mere statement of such a claim must seem a piece of intolerable arrogance. Nor is the Catholic himself unaware of the stupendous assertions it involves. But there seems no other way of explaining the texts in the New Testament upon which that claim is based. "I have come so that they may have life, and have it more abundantly." (John X.10.) "You have only to live on in me and I will live on in you. . . . If a man lives on in me and I in him, then he will yield abundant fruit. . . . The task I have appointed to you is to go out and bear fruit, fruit which will endure. . . ." (John XV.3–16.) "Thou hast sent me into the world on thy errand, and I have sent them into the world on my errand." (John XVII.18.) "I pray for those who are to find faith in me through their word." (John XVII.20.) "You therefore must go out, making disciples of all nations . . . teaching them to observe all the commandments which I have given you." (Matt. XXVIII.19–20.)

The basis of this whole doctrine of the propagation of the divine life in the world is that truth which is central to the whole Christian tradition, the doctrine of the Incarnation. This is no place to discuss the content of that truth, which Catholic and many non-Catholic Christians alike share; but it is relevant to our task to point out that the Catholic Church has, from the first, insisted on an acceptance of the truth in its fullest and most complete form. She holds, in the first place, that, at a certain moment in history, a man was born who was, besides being wholly human, not less really divine, divine in the full sense of the word: he was God. This act by which God chose to share the human experience of the creatures he had created was a further manifestation of that incomprehensible and infinite love which not only "moves the sun and moon and other stars" but must be invoked as the only feasible explanation of God's dealings with the world. "God," in the favourite aphorism of the Greek Fathers "became man in order that men might become gods." The reality of our supernaturalisation is proportionate to the truth of God's Incarnation. But how was this process of supernaturalisation to be achieved? Clearly, so the Catholic holds, if all men born into the world in time are to be enabled to draw near to the source of life, there must be some visible, recognizable system or institution which will make this possible. Is there such an institution and, if so, where is it to be found?

Since practically all that we know about Jesus Christ is to be derived ultimately from the New Testament records, we naturally turn to them for our knowledge of the plan and purpose of the Incarnational system. The facts about Christ's life, in broad outline, are not seriously in dispute. The tendentious and unscientific speculations of nineteenth century 'criticism' are being rapidly discredited, and as the dust of controversy settles, the traditional outlines of Christ's story are seen again with even greater clarity. And the solid factual basis of the events of his life and of the incidents outlined in the Acts of the Apostles is borne out by all that we know of contemporary political and social history. It is certain that, after his death, a chain of interconnected groups of men and women came into being in the

Levant and beyond, basing the principles of their conduct on belief in the existence of Jesus Christ and in the reality of his continuing power. That power meant for them not merely inspiration and instruction, but literal invigoration. He continued his own individual existence, it was true. But, in some profoundly actual sense, they lived by his life: he lived on in them. Plato, Aristotle, Zeno and the rest had established schools, in which their doctrine was handed on. But in none of these was it claimed that the disciples derived actual vitality, literally from the principle of life that had been present in the founder. The Apostles claimed, indeed, to teach what Christ had taught; but far more than that, they claimed—and their claim was accepted—that through their hands came an actual power, a force, by which all believers were enabled to live transformed lives.

As time went on, these inter-connected groups, loosely united at first in the possession of a common faith and a common way of life, developed a stronger organic unity. The 'churches' had become the 'Catholic Church.' From the beginning, there had been insistence on unity—the unity that comes from mutual love, the unity that comes from faith in a body of doctrine, the unity that comes from the possession of a common code of moral practice. Doubtless from Judaism was derived the notion of being a 'peculiar people,' and the early hostility both of non-Christian Jew and of pagan would help to bind Christians together. But the unity of the Church was something from within, fostered by men who had known the Master, who were filled at once with passionate devotion to his person and his ideals and with a consuming hatred for all that might appear to be treachery to the truth as taught by him and to the mission which he had laid upon them.

It was then from this personal knowledge and love that the source of that early unity springs. "Where Christ is, there is the Church Catholic," declared Ignatius of Antioch at the very dawn of the second century A.D. Yet for all that from the earliest times there had also been disloyalties and divisions. St. Paul could write: "Parties there must needs be among you, so that those who are true metal may be distinguished from the rest." (I Cor. XI.19.) From the very beginning, therefore, the Christian Church was concerned about the problem of maintaining unity of belief. "Has Christ been divided up?" (I Cor. I.13.) Since Christ and his truth was the sole burden of the Gospel message, it was intolerable, impossible, that a mere medley of contradictions should be all that survived of Christ's teaching in a Church that believed itself to be the vehicle and organ of his continuing life. Hence the story of St. John, fleeing in horror from the baths where the heretic Cerinthus was present. Hence the growing systematisation and organisation, beginning with the local establishments, churches with their elders, ordained by the Apostles themselves, to hand on the new life and to safeguard the faith and teaching of Christ's own commissioned teachers. "It is for thee, Timothy, to keep safe what has been entrusted to thee, avoiding these new, intruding forms of speech . . . there are those who profess them, and in professing them have shot wide of the mark which faith sets us." (I Tim. VI.20–21.)

To the Catholic, then, it seems entirely natural to suppose that such unity could not be preserved without a teaching authority, clearly recognized and freely acknowledged. Nor, in the circumstances of the time, when all roads led to and from Rome, could any other centre for what was professedly a universal religion be more natural than the capital of the world Empire. The centre of the Christian Church was early established in Rome—how early is a matter for historians to debate—and there it has remained. That is why 'Roman' is not normally employed by Roman Catholics amongst themselves. For them it is either misleading or tautologous: misleading if it implies that there can be more than one centre of truth; if not, tautologous.

Here, of course, we are at the heart of controversy, but for our purposes, it is unnecessary to pursue the subject. Suffice it to say that the Roman Catholic is convinced that, in his insistence on the need for a centre of doctrinal authority, he is not only being faithful to the apostolic tradition but is in the line of full historical development. Believing as he does that a clear primacy was conferred on Peter in the famous words of Christ: "Upon this rock I will build my Church" (Matt. XVI.18), he finds in Gospels and Acts clear evidence that Peter's pre-eminence was accepted by his fellow Apostles, whilst the fragmentary evidence of such writings as have survived is only explicable on the supposition that by the end of the first century A.D. some special dignity attached to the Church established at Rome. Certainly in the course of the second century, doctrinal and other disputes began to be referred to the bishop of the Roman Church. The witness of Clement of Rome and Ignatius of Antioch, of Hermes and Hegesippus, of Irenaeus and Tertullian, points in the same direction. Admittedly, the evidence is scanty and, in detail, inconclusive. But the most natural explanation of such indications as we find is to be found in the view that, increasingly, the Church of Christ looked towards Rome for guidance and instruction.

It might seem to the reader that we have moved far from a discussion of the function of Roman Catholicism, with which this chapter is allegedly dealing. Yet it will be seen that a discussion of function necessarily leads on to some consideration of the nature of the functioning organism. At any rate, it is to be hoped that nothing which has been said so far will obscure the fundamental notion that what the Church exists for is the supernatural fulfilment of the human individual, that is to say, she exists to enable man to become a partaker of that divine life which, far beyond his unaided capacity, is yet offered to him by the unimaginable goodness of God. In a word, the function of the Church is the sanctification of mankind. Again, it is necessary to recall that this process of 'sanctification' is not to be conceived of in terms of some purely human self-betterment or vague moral uplift. Sanctification, as the Catholic Church conceives it, is an effect, not of human effort, though it requires human co-operation, but of divine action. But that divine action is mediated by the divinely-ordained institution, the Church of Christ, the Church founded by Christ, developed by Christ through the activities of his Apostles, the Church which remains true to itself only in so far as it remains true to Christ and his teaching, propagated by his Apostles, the Church which exists in order that all men may have the opportunity and the means to receive of the fullness of life which Christ came on earth to bring.

All this is summed up for the Roman Catholic in the statement that the true Church is One—or else Christ is 'divided up'; she is Holy—or else she has failed in her purpose; she is Catholic, in other words addressing herself to all men whatsoever—or else she has failed to listen to the command of her Founder; she is Apostolic, since it was through the teaching and activity of the Apostles that, in the course of history, she developed into a widespread visible institution. . . .

. . . For the present . . . we must content ourselves with the statement that the Roman Catholic Church claims to be the divinely-appointed means for the continuation in time of the work of Redemption, which is the chief work of the Incarnate Word.

9

TRADITION IN
THE ORTHODOX CHURCH*

Timothy Ware

ORTHODOX history is marked outwardly by a series of sudden breaks: the capture of Alexandria, Antioch, and Jerusalem
by Arab Mohammedans; the burning of Kiev by the Mongols;
the two sacks of Constantinople; the October Revolution in
Russia. Yet these events, while they have transformed the
external appearance of the Orthodox world, have never broken
the inward continuity of the Orthodox Church. The thing that
first strikes a stranger on encountering Orthodoxy is usually its
air of antiquity, its apparent changelessness. He finds that
Orthodox still baptize by threefold immersion, as in the primitive Church; they still bring babies and small children to receive
Holy Communion; in the Liturgy the deacon still cries out: 'The
doors! The doors!'—recalling the early days when the church's
entrance was jealously guarded, and none but members of the
Christian family could attend the family worship; the Creed is
still recited without any additions.

These are but a few outward examples of something which
pervades every aspect of Orthodox life. Recently when two
Orthodox scholars were asked to summarize the distinctive
characteristic of their Church, they both pointed to the same

* Reprinted with permission from *The Orthodox Church,* by Timothy
Ware (Baltimore: Penguin Books, 1963), pp. 203–8. Footnotes omitted.

thing: its changelessness, its determination to remain loyal to the past, its sense of *living continuity* with the Church of ancient times. Two and a half centuries before, the Eastern Patriarchs said exactly the same to the Non-Jurors:

We preserve the Doctrine of the Lord uncorrupted, and firmly adhere to the Faith he delivered to us, and keep it free from blemish and diminution, as a Royal Treasure, and a monument of great price, *neither adding any thing, nor taking any thing from it.*

This idea of living continuity is summed up for the Orthodox in the one word *Tradition*. 'We do not change the everlasting boundaries which our fathers have set,' wrote John of Damascus, 'but *we keep the Tradition, just as we received it.*'

Orthodox are always talking about Tradition. What do they mean by the word? A tradition, says the Oxford Dictionary, is an opinion, belief, or custom handed down from ancestors to posterity. Christian Tradition, in that case, is the faith which Jesus Christ imparted to the Apostles, and which since the Apostles' time has been handed down from generation to generation in the Church. But to an Orthodox Christian, Tradition means something more concrete and specific than this. It means the books of the Bible; it means the Creed; it means the decrees of the Ecumenical Councils and the writings of the Fathers; it means the Canons, the Service Books, the Holy Icons—in fact, the whole system of doctrine, Church government, worship, and art which Orthodoxy has articulated over the ages. The Orthodox Christian of today sees himself as heir and guardian to a great inheritance received from the past, and he believes that it is his duty to transmit this inheritance unimpaired to the future.

Note that the Bible forms a part of Tradition. Sometimes Tradition is defined as 'the oral teaching of Christ, not recorded in writing by his immediate disciples' (Oxford Dictionary). Not only non-Orthodox but many Orthodox writers have adopted this way of speaking, treating Scripture and Tradition as two different things, two distinct sources of the Christian faith. But in reality there is only one source, since Scripture exists *within* Tradition. To separate and contrast the two is to impoverish the idea of both alike.

Orthodox, while reverencing this inheritance from the past, are also well aware that not everything received from the past is of equal value. Among the various elements of Tradition, a unique pre-eminence belongs to the Bible, to the Creed, to the doctrinal definitions of the Ecumenical Councils: these things the Orthodox accept as something absolute and unchanging, something which cannot be cancelled or revised. The other parts of Tradition do not have quite the same authority. The decrees of Jassy or Jerusalem do not stand on the same level as the Nicene Creed, nor do the writings of an Athanasius, or a Symeon the New Theologian, occupy the same position as the Gospel of Saint John.

Not everything received from the past is of equal value, nor is everything received from the past necessarily true. As one of the bishops remarked at the Council of Carthage in 257: 'The Lord said, I am truth. He did not say, I am custom.' There is a difference between 'Tradition' and 'traditions': many traditions which the past has handed down are human and accidental— pious opinions (or worse), but not a true part of the one Tradition, the essential Christian message.

It is necessary to question the past. In Byzantine and post-Byzantine times, Orthodox have not always been sufficiently critical in their attitude to the past, and the result has frequently been stagnation. Today this uncritical attitude can no longer be maintained. Higher standards of scholarship, increasing contacts with western Christians, the inroads of secularism and atheism, have forced Orthodox in this present century to look more closely at their inheritance and to distinguish more carefully between Tradition and traditions. The task of discrimination is not always easy. It is necessary to avoid alike the error of the Old Believers and the error of the 'Living Church': the one party fell into an extreme conservatism which suffered no change whatever in traditions, the other into a Modernism or theological liberalism which undermined Tradition. Yet despite certain manifest handicaps, the Orthodox of today are perhaps in a better position to discriminate aright than their predecessors have been for many centuries; and often it is precisely their contact with the west which is helping them to see more and more clearly what is essential in their own inheritance.

True Orthodox fidelity to the past must always be a *creative* fidelity; for true Orthodoxy can never rest satisfied with a barren 'theology of repetition,' which, parrot-like, repeats accepted formulae without striving to understand what lies behind them. Loyalty to Tradition, properly understood, is not something mechanical, a dull process of handing down what has been received. An Orthodox thinker must see Tradition *from within,* he must enter into its inner spirit. In order to live within Tradition, it is not enough simply to give intellectual assent to a system of doctrine; for Tradition is far more than a set of abstract propositions—it is a life, a personal encounter with Christ in the Holy Spirit. Tradition is not only kept by the Church—it lives in the Church, it is the life of the Holy Spirit in the Church. The Orthodox conception of Tradition is not static but dynamic, not a dead acceptance of the past but a living experience of the Holy Spirit in the present. Tradition, while inwardly changeless (for God does not change), is constantly assuming new forms, which supplement the old without superseding them. Orthodox often speak as if the period of doctrinal formulation were wholly at an end, yet this is not the case. Perhaps in our own day new Ecumenical Councils will meet, and Tradition will be enriched by fresh statements of the faith.

This idea of Tradition as a living thing has been well expressed by Georges Florovsky:

Tradition is the witness of the Spirit; the Spirit's unceasing revelation and preaching of good tidings. . . . To accept and understand Tradition we must live within the Church, we must be conscious of the grace-giving presence of the Lord in it; we must feel the breath of the Holy Ghost in it. . . . Tradition is not only a protective, conservative principle; it is, primarily, the principle of growth and regeneration. . . . Tradition is the constant abiding of the Spirit and not only the memory of words.

Tradition is the witness of the Spirit: in the words of Christ, 'When the Spirit of truth has come, he will guide you into all truth' (John xvi, 13). It is this divine promise that forms the basis of the Orthodox devotion to Tradition. . . .

. . . The Christian Church is a Scriptural Church: Orthodoxy believes this just as firmly, if not more firmly than Protestantism. The Bible is the supreme expression of God's revelation to man, and Christians must always be 'People of the Book.' But if Christians are People of the Book, the Bible is the Book of the People; it must not be regarded as something set up *over* the Church, but as something that lives and is understood *within* the Church (that is why one should not separate Scripture and Tradition). It is from the Church that the Bible ultimately derives its authority, for it was the Church which originally decided which books form a part of Holy Scripture; and it is the Church alone which can interpret Holy Scripture with authority. There are many sayings in the Bible which by themselves are far from clear, and the individual reader, however sincere, is in danger of error if he trusts his own personal interpretation. 'Do you understand what you are reading?' Philip asked the Ethiopian eunuch; and the eunuch replied: 'How can I, unless someone guides me?' (Acts viii, 30–1). Orthodox, when they read the Scripture, accept the guidance of the Church. When received into the Orthodox Church, a convert promises: 'I will accept and understand Holy Scripture in accordance with the interpretation which was and is held by the Holy Orthodox Catholic Church of the East, our Mother.'

10

WHO ARE THE EVANGELICALS?*

Harold Lindsell

CHRISTIAN history at its best is the lengthened shadow of evangelical Christianity. When the evangel has been central in the life of the Church, the Church has flourished. When it has been marginal, the Church has suffered. Evangelical Christianity has always had Jesus Christ as its chief cornerstone, the Apostles as its chief spokesmen, and the Word of God written as the only source and authority of its witness. The witnesses to the apostolicity and truth of God's divine revelation change from age to age. But the Word of God incarnate, Jesus Christ, and the Word of God written, the Holy Scriptures, do not change; they belong to the Church forever. We know that the apostolic foundation laid by Christ and the Apostles was lost after the first century and not recaptured until the days of the Reformers, when once again the message and the spirit of the Gospel became regnant. . . .

In 1846 the Evangelical Alliance was formed in England, and it spread rapidly to other countries. In the United States its twentieth-century counterpart was to be the National Association of Evangelicals (1942), and most European countries saw the rise of evangelical alliances of their own. Close ties have been developed among evangelical fellowships in India, Cey-

* Reprinted with permission from an article by the same title in *Christianity Today*, IX, 19 (June 18, 1965), 3–6. Copyright © 1965 by *Christianity Today*.

lon, other Asian countries, and the Western world. The result was the formation, in 1951, of the World Evangelical Fellowship. The Evangelical Alliance of 1846 followed the grand tradition of the Evangelical Awakening of the eighteenth century. It was ecumenical in outlook, ignoring denominational lines and attesting to the spiritual unity that believers have in Jesus Christ. The unity the members confessed was not, however, simply a gathering of people who professed Christianity, but rather a gathering based upon common theological convictions. They assembled "not to create Christian union, but to confess the unity which the Church of Christ possessed as His Body." The doctrinal basis of the alliance was as follows:

1. The Divine inspiration, authority, and sufficiency of the Holy Scriptures.

2. The right and duty of private judgment in the interpretation of the Holy Scriptures.

3. The Unity of the Godhead, and the Trinity of the persons therein.

4. The utter depravity of human nature in consequence of the Fall.

5. The incarnation of the Son of God, his work of atonement for the sins of mankind, and his mediatorial intercession and reign.

6. The justification of the sinner by faith alone.

7. The work of the Holy Spirit in the conversion and sanctification of the sinner.

8. The immortality of the soul, the resurrection of the body, the judgment of the world by our Lord Jesus Christ, with the eternal blessedness of the righteous, and the eternal punishment of the wicked.

9. The divine institution of the Christian ministry, and the obligation and perpetuity of the ordinances of Baptism and the Lord's Supper.

It was distinctly stated that this brief summary was "not to be regarded in any formal or ecclesiastical sense as a creed or confession, nor the adoption of the right authoritatively to define the limits of Christian brotherhood, but simply as an indication of the class of persons whom it is desirable to embrace within the Alliance"; and it was also stated that "the selection of certain tenets, with the omission of others, is not to be held as implying that the former constitute the whole body of important truth, or that the latter are unimportant." Like many other great confessions of faith, such as the Westminster and the New Hampshire, that of the Evangelical Alliance began with the Scriptures.

In the twentieth century, particularly in the United States, evangelical Christianity generally came to be known as "fundamentalism." Fundamentalists have often been labeled obscurantist, heretical, sectarian, schismatic, crude, and atavistic. They have been assailed by critics for failure to relate the Gospel to the social milieu, and even more for their theological fundamentalism. Some evangelicals disavowed the term "fundamentalist," although they were in general theological agreement with it. J. Gresham Machen, an ardent evangelical, never wanted to be known as a fundamentalist. In *Fundamentalism and the Word of God,* the British theologian J. I. Packer decries the use of the word "fundamentalist" because of its connotations. Fundamentalism is continuous with evangelical Christianity, even though it may have been colored by (1) a failure to relate the Gospel to the social structures as did nineteenth-century evangelicism in England; (2) the addition of particularistic elements that have often given fundamentalism a cultic stance; (3) a legalism and a system of interpretation that have codified concepts of personal conduct and raised them to the level of basic theological presuppositions; (4) lapses into anti-intellectualism or obscurantism. Nonetheless fundamentalists, like other evangelicals, including those of dispensational leanings, agree with all the theological tenets in the doctrinal platform of the Evangelical Alliance.

Foundational to evangelical Christianity is its view of the Scriptures as inspired, authoritative, and sufficient. . . . While the evangelical view of Scripture has not always included inerrancy, the consensus leaves no doubt that inerrancy has generally been normative. The *Concise Oxford Dictionary* defines fundamentalism as the "maintenance, in opposition to modernism, of *traditional orthodox beliefs* [my italics] such as the inerrancy of Scripture. . . ." Here it is claimed that inerrancy *is* the traditional viewpoint. J. I. Packer says: "The defenders of revelation in Eighteenth-century England had defeated their deist opponents and preserved the general English belief in the verbal infallibility of the Bible" (*Fundamentalism and the Word of God,* p. 72). Professor Alan Richardson, in the 1950 and 1957 editions of *Chambers' Encyclopedia,* makes the remarkable but palpably false statement that fundamentalism supports a mode of biblical inspiration "which regards the written words of the Bible as divinely dictated." This would be humorous, were not this libel commonly believed by many scholars ignorant of the facts. No evangelical or fundamentalist scholars entertain the notion of dictation in their views of Scripture; they do believe in verbal inspiration, which should never be identified as synonymous with dictation, mechanical or otherwise.

Evangelicalism has a theology consonant with that of the Reformation and rooted in the Scriptures. The same Gospel that was recovered in the Reformation, then lost in lifeless churches, was recovered again by evangelicalism in the eighteenth century. In the twentieth century evangelical Christianity is once more re-articulating the Gospel lost in the mire of liberalism, neo-orthodoxy, existentialism, and other current forms of theological expression. It is crystal clear that historic orthodoxy and evangelical Christianity are essentially one in theological outlook and content. In distinction from the views of modern theologians like Barth, Bultmann, and Tillich, evangelicals have always reposed high confidence in the Bible as the final religious authority, as propositional truth, as revealed knowledge. . . .

Surely an evangelical is one who believes that the Bible is truly the Word of God written. He can, therefore, subscribe to the theological fundamentals of the Christian faith as embraced by the Reformers and affirmed in their creeds, and can accept the convictions expressed by the Evangelical Alliance. The word "evangelical" stands for the Gospel of Christ mediated by grace through faith alone. Evangelicals are those who hold to such convictions and who believe and preach and teach that all men are lost and, in order to be rightly related to God, must be regenerated by the Holy Spirit through personal faith in the vicarious atoning work of the crucified and risen Christ.

11

IN WHAT SENSE IS THE BIBLE
THE WORD OF GOD?*

Bernhard W. Anderson

THE Bible is meant to be read and understood in times [of crisis] like these. The literature of the Old and New Testaments is the deposit of a succession of historical crises in which men were faced with the question of the meaning of their existence. With stark realism the Bible describes events which rocked the very foundation of life, which destroyed nations and displaced populations, which wrought havoc, suffering, and anxiety. This drama of faith was enacted upon a stage where poor people were the victims of the rich, where Palestinian rulers were drawn into the maelstrom of international events, and where one great nation after another sought to create a world empire by the power of the sword. Situated strategically at the cross-roads of the ancient world, Palestine was the very storm center of life. The Bible, therefore, does not come from a sheltered valley of Shangri-la; its message was forged out of circumstances in which people felt the maximum of tension and suffering. This book speaks out of the immediate and concrete realities of history, where men doubted and believed, hated and loved, despaired and hoped. Its message comes from the depth of life and speaks to the depth within us. It finds us where we are

* Reprinted with permission from *Rediscovering the Bible* (New York: Association Press, 1951), pp. 5–22. Footnotes omitted.

living. Therefore it is understandable that as modern people wrestle with the issues of destiny in their own contemporary situation, they often find themselves in rapport with the prophets and apostles of the Bible. Perhaps the Bible is most deeply understood only by shipwrecked men.

THE HUMANITY OF SCRIPTURE

From one point of view the Bible is a very human book. The word "bible," derived from a Greek plural word meaning "booklets," is descriptive of its diverse character. Here is a *library* of sacred writings. Protestants count sixty-six books: thirty-nine in the Old Testament and twenty-seven in the New. In this, Protestants differ from Roman Catholics who include in the Old Testament several additional writings which were admitted at the time when the first Greek translation, known as the Septuagint, was made by Greek-speaking Jews of Alexandria (about 250 B.C. and on). Since these books were never included in the *Hebrew* Bible, Protestants relegate them to the "Apocrypha" and consider them to be outside the limits of sacred scripture.

This library covers a long period of time. In fact, if we begin with Abraham, it includes almost two thousand years of historical remembrance. We would have some idea of the time span covered by the Bible if we could imagine a similar book of writings and traditions produced in the course of Western history from the period of Julius Caesar to the period of Joseph Stalin. The diversity of the Bible, therefore, is the kaleidoscopic diversity of Israelite history in the long and inexorable march of time.

Moreover, the Bible mirrors the experience of a great variety of people who were involved personally in these events. Many who contributed to the biblical epic are unknown to us by name; the Bible, however, bears the imprint of their lives. Prophets and apostles, kings and priests, wise men and scribes, have made their individual contribution. Side by side in this library, and often intermingled in separate books, are poetry and prose, law and prophecy, history and fiction, wisdom literature and devotional hymns, sermons and epistles. Sometimes the language moves in the majestic cadences of stately prose (as in Genesis 1), sometimes in the balanced rhythms of poetry (as in Isaiah 40–55), sometimes in the vivid style of narrative (as in the story of the Exodus, or the Nativity stories), sometimes in symbolic flights of religious imagination (as in Daniel and Revelation). All of the available literary forms and all of the rich variety of human expression enter into the proclamation of the biblical message.

In this library the human situation is presented with the utmost realism. Nothing human is alien to its range of interest. Stories about murder, rape, trickery, war, religious persecution, and church jealousies are mingled with accounts of divine action, heavenly visions, ventures of faith and hymns of hope. . . . In fact, there are whole tracts of Scripture in which the sacred element is not readily obvious, as, for instance, in the book of Esther where the name of God is not clearly mentioned even once, or the Song of Songs where sexual passion seems to predominate. . . . In its original form, however, the Bible gives an uncensored description of the human situation. The picture of human life is not "touched up" to make it appear better than it is. Many of the biblical stories verify a central truth of the biblical revelation, namely, that man is a sinner who often attempts to justify himself in his sin by means of his religion. In one sense a more human library has never been written.

Presently we shall look at the other side of the picture: the Bible as the witness to God's revelation. Now, however, it is important to notice that the human aspect of the Bible has enabled scholars to study it with the same critical methodology which is applicable in the study of other literature, like the Hindu Vedas, the Homeric poems, or the plays of Shakespeare. In fact, there is probably no other literature which has been studied more earnestly and intensively than the Bible.

The beginnings of biblical criticism can be traced back to the very dawn of the Christian era, when scholars began to raise questions as to the accuracy of the received text of the Bible and to notice difficulties that the rigid dogmas of the faith could not eliminate. The Renaissance, bringing a new sense of mental freedom and reviving an interest in the documents of the past, gave a fresh impetus to the study. Likewise the Protestant Reformation made its contribution by emphasizing the sole authority of Scripture in the Christian faith and by insisting upon making the Bible accessible to the masses. Finally, the rise of the scientific movement brought to the investigation both a passion for the attainment of truth and a critical methodology, by the use of which men sought to purge Christianity of error and superstition. Here we cannot go into the fascinating story of the many scholars who added their creative labors, often at the price of ostracism or excommunication from the Christian community. Many of the scientific hypotheses proposed were fanciful; many of the interpretations set forth were more expressive of the spirit of the age in which the scholar lived than representative of the biblical faith itself. But today we have the advantage of standing on the shoulders of these men of the past. Thanks to the labors of experts in Hebrew and Greek, it is now possible to present a translation of the Bible which overcomes some of the limitations of the classical King James Version. Archaeologists have excavated many places in the Near East and have thrown new light on the historical period and cultural situation in which the Bible was written. Historians have enabled us to read the writings of the Bible in the approximate chronological order in which they were composed, and have helped us to understand the message of each book in the light of the circumstances of its composition. Because of these critical labors, our knowledge of the human aspect of Scripture is far in advance of that of past theological leaders like Augustine, Aquinas, Luther, or Calvin.

THE BIBLE AS THE WORD OF GOD

The uniqueness of the Bible, however, cannot be understood adequately by treating it merely as a human book. The Bible was never designed to be read as great literature, sober history, naïve philosophy, or primitive science. Men remembered stories, treasured traditions, and wrote in various forms of literature because of one inescapable conviction: they had been confronted by God in events which had taken place in their history. Though hidden from mortal sight in light unapproachable, the holy God had revealed himself to mankind. He had taken the initiative to establish a relationship with his people. He had spoken his Word of judgment and of mercy. "In many and various ways God spoke of old to our fathers by the prophets; but in these last days he has spoken to us by a Son." These opening words of the Letter to the Hebrews strike the keynote of the Bible. It is this central conviction which gives the Bible, both Old and New Testaments, the status of sacred scripture in the Christian Church.

This faith is a stumbling block to the modern mind. It would be more honest, however, to reject the biblical claim outright than to insist that the message of God's revelation is peripheral and that these people actually meant to say something other than they seem to say. The Bible has suffered seriously from readers who, like the legendary highwayman of ancient Greece, have attempted to force its message into the Procrustean bed of modern ways of thinking. As a consequence, some people have dismissed the theology of the Bible as a poetic or mythical embellishment of men's maturing awareness of the distinction between right and wrong. Others have treated it as elementary philosophy, the first efforts of the Hebrews reflectively to understand Reality. These approaches to the meaning of human existence may be adequate outside the Bible. But the men of the Bible say something very different. It is their claim that God himself has spoken with a decisiveness, a once-for-allness. They do not tell us about searching for moral values, or attempting to reach a more satisfying philosophy by standing a bit taller on their intellectual tiptoes. Rather, they bear witness to their encounter with God in the midst of crucial events of history, their engagement with him in moments of historical crisis. And, above all, this revelation was not peripheral or incidental to their message; it was the vantage point from which they viewed everything else—politics, social injustice, and war; past, present, and future. They do not argue this faith; they proclaim it with confessional language: "Here I stand, I cannot do otherwise."

The subject matter of the Bible, then, is God's self-revelation to men. Because of this stupendous theme, traditional Christianity has described the Bible as the "Word of God" and has insisted upon the divine authorship of Scripture. Says a New Testament writer: "All Scripture is given by inspiration of God," that is, as the Greek word suggests, it is "God-breathed" or "filled with the breath of God" (II Timothy 3:16). However seriously one may take the human dimension of Scripture, he cannot easily disregard the central claim of the Bible itself to be the record and witness of revelatory events in which God has spoken. This is sacred scripture because the Holy Spirit breathes through the ancient words and reveals to men in every age the Word of truth.

THE INSPIRATION OF THE BIBLE

What does it mean to say that the Bible is inspired? This is the heart of our problem. It is no easy task to deal with the Bible in such a manner that one does justice both to its humanity and its divine authorship. Much confusion has been brought about by those who would oversimplify the matter, either by emphasizing the human element in Scripture to the point of stultifying its divine authorship, or by emphasizing the divine character of the Bible to the point of ignoring that it is a human book. The major cleavage in the Protestant churches in America is no longer denominational, geographical, or even doctrinal. The line is drawn at the point of the authority of the Bible, and in general Protestants can be divided according to which side they take in the debate over biblical inspiration.

Many Protestants have adopted a position which has been labeled "liberalism." Instead of hiding their heads, ostrichlike, in the barren sands of the past, these Christians sincerely and devoutly have attempted to make the Bible speak relevantly to the modern situation. A Christian cannot believe one set of ideas on Sunday and then live by another set of assumptions the rest of the week. Such religious "schizophrenia" is intolerable, for the Christian faith jealously demands the allegiance of the whole man. Therefore, liberals sought to adjust the inherited faith to the bewildering modern world whose outlook had been defined by the achievements of science. It was their intention to remain loyal to the biblical faith, but to make this faith relevant by translating its truths into the language of the modern age. This point of view was championed brilliantly by Harry Emerson Fosdick, who popularized the phrase, "abiding experiences in changing categories," and insisted that biblical truth could be lifted out of the biblical framework of expression and reinterpreted in the categories of modern thought.

Specifically, this meant reinterpreting the Bible in terms of the concept of evolution, a scientific hypothesis which originally was applied in the field of biology but which soon was transferred to other fields of investigation until it became the dominant philosophical point of view on the American scene. This outlook found theological expression in the toning down or outright rejection of supernaturalism in favor of the idea of divine immanence, that is, God's indwelling in man and nature. For instance, creation by supernatural fiat was reinterpreted to mean God's continuing creation, his immanence in the long evolutionary upthrust. In "Each in His Own Tongue," William Herbert Carruth gave poetic expression to the new interpretation of creation:

> A fire-mist and a planet,
>   A crystal and a cell,
> A jelly-fish and a saurian,
>   And caves where the cave-men dwell;
> Then a sense of law and beauty
>   And a face turned from the clod,—
> Some call it Evolution,
>   And others call it God.

Applied to religious knowledge, the evolutionary interpretation found expression in the idea of "progressive revelation." That is to say, God works immanently within the historical process, revealing his timeless truths up to man's ability to understand; on man's side, this progressive illumination yields increasing "discovery" or expanding "insight." The Bible allegedly gives evidence of such progress. The religion of Moses is said to be comparatively primitive. But under the influence of the prophetic "genius," crude and barbarous elements were gradually removed, until Jesus finally came as the great discoverer of God and the teacher of the loftiest ethical principles. Since all humanity is involved in the evolutionary process, it is no more surprising that religions outside the biblical tradition should arrive at the same insights than it is that both Russia and America, working independently, should unlock the secret of the atom. According to this view, the greatness of Jesus is that he saw what many others had seen, or could have seen, but by his forceful teaching and sacrificial death he helped men to take truth seriously.

This modern view of the Bible enabled Christians to keep their heads erect in a world where only fools or fanatics would dare to challenge the assured results of science. Of course, liberals were also children of their time, and therefore fell into the temptation of revising the Bible in accordance with their own presuppositions. Nevertheless, liberalism at its best was governed by the spirit of evangelical Christianity. This is noticeable, for example, in one of the characteristic elements of the liberal attitude: devotion to truth. A critical principle lies at the heart of the liberal attitude, the fearless application of which is akin to the spirit of ancient prophets who challenged all human securities. Just as the Protestant Reformation broke upon the world in protest against a Church which had identified itself with God's Kingdom on earth, so liberalism emerged as a prophetic challenge to a decadent Protestantism that had prematurely congealed Christian truth into a static system of belief. According to liberalism, all conclusions must be judged by truth itself. This attitude, when applied to biblical study, has aided in our rediscovery of the Bible by enabling us to read it in the light of the circumstances in which it was written.

Moreover, Protestant liberalism was a healthy relief from the one-sided emphasis upon the salvation of the individual soul. Liberalism flowered in the "social gospel" movement, as ably represented by men like Walter Rauschenbusch. If the liberal's expectancy of building a Christian society on earth was too much under the influence of the faith of the Enlightenment, it was certainly akin to the this-worldly religion of the Bible according to which all of life must be brought under the sovereignty of God. Finally, liberalism at its best was motivated by a vivid and vital rediscovery of Christian experience. If, as Luther said, "every Christian must do his own believing, just as he must do his own dying," then likewise each age must make its own discovery of Christ and express its faith in its unique way. Liberalism did this for the late nineteenth and early twentieth centuries. Indeed, future historians undoubtedly will appraise liberalism as one of the most dynamic movements in the history of Christianity.

Although liberalism was swept along by a powerful current of evangelical Christianity, the theology of liberalism came too much under the influence of the modern world-view. It is one thing to attempt to translate the biblical faith into categories which modern man can understand; it is quite another thing to adopt modern categories as ruling principles of interpretation. In attempting to bring Christianity up to date, liberals virtually capitulated to the prevailing world-view of the day, so much so that the dividing line between liberal Protestantism and secularism became increasingly dim. Reaction was inevitable.

The reaction came in the form of a movement known as fundamentalism. Beginning during the period 1910–20 on an organized interdenominational basis, it was led by conservative Protestants who felt that "modernists" were "throwing out the baby with the bath" in their streamlining of the Christian faith. The historian will point out precedents for this movement in the sterile orthodoxy which set in shortly after the outburst of the Protestant Reformation, and in the decadent Calvinism which persisted in America, especially in rural areas, throughout the eighteenth and nineteenth centuries. Fundamentalism as such, however, is a distinctly twentieth-century phenomenon, and is properly regarded as essentially a reactionary protest against the excesses of the modernizing of the Bible. Precipitated by the crisis occasioned by the introduction of the theory of evolution, it was aimed at restoring and preserving the fundamentals of the Faith. The movement gained national and even international attention through the "heresy" investigation of Harry Emerson Fosdick in 1923, and the infamous Scopes "monkey" trial at Dayton, Tennessee, in 1925 where the anti-evolution case was championed eloquently by William Jennings Bryan. Even yet, fundamentalism is a powerful force in the American religious scene. Young people become familiar with crusading fundamentalism through the "Youth for Christ" movement or, on the college campus, through the "Inter-Varsity Fellowship."

The key "fundamental" of the faith, according to this group, is the inerrancy of Scripture. In the words of a representative statement, it is "an essential doctrine of the Word of God and our standards that the Holy Spirit did so inspire, guide, and move the writers of the Holy Scripture as to keep them from error." This means that the words of the Bible are the very words of God himself. The writers of the Bible were mere passive secretaries who mechanically transcribed the divine words, these words being the media for conveying the thoughts of the Infinite Intelligence who knows everything past, present, and future. Because God is literally the author of Holy Scripture, the whole Bible "from cover to cover" is held to be absolutely infallible. In popular practice fundamentalists have claimed infallibility for a particular version of the Bible: the King James Version of 1611! Apparent contradictions in Scripture, they say, are not real and are made to vanish by the magic of an interpretative method which weaves together texts from all over the Bible. It is supposedly a matter of faith for the Christian to take the Bible exactly for what it says. If the Bible says that the world was created in six days, that God made a woman out of Adam's rib, that Joshua commanded the sun to stand still, that Balaam's ass talked, or that Jesus turned water into wine, then these matters must be accepted as facts. Many young people have gone away to college burdened with the anxiety that it is a sin to question the literal accuracy of the biblical stories.

Fundamentalists argue that the doctrine of the inerrancy of Scripture is a Christian belief of long standing. It is quite true that both Protestantism and Roman Catholicism have spoken of the Bible in the highest terms. Calvin, for instance, referred to the Bible as the infallible Word of God, and described it by such phrases as "God's own voice," "dictated by the Holy Spirit," and so on. Moreover, a recent Vatican Council declared that the books of the Bible are sacred "not because, having been composed by human industry, they were afterward approved by her [the Church's] authority, nor merely because they contain revelation without error, but because having been written under the inspiration of the Holy Spirit, they have God for their author, and as such were handed down to the Church herself." But in neither case did insistence upon the divine authorship of Scripture carry with it a slavish devotion to the letter of the Scriptures or involve the belief that the Bible is the sole norm for everything under the sun. It is a great mistake to identify fundamentalism with the thinking of men like Luther or Calvin. Unlike classical Christian orthodoxy, fundamentalism is slavishly bound to the literal text of the Bible, and manifests open hostility to anything which goes under the name of biblical criticism. The point bears repetition that fundamentalism is a twentieth-century reactionary movement.

To the credit of fundamentalism it should be said that these conservative Christians have been sincere and devout in their attempt to defend the fundamentals of Christianity behind a Maginot line of biblical literalism. As we have observed, liberalism tended to veer away from the main stream of evangelical Christianity and to become a "modernism" carried along by the current of secularism. Thus one may say that fundamentalists, in their dogmatic way, have been making a valid protest against a secularized Christianity which failed to remember Paul's advice: "Be not conformed to this world. . . ." The protest, however, has had little effect on the real frontiers of theological thinking. . . .

The real strength of fundamentalism lies in its weaknesses. When the securities of life are threatened, men seek an authority which is visible and absolute. The Bible, therefore, came to be an Ark of salvation in which, like Noah and his family, the faithful could find refuge from the storms of agnosticism and change which were sweeping the world. Fundamentalism is really a form of bibliolatry, that is, it is a faith in the Bible itself, rather than faith in the God who speaks his Word through the Bible. Despite its high regard for the Bible, this movement offers men a false and—paradoxical though this may seem—an *unbiblical* authority.

Moreover, part of the appeal of fundamentalism lies in its reactionary social position. Too often the defense of the Bible has been allied curiously with a reactionary defense of the status quo. It is hardly accidental that frequently the fundamentalist leadership has been recruited from, and the financial support for the movement given by, successful businessmen who have been more concerned about "saving souls" for eternity than about redeeming society in the name of Jesus Christ. The biblical justification for this escape from social radicalism has been the "premillennial" hope, that is, the belief that Christ must come again before the millennium of justice and peace can be introduced; in the meantime, the evils of society must continue and even become worse. The belief that "Jesus is coming soon"—as one reads on signs along our highways—produces evangelists, but does not inspire a "social gospel." If liberalism has capitulated to secularism, it is equally true that fundamentalism in its own way has made even more dangerous concessions to the status quo.

In summary, fundamentalism and liberalism are both partly right and partly wrong. Fundamentalists are right in insisting that the Bible on its own witness presents men with the Word of God. When liberals equate "progressive revelation" with "increasing discovery," the word revelation is virtually emptied of meaning. The reality has gone, leaving behind only the empty word, like the lingering grin after the disappearance of the Cheshire cat; for that which men can discover potentially—like the secret of the atom—is scarcely the traditional meaning of "revelation." If there is revelation, God must reveal to man what man in his blindness cannot or will not see. He must shed eternal light upon the mystery of life. He must offer a divine solution to an otherwise insoluble human problem. Fundamentalists are keen enough to see this. But unfortunately they make so much of the divine authorship of Scripture that the human element is virtually eliminated, the human secretary being only a mechanical or passive transmitter of God's revelation.

Liberalism, on the other hand, is right in emphasizing the humanity of Scripture—"the warp of human life on the loom of Scripture, across which the shuttle of the Spirit of God so constantly moved," as H. Wheeler Robinson has put it. Whatever the inspired content of the Bible is, "we have this treasure in a frail earthen vessel." If God speaks his Word, men must hear it and respond within the limitations of concrete historical situations. Since the men of the Bible were men and not God they inevitably used the language of their time to communicate their faith. These things liberalism emphasized and brilliantly verified by means of historical criticism. Unfortunately, however, the human element of Scripture was overemphasized, especially under the influence of the dominant evolutionary philosophy, with the result that "God" became little more than a force at work in the social process, leading men to the formulation of loftier ideas and sounder ethical insights. Thus the uniqueness of the biblical revelation was often discounted and the divine authorship of Scripture reduced to an empty figure of speech. As liberal scholars are now recognizing increasingly, the weakness of the liberalism of the past was not in the use of the method of historical criticism, but rather the fault lay in the dubious presuppositions about the nature of man and history which governed the use of the method. . . .

What do we mean when we speak of the Bible as the "Word of God"? Let us recognize at the outset that we are using the language of metaphor. When the prophets exclaimed "thus saith the Lord" they were not putting quotation marks around the actual words which had been spoken by God; and when they exhorted their countrymen to "hear the Word of the Lord" they did not refer to a Voice which was carried to them on the sound waves. Speaking and hearing are the ways in which persons become related to one another. If my friend speaks to me and I hear his word, a bridge of communication is thrown out from his life to mine, with the result that a relationship exists between us. Analogously, the Word of God, when heard in a historical crisis, is the medium through which God enters into *relationship* with men. Thus it is proper to speak of God revealing himself by his Word—the word of the prophets of old, and Jesus Christ, "the Word made flesh."

According to the Bible, man encounters God in history. Sometimes we say that we are most aware of God as we behold the beauties of nature. So Wordsworth—that mystic lover of nature—has caught our poetic fancy:

> And I have felt
> A presence that disturbs me with the joy
> Of elevated thoughts; a sense sublime
> Of something far more deeply interfused,
> Whose dwelling is the light of setting suns,
> And the round ocean, and the living air,
> And the blue sky, and in the mind of men.

The men of the Bible testify that the heavens and earth declare the glory of God, but to them nature was not the *primary* sphere of God's revelation. They first heard God's Word in moments of historical crisis, in events which were experienced with a unique meaning. To be sure, the encounter with God often took place in a setting of nature. Moses heard the divine call in the severe grandeur and serene solitude of the desert of Sinai; Elijah was addressed by God in the silence which followed nature's tumultuous display of earthquake, wind, and fire; and Amos received the divine summons as he was tending his flocks in the rugged wilderness of Tekoa. But in each of these cases there was an acute awareness of the historical crisis in which Israel was involved at the moment. Thus the "Word of God" was essentially the interpretation of a historical crisis in which men were grasped by God's claim upon them. In order to communicate the discerned meaning of events, the writers of the

Bible employed words, but words, of course, are only symbols for the conveyance of meaning. Therefore the biblical interpreter must go beyond the letter of Scripture to the meaning. He must seek "the Word behind the words," as someone has put it.

In the strict sense, then, it is inaccurate to speak of the Bible itself as the Word of God. Properly speaking, the Bible *contains* the Word of God. The subject matter of the Bible is God's approach to man in history, in particular the stream of Hebraic-Christian history which begins with the Exodus and culminates in the coming of Jesus Christ. Though this book is characterized by great diversity and variety, both in literary form and religious content, its internal unity is the drama of the working out of God's purpose in the events of Israel's history. As someone has said, this biblical history is His-Story, in which he reveals his judgment upon men's sin and his intention and power to re-create mankind. The plot has God's purpose at the beginning, God's ultimate triumph at the conclusion, and—at the tragic and victorious climax—a Cross, the sign of God's omnipotent love. Because the Bible is both the record of these unique events and the witness to their divine meaning, it may be called the Word of God.

If we are to hear God's Word spoken through the Bible to our situation today, our first task is to put ourselves within the world of the Bible. No casual or superficial reading of Scripture can accomplish this. We must avail ourselves of the results of historical criticism and biblical theology so that we may imaginatively relive the actual historical situation in which an Amos or a Paul heard the high calling of God. We must, as it were, sit where these ancient people sat and learn to look at the human scene from their unique point of view. We must live with the Bible until it becomes part of us, just as the actor identifies himself with the role that he plays. It is then, perhaps, that the Holy Spirit, breathing through the ancient words of the sacred page, will lead us to know that the "Word of the Lord" spoken by the prophets and embodied in Jesus Christ is actually the deepest interpretation of our own life situation and our world crisis in the twentieth century.

PART IV

THE HUMAN PLACE

Man and God as protagonists. In this section and the next, theology is addressing itself to the human situation. Part IV focuses upon certain fundamental problems of man as man while Part V concentrates upon specific challenges occasioned by recent historical developments within and beyond theology. The human place is a classical and inevitable subject of theological discussion, although always as part of the question of faith in God and of the divine authority.

The initial passage from *Paul Tillich* serves both as a transition from the emphases in Parts II and III and as an independent argument that faith and doubt are not antithetical but interrelated. However Tillich's general theological position may be evaluated, he has succeeded in making central to contemporary theological discussion the question, Is man intrinsically religious?

In the work of the playwright *Rolf Hochhuth* is exemplified the truth that one does not have to be a professional theologian to grapple with theological problems. In the scene from *The Deputy* (*Der Stellvertreter*) reproduced here, the Doctor tries to humiliate Father Riccardo for his faith. The scene is part of the Act bearing the unqualifiedly fitting title, "Auschwitz or the Question Asked of God." Thus, the issue is not in the first instance that of human diabolism but one of *theodicy:* In the presence of ultimate evil, can a man still trust God? Even more shatteringly, *ought* he then trust God? In other words, *is the suffering of Auschwitz an unredeemable horror?* The Doctor places God, not man, on the stand of the accused. Yet Hochhuth does not discount the relevance of human diabolism. For days on end the Doctor, by simple waves of the hand, had been dispatching whomever he wished to the crematoria, while "sparing" others. But the inescapable choices are present: Must the trial of God mean the defeat of God? Or are the Doctor's allocations of human beings a dread instance of what happens

129

to a man when he seeks to capture God's place? Which one is dead, dead inside, God or the Doctor? Strangely enough, the Doctor seems himself to show an affinity for the second option, for he has already confessed that he is the devil. At the end of the dialogue cited, he calls Riccardo a fanatic (in the original German version; the translation wrongly uses "idealist"). But which of the two has in fact earned the label of fanatic?

Hochhuth does not attempt a positive theodicy. For possible aid here, although in a way restricted to a Christian outlook, we may turn to the second body of materials from Paul Tillich. As Lord Keynes put it, "in the long run, we shall all be dead." Yet faith in God carries the hope that the Lord of life and death will not finally abandon us, and those who count to us, to a terrible nothingness.

In the passages from *Reinhold Niebuhr* our attention is directed to the uniqueness of the human "spirit," which in its sinfulness willfully compounds evil and suffering. Spokesmen for Judaism will dispute Niebuhr's conclusion that "it is impossible without the presuppositions of the Christian faith to find the source of sin within man himself." But most Jewish and Christian—as well as Muslim—thinkers will agree with Niebuhr that men find their true end only in the will of God, whose judgments and mercy are sure, within but also beyond the history of man and the world.

The following questions are among those arising from the present phase of our deliberations: Is it possible to live as a man and to have no faith whatsoever? Is faith in God a means of abolishing evil and suffering, or is it primarily a way of living with and despite these threats? Does death fall of necessity within the category of evil? In what ways does the persuasion of "resurrection of the dead" differ from that of "immortality of the soul"? What major consequences may be found in the view that God is creator, judge, and redeemer for one's understanding of the world and of the nature and destiny of man? In what respects, if any, is man totally responsible for his wrongdoing?

12

FAITH AND DOUBT*

Paul Tillich

[We turn to a] description of faith as an act of the human personality, as its centered and total act. An act of faith is an act of a finite being who is grasped by and turned to the infinite. It is a finite act with all the limitations of a finite act, and it is an act in which the infinite participates beyond the limitations of a finite act. Faith is certain in so far as it is an experience of the holy. But faith is uncertain in so far as the infinite to which it is related is received by a finite being. This element of uncertainty in faith cannot be removed, it must be accepted. And the element in faith which accepts this is courage. Faith includes an element of immediate awareness which gives certainty and an element of uncertainty. To accept this is courage. In the courageous standing of uncertainty, faith shows most visibly its dynamic character.

If we try to describe the relation of faith and courage, we must use a larger concept of courage than that which is ordinarily used. Courage as an element of faith is the daring self-affirmation of one's own being in spite of the powers of "non-being" which are the heritage of everything finite. Where there is daring and courage there is the possibility of failure. And in every act of faith this possibility is present. The risk must be

* Reprinted with permission from *Dynamics of Faith,* by Paul Tillich (New York: Harper & Brothers, 1957), pp. 16–22. Copyright © 1957 by Paul Tillich.

taken. Whoever makes his nation his ultimate concern needs courage in order to maintain this concern. Only certain is the ultimacy as ultimacy, the infinite passion as infinite passion. This is a reality given to the self with his own nature. It is as immediate and as much beyond doubt as the self is to the self. It *is* the self in its self-transcending quality. But there is not certainty of this kind about the content of our ultimate concern, be it nation, success, a god, or the God of the Bible: they all are contents without immediate awareness. Their acceptance as matters of ultimate concern is a risk and therefore an act of courage. There is a risk if what was considered as a matter of ultimate concern proves to be a matter of preliminary and transitory concern—as, for example, the nation. The risk to faith in one's ultimate concern is indeed the greatest risk man can run. For if it proves to be a failure, the meaning of one's life breaks down; one surrenders oneself, including truth and justice, to something which is not worth it. One has given away one's personal center without having a chance to regain it. The reaction of despair in people who have experienced the breakdown of their national claims is an irrefutable proof of the idolatrous character of their national concern. In the long run this is the inescapable result of an ultimate concern, the subject matter of which is not ultimate. And this is the risk faith must take; this is the risk which is unavoidable if a finite being affirms itself. Ultimate concern is ultimate risk and ultimate courage. It is not risk and needs no courage with respect to ultimacy itself. But it is risk and demands courage if it affirms a concrete concern. And every faith has a concrete element in itself. It is concerned about something or somebody. But this something or this somebody may prove to be not ultimate at all. Then faith is a failure in its concrete expression, although it is not a failure in the experience of the unconditional itself. A god disappears; divinity remains. Faith risks the vanishing of the concrete god in whom it believes. It may well be that with the vanishing of the god the believer breaks down without being able to re-establish his centered self by a new content of his ultimate concern. This risk cannot be taken away from any act of faith. There is only one point which is a matter not of risk but of immediate certainty and herein lies the greatness and the pain of being human; namely, one's standing between one's finitude and one's potential infinity.

All this is sharply expressed in the relation of faith and doubt. If faith is understood as belief that something is true, doubt is incompatible with the act of faith. If faith is understood as being ultimately concerned, doubt is a necessary element in it. It is a consequence of the risk of faith.

The doubt which is implicit in faith is not a doubt about facts or conclusions. It is not the same doubt which is the lifeblood of scientific research. Even the most orthodox theologian does not deny the right of methodological doubt in matters of empirical inquiry or logical deduction. A scientist who would say that a scientific theory is beyond doubt would at that moment cease to be scientific. He may believe that the theory can be trusted for all practical purposes. Without such belief no technical application of a theory would be possible. One could attribute to this kind of belief pragmatic certainty sufficient for action. Doubt in this case points to the preliminary character of the underlying theory.

There is another kind of doubt, which we could call skeptical in contrast to the scientific doubt which we could call methodological. The skeptical doubt is an attitude toward all the beliefs of man, from sense experiences to religious creeds. It is more an attitude than an assertion. For as an assertion it would conflict with itself. Even the assertion that there is no possible truth for man would be judged by the skeptical principle and could not stand as an assertion. Genuine skeptical doubt does not use the form of an assertion. It is an attitude of actually rejecting any certainty. Therefore, it cannot be refuted logically. It does not transform its attitude into a proposition. Such an attitude necessarily leads either to despair or cynicism, or to both alternately. And often, if this alternative becomes intolerable, it leads to indifference and the attempt to develop an attitude of complete unconcern. But since man is that being who is essentially concerned about his being, such an escape finally breaks down. This is the dynamics of skeptical doubt. It has an awakening and liberating function, but it also can prevent the development of a centered personality. For personality is not possible without faith. The despair about truth by the skeptic shows that truth is still his infinite passion. The cynical superiority over every concrete truth shows that truth is still taken seriously and that the impact of the question of an ultimate concern is strongly felt. The skeptic, so long as he is a serious skeptic, is not without faith, even though it has no concrete content.

The doubt which is implicit in every act of faith is neither the methodological nor the skeptical doubt. It is the doubt which accompanies every risk. It is not the permanent doubt of the scientist, and it is not the transitory doubt of the skeptic, but it is the doubt of him who is ultimately concerned about a concrete content. One could call it the existential doubt, in contrast to the methodological and the skeptical doubt. It does not question whether a special proposition is true or false. It does not reject every concrete truth, but it is aware of the element of insecurity in every existential truth. At the same time, the doubt which is implied in faith accepts this insecurity and takes it into itself in an act of courage. Faith includes courage. Therefore, it can include the doubt about itself. Certainly faith and courage are not identical. Faith has other elements besides courage and courage has other functions beyond affirming faith. Nevertheless, an act in which courage accepts risk belongs to the dynamics of faith.

This dynamic concept of faith seems to give no place to that restful affirmative confidence which we find in the documents of all great religions, including Christianity. But this is not the case. The dynamic concept of faith is the result of a conceptual analysis, both of the subjective and of the objective side of faith. It is by no means the description of an always actualized state of the mind. An analysis of structure is not the description of a state of things. The confusion of these two is a source of many misunderstandings and errors in all realms of life. An example, taken from the current discussion of anxiety, is typical of this confusion. The description of anxiety as the awareness of one's finitude is sometimes criticized as untrue from the point of view of the ordinary state of the mind. Anxiety, one says, appears under special conditions but is not an ever-present implication of man's finitude. Certainly anxiety as an acute experience appears under definite conditions. But the underlying structure of finite life is the universal condition which makes the appearance of anxiety under special conditions possible. In the same way doubt is not a permanent experience within the act of faith. But it is always present as an element in the structure of faith. This is the difference between faith and immediate evidence either of perceptual or of logical character. There is no faith without an intrinsic "in spite of" and the courageous affirmation of oneself in the state of ultimate concern. This intrinsic element of doubt breaks into the open under special individual and social conditions. If doubt appears, it should not be considered as the negation of faith, but as an element which was always and will always be present in the act of faith. Existential doubt and faith are poles of the same reality, the state of ultimate concern.

The insight into this structure of faith and doubt is of tremendous practical importance. Many Christians, as well as members of other religious groups, feel anxiety, guilt and despair about what they call "loss of faith." But serious doubt is confirmation of faith. It indicates the seriousness of the concern, its unconditional character. This also refers to those who as future or present ministers of a church experience not only scientific doubt about doctrinal statements—this is as necessary and perpetual as theology is a perpetual need—but also existential doubt about the message of their church, e.g., that Jesus can be called the Christ. The criterion according to which they should judge themselves is the seriousness and ultimacy of their concern about the content of both their faith and their doubt.

13

AUSCHWITZ OR THE QUESTION ASKED OF GOD*

Rolf Hochhuth

DOCTOR (*threateningly, as if speaking to a dog*): Come here, I say.

RICCARDO *again follows him a short distance. They now stand face to face, far downstage.* RICCARDO'S *forehead and face are bleeding. He has been beaten.*

DOCTOR (*in a sarcastically friendly tone*): That pretty brat your own?

RICCARDO (*with pent fury*): The Germans beat her father to death. They thought it funny because he wore glasses.

DOCTOR: Such brutes, these Germans. (*With his stick, which he handles with the air of a dandy, he gives* RICCARDO *a brief and almost comradely tap on the chest.*) Where is your yellow star?

RICCARDO: I threw it away because I wanted to escape.

DOCTOR: What's this about your not being a Jew? On the railroad platform, I am told, you claimed the Pope assigned you to care for the Jews.

RICCARDO: I said that only to escape. They believed me and let me go. I am a Jew like the others.

* From *The Deputy*, by Rolf Hochhuth, Act Five, Scene Two. Translated by Richard and Clara Winston. Reprinted with the permission of Grove Press, Inc. Copyright © 1964 by Grove Press, Inc.

DOCTOR: Congratulations. A subtle Jesuit trick. How is it they caught up with you again?

RICCARDO (*contemptuously*): Nobody caught me. I joined my companions of my own accord, when nobody was looking.

DOCTOR (*scornfully*): My, how noble! We've needed volunteers. Priests too. Just in case someone should die here. The climate can be nasty in Auschwitz. Of course you're not a Jew . . .

RICCARDO *does not answer. The* DOCTOR *sits down on the bench. He says sarcastically:* A martyr, then. If that's the case, why did you run away?

RICCARDO: Wouldn't you be afraid if you were sent here?

DOCTOR: Afraid of what? An internment camp. Why should a man so close to God as you be afraid!

RICCARDO (*insistently*): People are being burned here . . . The smell of burning flesh and hair—

DOCTOR (*addressing him more as an equal*): What foolish ideas you have. What you see here is only industry. The smell comes from lubricating oil and horsehair, drugs and nitrates, rubber and sulphur. A second Ruhr is growing up here. I. G. Farben, Buna, have built branches here. Krupp will be coming soon. Air raids don't bother us. Labor is cheap.

RICCARDO: I've known for a year what this place is used for. Only my imagination was too feeble. And today I no longer had the courage—to go along.

DOCTOR: Ah, then you know about it. Very well. I understand your ambition to be crucified, but in the name of God the Father, the Son and the Holy Ghost, I intend to have a little sport deflating your self-importance. I have something quite different in mind for you.

RICCARDO *has placed the child he was carrying at his side. She snuggles close to him.*

DOCTOR (*to the child*): Uncle Doctor has some candy for you. Come here!

He takes a bag from his pocket. The child reaches out eagerly.

THE GIRL (*shyly*): Thank you.

The DOCTOR *picks up the little girl and attempts to seat her on the bench. But the child scrambles off and clings to* RICCARDO.

DOCTOR (*scornfully*): So affectionate! (*Pleasantly, to the child*) What's your name? (*The child does not answer*) A pity the little girl has no twin brother. Research on twins is my special hobby. Other children here never live more than six hours, even when we're rushed. Nor their mothers either—we have enough workhorses and we're sufficiently accommodating to gas children under fifteen together with their mothers. It saves a lot of screaming. What's wrong? You did say you knew what we do here.

RICCARDO (*hoarse from horror*): Get it over with.

DOCTOR: Don't tell me you want to die right now! You'd like that, wouldn't you; inhaling for fifteen minutes, and then sitting at God's right hand as saint! No! I cannot give you such preferential treatment while so many others go up in smoke without that consolation. As long as you can *believe,* my dear priest, dying is just a joke.

A scuffle in the background; the deportees are being made to move forward. The line advances. SIGNORA LUCCANI *tries to break out of it, to go to* RICCARDO. *She screams:*

JULIA: Let us stay together. I won't.—My child!

A Kapo runs up and tries to push her back into the line. LUCCANI *clumsily intervenes.*

LUCCANI: Don't! Don't hit the women. Don't hit their children.

The little GIRL *tries to pull* RICCARDO *over to her mother.* RICCARDO *hesitates. The* DOCTOR *interferes.*

DOCTOR: Let her go! (*To* JULIA) What's this weeping over a brief separation?

The deportees move forward; old LUCCANI *tries to stay back, is pushed on. He calls out in a feeble voice:*

LUCCANI: Julia—Julia—I'm waiting—do come.

He is pushed out of sight. The whole group, including the MANUFACTURER, *who is supporting old* LUCCANI, *and a pregnant woman, disappear off right. The back of the stage is left empty. Soon the cement mixer falls silent.*

JULIA (*pleading with the* DOCTOR): Let us stay with the priest!
You can see how attached the child is to him. He calmed us
so on the train. Please, let us die together, the priest and us—

DOCTOR (*to* JULIA): Now, now, nobody's dying here. (*to*
RICCARDO) Tell the woman the truth! That those are factory
chimneys over there. You'll have to turn out work here, work
hard. But nobody will do you any harm. (*He strokes the little
boy's hair reassuringly.*) Come along, my boy. It's time for
lunch, and there's pudding for dessert.

JULIA (*a moment before half-mad with fear, is now full of
confidence in the* DOCTOR): Do you know where my husband
is? Where my husband was taken to?

DOCTOR: Run along now. Here, take your sister with you. Your
husband? Still in Rome, I think. Or perhaps in another camp.
I don't know everybody here. (*To* RICCARDO) Let go—give
the woman her child! (*To* JULIA) Here, take your little girl.
The priest and I have some things to discuss.

JULIA (*to* RICCARDO): Stay with us, please stay! You disappeared so suddenly this morning, were gone so long. I was
so relieved when you returned.

RICCARDO (*strokes the little girl, kisses her and gives her to her
mother*): I'll come afterwards—I'll come, as surely as God
is with us.

DOCTOR: Please, now—in fifteen minutes your friend will be
with you again.

He beckons to the KAPO, *who herds the family along.* Those who
don't keep up get nothing more to eat. Hurry—move on!

All go out except the DOCTOR *and* RICCARDO. RICCARDO *sways.*

The DOCTOR *addresses him patronizingly:* You're very tired,
I see. Do sit down.

*He points to the bench and walks back and forth with little
tripping steps.* RICCARDO, *exhausted, sits down.*

RICCARDO: What a devil you are!

DOCTOR (*extremely pleased*): Devil—wonderful! I am the devil.
And you will be my private chaplain. It's a deal: save my

soul. But first I must see to those scratches. Oh dear—however did it happen?

While the DOCTOR *goes into the hut,* RICCARDO *remains seated on the bench, holding the bloodstained handkerchief to his forehead to check the flow. The* DOCTOR, *in the doorway, calls:* Come here. I have great plans for you, Chaplain.

RICCARDO: What do you want of me?

DOCTOR: I mean my offer seriously. Do you really know what awaits you otherwise?

He goes inside the hut, and is rummaging in a medicine chest. RICCARDO *has dragged himself up the steps. He drops into the nearest chair. The* DOCTOR *applies a dressing and adhesive tape to his wounds, meanwhile saying reassuringly, and almost seriously:* Not long ago the brutal idiots here had their fun with a certain Polish priest who said he wanted to die in place of another prisoner—a man with a family. A voluntary offering, in short, like yours. They kept him in a starvation cell ten days, then even put a barbed wire crown on him. Oh well, he had what he wanted, what your kind wants: suffering in Christ—and Rome will surely canonize him some day. He died as an individual, a fine, old-fashioned, personal death. You, my dear friend, would be merely gassed. Quite simply gassed, and *no one,* no man, Pope or God, will ever find out. At best you may be missed like an enlisted man on the Volga, or a U-boat sailor in the Atlantic. If you insist on it, you'll die here like a snail crushed under an auto tire—die as the heroes of today do die, namelessly, snuffed out by powers they have never known, let alone can fight. In other words, meaninglessly.

RICCARDO (*scornfully*): Do you think God would overlook a sacrifice, merely because the killing is done without pomp and circumstance? Your ideas can't be as primitive as that!

DOCTOR: Aha, you think God does not overlook the sacrifice! Really? You know, at bottom all my work's concerned entirely with this one question. Really, now, I'm doing all I can. Since July of '42, for fifteen months, weekdays and Sabbath,

I've been sending people to God. Do you think He's made the slightest acknowledgment? He has not even directed a bolt of lightning against me. Can you understand that? *You* ought to know. Nine thousand in one day a while back.

RICCARDO (*groans, says against his better knowledge*): That isn't true, it can't be . . .

DOCTOR (*calmly*): Nine thousand in one day. Pretty little vermin, like that child you were holding. All the same, in an hour they're unconscious or dead. At any rate ready for the furnace. Young children often go into the furnaces still alive, though unconscious. An interesting phenomenon. Infants, especially. A remarkable fact: the gas doesn't always kill them.

RICCARDO *covers his face with his hand. Then he rushes to the door. Laughing, the* DOCTOR *pulls him back.*

DOCTOR: You cannot always run away. Stop trembling like that. My word of honor, I'll let you *live* . . . What difference does it make to me, one item more or less puffing up the chimney.

RICCARDO (*screams*): Live—to be *your* prisoner!

DOCTOR: Not my prisoner. My partner.

RICCARDO: I assure you, leaving a world in which you and Auschwitz are possible, is scarcely harder than to live in it.

DOCTOR: The martyr always prefers dying to thinking. Paul Valéry was right. The angel, he said—who knows, you may be an angel—(*laughs*) is distinguishable from me, the devil, only by the act of thought that still awaits him. I shall expose you to the task of thinking like a swimmer to the ocean. If your cassock keeps you above water then I promise I'll let you fetch me back home into the bosom of Christ's Church. (*Laughs.*) Who knows, who knows. But first you have to practice the celebrated patience of Negation. First you can watch me for a year or so conducting this, the boldest experiment that man has ever undertaken. Only a theological mind like my own—(*he taps* RICCARDO's *clerical collar*) I too once wore the iron collar for a while—could risk loading himself with such a burden of sacrilege.

RICCARDO (*beating his forehead in despair, cries*): Why . . . why? Why do you do it?

DOCTOR: Because I wanted an answer! And so I've ventured what no man has ever ventured since the beginning of the world. I took the vow to challenge the Old Gent to provoke him so limitlessly that He would have to give an answer. Even if only the negative answer which can be His sole excuse, as Stendhal put it: that He doesn't exist.

RICCARDO (*bitingly*): A medical student's joke—for which millions are paying with their lives. Can it be that you are not even a criminal? Are you only a lunatic? As primitive as Virchow when he said he had dissected ten thousand cadavers and never found a soul?

DOCTOR (*offended*): Soul! Now *that's* what I call primitive! What utter flippancy to be forever taking cover behind such empty words! (*He imitates a priest praying.*) *Credo quia absurdum est*—still? (*seriously*) Well, hear the answer: not a peep came from Heaven, not a peep for fifteen months, not once since I've been giving tourists tickets to Paradise.

RICCARDO (*ironically*): So much sheer cruelty—merely to do what every harmless schoolmaster manages without all this effort, if he happens to be stupid enough to want to prove that the Incomprehensible isn't there.

DOCTOR: Then do you find it more acceptable that God in person is turning the human race on the spit of history? History! The final vindication of God's ways to man? Really? (*He laughs like a torturer.*) History: dust and altars, misery and rape, and all glory a mockery of its victims. The truth is, Auschwitz refutes creator, creation, and the creature. Life as an idea is dead. This may well be the beginning of a great new era, a redemption from suffering. From this point of view only one crime remains: cursed be he who creates life. I cremate life. That is modern humanitarianism—the sole salvation from the future. I mean that seriously, even on the personal level. Out of pity, I have always buried my own children right away—in condoms.

RICCARDO (*attempts mockery, but shouts in order to keep himself from weeping*): Redemption from suffering! A lecture on humanism from a homicidal maniac! Save someone—save just a single child!

DOCTOR (*calmly*): What gives priests the right to look down on the SS? We are the Dominicans of the technological age. It is no accident that so many of my kind, the leaders, come from good Catholic homes. Heydrich was a Jew—all right. Eichmann and Göring are Protestants. But Hitler, Goebbels, Bormann, Kaltenbrunner . . . ? Höss, our commandant, studied for the priesthood. And Himmler's uncle, who stood godfather to him, is nothing less than Suffragan Bishop in Bamberg! (*He laughs.*) The Allies have solemnly sworn to hang us all if they should catch us. So after the war, it's only logical, the SS tunic will become a shroud for gallows birds. The Church, however, after centuries of killing heretics throughout the West now sets itself up as the exclusive moral authority of this Continent. Absurd! Saint Thomas Aquinas, a mystic, a god-crazed visionary like Heinrich Himmler, who also babbles well-meant nonsense, Thomas condemned the innocent for heresy just as these morons here condemn the Jews . . . But you do not cast him out of your temple! The readers that they use in German schools in centuries to come may well reprint the speeches Himmler made in honor of the mothers of large families—why not? (*He is royally amused.*) A civilization that commits its children's souls into the safeguard of a Church responsible for the Inquisition comes to the end that it deserves when for its funeral pyres it plucks the brands from our furnaces for human bodies. Do you admit that? Of course not. (*Spits and pours a glass of brandy for himself.*) One of us is honest—the other credulous. (*Malignantly*) Your Church was the first to show that you can burn men just like coke. In Spain alone, without the benefit of crematoria, you turned to ashes three hundred and fifty thousand human beings, most of them while alive, mind you. Such an achievement surely needs the help of Christ.

RICCARDO (*furious, loudly*): I know as well as you—or I would not be here—how many times the Church has been guilty, as it is again today. I have nothing more to say if you make God responsible for the crimes of His Church. God does not stand *above* history. He shares the fate of the natural order. In Him all man's anguish is contained.

DOCTOR (*interrupting*): Oh yes, I also learned that drivel once. His suffering in the world fetters the evil principle. Prove it. Where—when have I ever been fettered? Luther did not fool himself so badly. Not man, he said, but God hangs, tortures, strangles, wars . . .

Laughing, he slaps RICCARDO *on the back*. RICCARDO *shrinks from him.*

Your anger amuses me—you'll make a good partner. I saw that right off. You'll help in the laboratory, and at night we'll wrangle about that product of neurosis which for the present you call God or about some other philosophical rot.

RICCARDO: I don't intend to act your court jester, to cheer the hours when you are face to face with your own self. I have never seen a man so wretched, for you know what you do . . .

DOCTOR (*painfully jarred*): Then I must disappoint you once again. Just as your whole faith is self-deception and despera- tion, so is your hope that I feel wretched. Of course boredom has always plagued me. That is why I find our dispute so re- freshing, and why you are to stay alive. But wretched? No. At present I am studying *homo sapiens*. Yesterday I watched one of the workers at the crematorium. As he was chopping up the cadavers to get them through the furnace doors he discovered the body of his wife. *How* did he react?

RICCARDO: You do not look as if this study made you especially cheerful . . . I think you too feel no easier than that worker.

DOCTOR: Don't I? Well then, I still have my books. Napoleon, as you know, remarked to Metternich he did not give a damn about the death of a million men. I've just been investigating how long it was before that scoundrel became the idol of posterity. Quite relevant, in view of Hitler's . . . Of course, that disgusting vegetarian has not, like Napoleon, seduced all of his sisters. He's quite devoid of such endearing traits. All the same I find him more likable—

He picks up a book; the name "Hegel" is on the cover.

than the philosophers who squeeze the horrors of world history through countless convolutions of their brains, until at last they look acceptable. I was recently rereading Nietzsche, that eternal schoolboy, because a colleague of mine had the honor of delivering to Mussolini Herr Hitler's present on his sixtieth birthday.

Laughs piercingly.

Just think: The complete works of Nietzsche on *Bible* paper.

RICCARDO: Is Nietzsche to blame if weak-headed visionaries, brutes and murderers have stolen his legacy? Only madmen take him literally . . .

DOCTOR: Right, only madmen, men of action. It suits *them* perfectly that Nietzsche looked to the beasts of prey for his criterion of manly virtues—presumably because he himself had so little of the beast in him, not even enough to lay a girl. Grotesque: the Blond Beast, or, The Consequences of Crippling Inhibitions, comes down to: a massacre of millions. (*He chuckles.*) No, what captivated Hitler was certainly not the finest critical mind in Europe. What Hitler fell for was the Beast, the beautiful beast of prey. No wonder, when the inventor of that monstrosity wrote in language so intoxicated, and with such sovereign arrogance, it seemed he had champagne instead of ink in his pen. (*Abruptly*) You can have champagne here too, and girls. This afternoon when those people there, the ones you came with, burn up in smoke, I shall be burning up myself between the legs of a nineteen-year-old girl. That's one amenity that beats your faith because it's something a fellow really has, with heart, mouth, and hands. And has it here on earth, where we need such things. But of course you know all that . . .

RICCARDO (*casually*): Oh yes, a fine amenity . . . only it doesn't last too long.

DOCTOR (*draws on his gloves, smiles with something close to triumph*): We understand each other splendidly. You'll have two nice girls in the laboratory. I suppose the newest books will interest you more. *Habent sua fata divini*—the saints fall on their faces. The light of reason falls on the Gospels. I made a pilgrimage last year to Marburg, to hear Bultmann. Daring, for a theologian, the way he throws out the clutter in the New Testament. Even evangelism no longer asks men to believe the mythical cosmogony of the past.

During these last sentences the rumble of the cement mixer resumes. As yet, no more deportees are visible. But upstage, far right, the glare of a mighty fire rises once more, high and menacing. Shrill whistles. RICCARDO *has leaped to his feet. He wrenches the door open and runs outside. He points to the underworld light and cries out contemptuously, as the* DOCTOR *slowly follows him*—

RICCARDO: Here—there—I'm in the midst of it. What need have I of believing in Heaven or Hell.

He comes closer to the DOCTOR, *speaks in a lower voice.*

You know that. You know that even St. John did not see the Last Judgment as a cosmic event.

Loudly, flinging the insult at the DOCTOR.

Your hideous face composed of lust and filth and gibberish sweeps all doubts away—all. Since the devil exists, God also exists. Otherwise *you* would have won a long time ago.

DOCTOR (*grips his arms, laughs ebulliently*): That's the way I like you. The idealist's St. Vitus dance. . . .

14

IS A THEODICY POSSIBLE?*

Paul Tillich

THE darkness into which the light of Christmas shines is above all the darkness of death. The threat of death, which shadows the whole road of our life, is the dark background of the Advent expectation of mankind. Death is not merely the scissors which cuts the thread of our life, as a famous ancient symbol indicates. It is rather one of those threads which are woven into the design of our existence, from its very beginning to its end. Our having to die is a shaping force through our whole being of body and soul in every moment. The face of every man shows the trace of the presence of death in his life, of his fear of death, of his courage toward death, and of his resignation to death. This frightful presence of death subjects man to bondage and servitude all his life. . . . So far as I stand in fear, I stand not in freedom; and I am not free to act as the situation demands, but am bound to act as the pictures and imaginations produced by my fear drive me to act. For fear is, above all, fear of the unknown; and the darkness of the unknown is filled with the images created by fear. This is true even with respect to events on the plane of daily life: the unknown face terrifies the infant; the unknown will of the parent and the teacher creates fear in the child; and all the unknown implications of any situation or

* Excerpts from *The Shaking of the Foundations,* by Paul Tillich, pp. 169–72, 165–68, 104–7 (Copyright © 1948 Charles Scribner's Sons), are reprinted with permission of Charles Scribner's Sons.

new task produce fear, which is the feeling of not being able to handle the situation. All this is true to an absolute degree with respect to death—the absolutely unknown; the darkness in which there is no light at all, and in which even imagination vanishes; that darkness in which all acting and controlling cease, and in which everything which we were is finished; the most necessary and impossible idea at the same time; the real and ultimate object of fear from which all other fears derive their power, that fear that overwhelmed even Christ at Gethsemane.

But we must ask what is the reason for this fear. Are we not finite, limited and unable to imagine or to wish for an infinite continuation of our finiteness? Would that not be more terrible than death? Is there not a feeling within us of fulfillment, of satisfaction, and of weariness with respect to life, as is evident in the words about the Old Testament Patriarchs? Is not the law "dust to dust" a natural law? But then why is it used as a curse in the Paradise story? There must be something more profoundly mysterious about death than the natural melancholy which accompanies the realization of our transitoriness. Paul points to it, when he calls death the wages of sin, and sin, the sting of death. And [the Epistle to the Hebrews], as well, speaks of "him that had the power of death, that is, the devil"—the organized power of sin and evil. Death, although natural to every finite being, seems at the same time to stand against nature. But it is man only who is able to face his death consciously; that belongs to his greatness and dignity. It is that which enables him to look at his life as a whole, from a definite beginning to a definite end. It is that which enables him to ask for the meaning of his life—a question which elevates him above his life, and gives him the feeling of his eternity. Man's knowledge that he has to die is also man's knowledge that he is above death. It is man's destiny to be mortal and immortal at the same time. And now we know what the sting of death is, and why the devil has the power of death: we have lost our immortality. It is not that we are mortal which creates the ultimate fear of death, but rather that we have lost our eternity beyond our natural and inescapable mortality; that we have lost it by sinful separation from the Eternal; and that we are guilty of this separation.

To be in servitude to the fear of death during our lifetime means being in servitude to the fear of death which is nature and guilt at the same time. In the fear of death, it is not merely the knowledge of our finiteness that is preserved, but also the knowledge of our infinity, of our being determined for eternity, and of our having lost eternity. We are slaves of fear, not because we have to die, but because we deserve to die.

Therefore, salvation is not a magic procedure by which we lose our finiteness. It is rather a judgment which declares that we do not deserve to die, because we are justified—a judgment which is not based on anything that we have done, for then certainly we would not have faith in it. But it is based on something that Eternity itself has done, something that we can hear and see, in the reality of a mortal man who by his own death has conquered him who has the power of death.

If Christmas has any meaning, it has that meaning. Ask yourself, as you listen to the prophecies of Advent and to the stories of Christmas, whether your attitude toward death has changed; whether you are any longer in servitude to the fear of death; and whether you can stand the image of your own death. Do not deceive yourself about the seriousness of death—not death in general, not the death of somebody else, but your own death—by nice arguments for the immortality of the soul. The Christian message is more realistic than those arguments. It knows that we, *really we,* have to die; it is not just a part of us that has to die. And within Christianity there is only one "argument" against death: the forgiveness of sins, and the victory over Him who has the power of death. It speaks of the coming of the Eternal to us, becoming temporal in order to restore our eternity. The whole man is mortal and immortal at the same time: the whole man is temporal and eternal at the same time; the whole man is judged and saved at the same time, because the Eternal took part in flesh and blood and fear of death. That is the message of Christmas.

. . . .

In the Nuremberg war-crime trials a witness appeared who had lived for a time in a grave in a Jewish grave-yard, in Wilna, Poland. It was the only place he—and many others—could live, when in hiding after they had escaped the gas chamber. During this time he wrote poetry, and one of the poems was a description of a birth. In a grave nearby a young woman gave birth to a boy. The eighty-year-old gravedigger, wrapped in a linen shroud, assisted. When the newborn child uttered his first cry, the old man prayed: "Great God, hast Thou finally sent the Messiah to us? For who else than the Messiah Himself can be born in a grave?" But after three days the poet saw the child sucking his mother's tears because she had no milk for him.

This story, which surpasses anything the human imagination could have invented, has not only incomparable emotional value, but also tremendous symbolic power. When I first read it, it occurred to me more forcefully than ever before that our Christian symbols, taken from the gospel stories, have lost a great deal of their power because too often repeated and too superficially used. It has been forgotten that the manger of Christmas was the expression of utter poverty and distress before it became the place where the angels appeared and to which the star pointed. And it has been forgotten that the tomb of Jesus was the end of His life and of His work *before* it became the place of His final triumph. We have become insensitive to the infinite tension which is implied in the words of the Apostles' Creed: "suffered . . . was crucified, dead, and buried . . . rose again from the dead." We already know, when we hear the first words, what the ending will be: "rose again;" and for many people it is no more than the inevitable "happy ending." The old Jewish gravedigger knew better. For him, the immeasurable tension implicit in the expectation of the Messiah was a reality, appearing in the infinite contrast between the things he saw and the hope he maintained.

The depth of this tension is emphasized by the last part of the story. After three days the child was not elevated to glory; he drank his mother's tears, having nothing else to drink. Probably he died and the hope of the old Jew was frustrated once more, as it had been frustrated innumerable times before. No consolation can be derived from this story; there cannot be a happy ending—and precisely this is the truth about our lives. In a remarkable passage of his book, *Credo,* Karl Barth writes about the word "buried" in the Creed: "By a man's being buried it is evidently confirmed and sealed—seemingly in his presence, actually already in his absence—that he has no longer a present, any more than a future. He has become pure past. He is accessible only to memory, and even that only so long as those who are able and willing to remember him are not themselves buried. And the future toward which all human present is running is just this: to be buried." These words describe exactly the situation in which the pious old Jew prayed: "Great God, hast Thou finally sent the Messiah to us?"

We often hide the seriousness of the "buried" in the Creed, not only for the Christ, but also for ourselves, by imagining that not *we* shall be buried, but only a comparatively unimportant part of us, the physical body. That is not what the Creed implies. It is the same subject, Jesus Christ, of Whom it is said that He suffered and that He was buried and that He was resurrected. *He* was buried, He—His *whole* personality—was removed from the earth. The same is true of us. *We* shall die, we—our *personality,* from which we cannot separate our body as an accidental part—shall be buried.

Only if we take the "buried" in the gospel stories as seriously as this, can we evaluate the Easter stories and can we evaluate the words of the gravedigger, "Who else than the Messiah can be born in a grave?" His question has two aspects. Only the Messiah can bring birth out of death. It is not a natural event. It does not happen every day, but it happens on the day of the Messiah. It is the most surprising, the most profound, and the most paradoxical mystery of existence. Arguments for the immortality of an assumedly better part of us cannot bring life out of the grave. Eternal life is brought about only with the coming of the "new reality," the eon of the Messiah, which, according to *our* faith, has already appeared in Jesus as the Christ.

But there is another side to the assertion that nobody other than the Messiah Himself can be born in a grave, a side which, perhaps, was less conscious to the pious Jew. The Christ *must* be buried in order to be the "Christ," namely, He Who has conquered death. The gospel story . . . assures us of the real and irrevocable death and burial of Jesus. The women, the high priests, the soldiers, the sealed stone—they are all called by the gospel to witness to the reality of the end. We ought to listen more carefully to these witnesses, to the ones who tell us with triumph or cynicism that He has been buried, that He is removed forever from the earth, that no real traces of Him are left in our world. And we ought also to listen to the others who say, in doubt and despair, "But we trusted that it had been He Who should have redeemed Israel." It is not hard to hear both these voices today, in a world where there are so many places like the Jewish cemetery in Wilna. It is even possible to hear them in ourselves, for each of us to hear them in himself.

And, if we hear them, what can we answer? Let us be clear about this. The answer of Easter is not a necessity. In reality, there is no inevitable happy ending as there is in perverted and perverting cinemas. But the answer of Easter has become possible precisely because the Christ has been buried. The new life would not really be *new* life if it did not come from the complete end of the old life. Otherwise, it would have to be buried again. But if the new life has come out of the grave, then the Messiah Himself has appeared.

.   .   .   .

[The well-known words of Paul in Romans 8:38–39] express the Christian faith in divine Providence. They are the first and fundamental interpretation of the disturbing words in the gospel of Matthew, where Jesus commands us not to take any thought about our life and food and clothing, and to seek first the Kingdom of God, for all of our daily life and needs are already known by God. We need such an interpretation. For there are few articles of the Christian faith which are more important for the daily life of every man and woman, and there are few more open to misunderstanding and distortion. And such misunderstanding necessarily leads to a disillusionment which not only turns the hearts of men away from God, but also creates a revolt against Him, against Christianity, and against religion. When I spoke to the soldiers between the battles of the last war, they expressed their denial of the Christian message in terms of an attack upon the belief in Providence—an attack which obviously drew its bitterness from fundamental disappointments. After reading a paper written by the great Einstein, in which he challenges the faith in a personal God, I concluded that there was no difference between his feeling and that of the unsophisticated soldiers. The idea of God seemed to be impossible, because the reality of our world seems to be in opposition to the all-mighty power of a wise and righteous God.

Once, when I tried to interpret to a group of Christian and Jewish refugees the paradoxical character of the divine world-government in terms of Second Isaiah, a formerly eminent Jew from Western Germany told me that he had received many cablegrams from Southern France informing him of the horrible story of the sudden evacuation, from Germany, of nearly ten thousand Jews, of the age of ninety or more, and of their transportation to the concentration camps. He said that the thought of this unimaginable misery prevented him from being able to find meaning in even the most powerful message concerning the divine Providence. What answer shall we give, what answer *can* we give to such a crucial problem—a problem in which Christianity as a whole is at stake, a problem which has nothing to do with a theoretical criticism of the idea of God, but rather which represents the anguish of the human heart which can no longer stand the power borne by the daemonic forces on earth?

Paul speaks of these forces. He knows them all: the horror of death and the anxiety of life; the irresistible strength of natural and historic powers; the ambiguity of the present and the inscrutable darkness of the future; the incalculable turns of fate from height to depth, and from depth to height; and the natural destruction of creature by creature. He knows them all as well as we do, who have, in our period, rediscovered them, after a short time in which Providence and reality seemed to be a matter of fact. But it never was, and never will be, a matter of fact. It is rather a matter of the most powerful, the most paradoxical, and the most venturing faith. Only as such has it meaning and truth.

What is its content? It is certainly not a vague promise that, with the help of God, everything will come to a good end; there are many things that come to a bad end. And it is not the maintenance of hope in every situation; there are situations in which there can be no hope. Nor is it the anticipation of a period of history, in which divine Providence will be proved by human happiness and goodness; there is no generation in which divine Providence will be less paradoxical than it is in ours. But the content of the faith in Providence is this: when death rains from heaven as it does now, when cruelty wields power over nations and individuals as it does now, when hunger and persecution drive millions from place to place as they do now, and when prisons and slums all over the world distort the humanity of the bodies and souls of men as they do now—we can boast in that time, and just in that time, that even all of this cannot separate us from the love of God. In this sense, and in this sense alone, all things work together for good, for the *ultimate* good, the eternal love, and the Kingdom of God. Faith in divine Providence is the faith that nothing can prevent us from fulfilling the ultimate meaning of our existence. Providence does not mean a divine planning by which everything is predetermined, as is an efficient machine. Rather, Providence means that there is a creative and saving possibility implied in every situation, which cannot be destroyed by any event. Providence means that the daemonic and destructive forces within ourselves and our world can never have an unbreakable grasp upon us, and that the bond which connects us with the fulfilling love can never be disrupted.

This love appears to us and is embodied in "Christ Jesus our Lord." By adding this, Paul does not use a merely solemn phrase, as we often do when we use the words. He uses them, rather, after he has pointed to the only thing that can destroy our faith in Providence, which is our disbelief in the love of God, our distrust of God, our fear of His wrath, our hatred of his Presence, our conception of Him as a tyrant who condemns us, and our feeling of sin and guilt. It is not the depth of our suffering, but the depth of our separation from God, which destroys our faith in Providence. Providence and the forgiveness of sins are not two separate aspects of the Christian faith; they are one and the same—the certainty that we can reach eternal life in spite of suffering and sin. Paul unites both words by saying, "Who is he that condemneth? It is Christ Jesus . . . who maketh intercession for us," and *therefore,* he continues, "Who shall separate us from the love of Christ? Shall tribulation, or anguish, or persecution, or famine, or nakedness, or peril, or sword . . . ? In all these things we are more than conquerors through him who loved us. . . ." *This* is the faith in Providence, and this alone.

15

HUMAN NATURE AND DESTINY*

Reinhold Niebuhr

. . . THE Christian faith in God as Creator of the world transcends the canons and antinomies of rationality, particularly the antinomy between mind and matter, between consciousness and extension. God is not merely mind who forms a previously given formless stuff. God is both vitality and form and the source of all existence. He creates the world. This world is not God; but it is not evil because it is not God. Being God's creation, it is good.

The consequence of this conception of the world upon the view of human nature in Christian thought is to allow an appreciation of the unity of body and soul in human personality which idealists and naturalists have sought in vain. Furthermore it prevents the idealistic error of regarding the mind as essentially good or essentially eternal and the body as essentially evil. But it also obviates the romantic error of seeking for the good in man-as-nature and for evil in man-as-spirit or as reason. Man is, according to the Biblical view, a created and finite existence in both body and spirit. Obviously a view which depends upon an ultra-rational presupposition is immediately endangered when rationally explicated; for reason which seeks to bring all

* Excerpts from *The Nature and Destiny of Man,* by Reinhold Niebuhr, Vol. 1, pp. 12–18; Vol. 2, pp. 287–96 (Copyright © 1941, 1943 Charles Scribner's Sons) are reprinted with the permission of Charles Scribner's Sons. Footnotes omitted.

things into terms of rational coherence is tempted to make one known thing the principle of explanation and to derive all other things from it. Its most natural inclination is to make itself that ultimate principle, and thus in effect to declare itself God. Christian psychology and philosophy have never completely freed themselves from this fault, which explains why naturalists plausibly though erroneously regard Christian faith as the very fountain source of idealism. . . .

The second important characteristic of the Christian view of man is that he is understood primarily from the standpoint of God, rather than the uniqueness of his rational faculties or his relation to nature. He is made in the "image of God." It has been the mistake of many Christian rationalists to assume that this term is no more than a religious-pictorial expression of what philosophy intends when it defines man as a rational animal. We have previously alluded to the fact that the human spirit has the special capacity of standing continually outside itself in terms of indefinite regression. Consciousness is a capacity for surveying the world and determining action from a governing centre. Self-consciousness represents a further degree of transcendence in which the self makes itself its own object in such a way that the ego is finally always subject and not object. The rational capacity of surveying the world, of forming general concepts and analysing the order of the world is thus but one aspect of what Christianity knows as "spirit." The self knows the world, insofar as it knows the world, because it stands outside both itself and the world, which means that it cannot understand itself except as it is understood from beyond itself and the world.

This essential homelessness of the human spirit is the ground of all religion; for the self which stands outside itself and the world cannot find the meaning of life in itself or the world. It cannot identify meaning with causality in nature; for its freedom is obviously something different from the necessary causal links of nature. Nor can it identify the principle of meaning with rationality, since it transcends its own rational processes, so that it may, for instance, ask the question whether there is a relevance between its rational forms and the recurrences and forms of nature. It is this capacity of freedom which finally prompts great cultures and philosophies to transcend rationalism and to seek for the meaning of life in an unconditioned ground of existence. But from the standpoint of human thought this unconditioned ground of existence, this God, can be defined only negatively. This is why mystic religions in general, and particularly the neo-Platonic tradition in western culture, have one interesting similarity with Christianity and one important difference in their estimate of human nature. In common with Christianity they measure the depth of the human spirit in terms of its capacity of self-transcendence. Thus Plotinus defines *nous* not as Aristotle defines it. For him it is primarily the capacity for self-knowledge and it has no limit short of the eternal. Mysticism and Christianity agree in understanding man from the standpoint of the eternal. But since mysticism leads to an undifferentiated ultimate reality, it is bound to regard particularity, including individuality, as essentially evil. All mystic religions therefore have the characteristic of accentuating individuality inasfar as individuality is inherent in the capacity for self-consciousness emphasized in mysticism and is something more than mere bodily particularity; but all mystic philosophies ultimately lose the very individuality which they first emphasize, because they sink finite particularity in a distinctionless divine ground of existence.

God as will and personality, in concepts of Christian faith, is thus the only possible ground of real individuality, though not the only possible presupposition of self-consciousness. But faith in God as will and personality depends upon faith in His power to reveal Himself. The Christian faith in God's self-disclosure, culminating in the revelation of Christ, is thus the basis of the Christian concept of personality and individuality. In terms of this faith man can understand himself as a unity of will which finds its end in the will of God. We thus have in the problem of human nature one of the many indications of the relation of general and special revelation, which concerns theology so perennially. The conviction that man stands too completely outside of both nature and reason to understand himself in terms of either without misunderstanding himself, belongs to general revelation in the sense that any astute analysis of the human situation must lead to it. But if man lacks a further revelation of the divine he will also misunderstand himself when he seeks to escape the conditions of nature and reason. He will end by seeking absorption in a divine reality which is at once all and nothing. To understand himself truly means to begin with a faith that he is understood from beyond himself, that he is known and loved of God and must find himself in terms of obedience to the divine will. This relation of the divine to the human will makes it possible for man to relate himself to God without pretending to be God; and to accept his distance from God as a created thing, without believing that the evil of his nature is caused by this finiteness. Man's finite existence in the body and in history can be essentially affirmed, as naturalism wants to affirm it. Yet the uniqueness of man's spirit can be appreciated even more than idealism appreciates it, though always preserving a proper distinction between the human and divine. Also the unity of spirit and body can be emphasized in terms of its relation to a Creator and Redeemer who created both mind and body. These are the ultra-rational foundations and presuppositions of Christian wisdom about man.

This conception of man's stature is not, however, the complete Christian picture of man. The high estimate of the human stature implied in the concept of "image of God" stands in paradoxical juxtaposition to the low estimate of human virtue in Christian thought. Man is a sinner. His sin is defined as rebellion against God. The Christian estimate of human evil is so serious precisely because it places evil at the very centre of human personality: in the will. This evil cannot be regarded complacently as the inevitable consequence of his finiteness or the fruit of his involvement in the contingencies and necessities of nature. Sin is occasioned precisely by the fact that man refuses to admit his "creatureliness" and to acknowledge himself as merely a member of a total unity of life. He pretends to be more than he is. Nor can he, as in both rationalistic and mystic dualism, dismiss his sins as residing in that part of himself which is not his true self, that is, that part of himself which is involved in physical necessity. In Christianity it is not the eternal man who judges the finite man; but the eternal and holy God who judges sinful man. Nor is redemption in the power of the eternal man who gradually sloughs off finite man. Man is not divided against himself so that the essential man can be extricated from the nonessential. Man contradicts himself within the terms of his true essence. His essence is free self-determination. His sin is the wrong use of his freedom and its consequent destruction.

Man is an individual but he is not self-sufficing. The law of his nature is love, a harmonious relation of life to life in obedience to the divine centre and source of his life. His sin is therefore spiritual and not carnal, though the infection of rebellion spreads from the spirit to the body and disturbs its harmonies also. Man, in other words, is a sinner not because he is one limited individual within a whole but rather because he is betrayed by his very ability to survey the whole to imagine himself the whole. . . .

. . . [It] is impossible without the presuppositions of the Christian faith to find the source of sin within man himself. . . . Only in a religion of revelation, whose God reveals Himself to man from beyond Himself and from beyond the contrast of vitality and form, can man discover the root of sin to be within himself. The essence of man is his freedom. Sin is committed in that freedom. Sin can therefore not be attributed to a defect in his essence. It can only be understood as a self-contradiction, made possible by the fact of his freedom but not following necessarily from it.

Christianity, therefore, issues inevitably in the religious expression of an uneasy conscience. Only within terms of the Christian faith can man not only understand the reality of the evil in himself but escape the error of attributing that evil to any one but himself. It is possible of course to point out that man is tempted by the situation in which he stands. He stands at the juncture of nature and spirit. The freedom of his spirit causes him to break the harmonies of nature and the pride of his spirit prevents him from establishing a new harmony. The freedom of his spirit enables him to use the forces and processes of nature creatively; but his failure to observe the limits of his finite existence causes him to defy the forms and restraints of both nature and reason. Human self-consciousness is a high tower looking upon a large and inclusive world. It vainly imagines that it is the large world which it beholds and not a narrow tower insecurely erected amidst the shifting sands of the world. . . .

. . . [The] Christian view of human nature is involved in the paradox of claiming a higher stature for man and of taking a more serious view of his evil than other anthropology.

.   .   .   .

Everything in human life and history moves toward an end. By reason of man's subjection to nature and finiteness this "end" is a point where that which exists ceases to be. It is *finis*. By reason of man's rational freedom the "end" has another meaning. It is the purpose and goal of his life and work. It is *telos*. This double connotation of end as both *finis* and *telos* expresses, in a sense, the whole character of human history and reveals the fundamental problem of human existence. All things in history move towards both fulfillment and dissolution, towards the fuller embodiment of their essential character and towards death.

The problem is that the end as *finis* is a threat to the end as *telos*. Life is in peril of meaninglessness because *finis* is a seemingly abrupt and capricious termination of the development of life before it has reached its true end or *telos*. The Christian faith understands this aspect of the human situation. It shares an understanding of the tension between time and eternity with all other religions. But it asserts that it is not within man's power to solve the vexing problem of his subjection to, and partial freedom of, the flux of time. It holds, furthermore, that evil is introduced into history by the very effort of men to solve this problem by their own resources.

The evil thus introduced by the "false eternals" of human

pride complicates the problem of historical fulfillment. The culmination of history must include not merely the divine completion of human incompleteness but a purging of human guilt and sin by divine judgment and mercy.

We have previously considered the implications of the revelation of God in Christ for the interpretation of history, and sought to establish that the Kingdom of God as it *has come* in Christ means a disclosure of the meaning of history but not the full realization of that meaning. That is anticipated in the Kingdom which *is to come,* that is, in the culmination of history. It must be remembered that a comprehension of the meaning of life and history from the standpoint of the Christian revelation includes an understanding of the contradictions to that meaning in which history is perennially involved.

Such an understanding by faith means that the world is in a sense already "overcome"; for none of the corruptions of history, its fanaticisms and conflicts, its imperial lusts and ambitions, its catastrophes and tragedies, can take the faithful completely unaware. The light of revelation into the meaning of life illumines the darkness of history's self-contradictions, its fragmentary realizations of meaning and its premature and false completions. But obviously such a faith points to an *end* in which history's incompleteness and corruption is finally overcome. Thus history as we know it is regarded as an "interim" between the disclosure and the fulfillment of its meaning. Symbolically this is expressed in the New Testament in the hope that the suffering Messiah will "come again" with "power and great glory." Men shall "see the Son of man sitting on the right hand of power, and coming in the clouds of heaven. . . ."

This hope of the *parousia* in New Testament thought is sometimes dismissed as no more than a projection of those elements of Jewish apocalypse to which the first coming of Christ did not conform and for the satisfaction of which a "second coming" had to be invented. On the other hand they have frequently been taken literally and have thus confused the mind of the church. The symbol of the second coming of Christ can neither be taken literally nor dismissed as unimportant. It participates in the general characteristic of the Biblical symbols, which deal with the relation of time and eternity, and seek to point to the ultimate from the standpoint of the conditioned. If the symbol is taken literally the dialectical conception of time and eternity is falsified and the ultimate vindication of God over history is reduced to a point in history. The consequence of this falsification is expressed in the hope of a millennial age. In such a millennial age, just as in a utopian one, history is supposedly fulfilled despite the persisting conditions of finiteness. On the other hand if the symbol is dismissed as unimportant, as merely a picturesque or primitive way of apprehending the relation of the historical to the eternal, the Biblical dialectic is obscured in another direction. All theologies which do not take these symbols seriously will be discovered upon close analysis not to take history seriously either. They presuppose an eternity which annuls rather than fulfills the historical process.

The Biblical symbols cannot be taken literally because it is not possible for finite minds to comprehend that which transcends and fulfills history. The finite mind can only use symbols and pointers of the character of the eternal. These pointers must be taken seriously nevertheless because they express the self-transcendent character of historical existence and point to its eternal ground. The symbols which point towards the consummation from within the temporal flux cannot be exact in the scientific sense of the word. They are inexact even when they merely define the divine and eternal ground of history in terms of contrast to the temporal. They are even more difficult to understand when they seek to express the Biblical idea of an eternity involved in, and yet transcending, the temporal.

The *eschata* or "last things" in New Testament symbolism are described in three fundamental symbols: the return of Christ, the last judgment and the resurrection. They must be considered in order.

1. *The Parousia*

The idea of the return of the triumphant Christ dominates the other two symbols. The judgment and the resurrection are a part of the vindication of God in the return of Christ. To believe that the suffering Messiah will return at the end of history as a triumphant judge and redeemer is to express the faith that existence cannot ultimately defy its own norm. Love may have to live in history as suffering love because the power of sin makes a simple triumph of love impossible. But if this were the ultimate situation it would be necessary either to worship the power of sin as the final power in the world or to regard it as a kind of second God, not able to triumph, but also strong enough to avoid defeat.

The vindication of Christ and his triumphant return is therefore an expression of faith in the sufficiency of God's sovereignty over the world and history, and in the final supremacy of love over all the forces of self-love which defy, for the moment, the inclusive harmony of all things under the will of God.

This return of Christ stands at the "end" of history in such a way that it would sometimes appear to be a triumph in history and to mean a redeemed temporal-historical process. But according to other, and usually later, interpretations, the fulfillment of the historical process is also its end in the quantitative sense; and the redemption of history would appear to be its culmination also. This twofold aspect of the final vindication of Christ implies a refutation in Biblical faith of both utopianism and a too consistent other-worldliness. Against utopianism the Christian faith insists that the final consummation of history lies beyond the conditions of the temporal process. Against otherworldliness it asserts that the consummation fulfills rather than negates, the historical process. There is no way of expressing this dialectical concept without running the danger of its dissolution. The dissolution has, in fact, taken place again and again in Christian history. Those who believed in the simple fulfillment of history have been arrayed against those who believed that historical existence was robbed of its meaning in the final consummation. Both parties to the debate used Christian symbols to express their half-Christian convictions.

If we analyse the meaning of the two subordinate symbols of the "last judgment" and the resurrection it becomes clear that, according to Biblical faith, some aspects of history are refuted

more positively while the meaning of historical existence as
such is affirmed more unequivocally than in alternative conceptions.

2. *The Last Judgment*

The symbol of the last judgment in New Testament escha-
tology contains three important facets of the Christian conception of life and history. The first is expressed in the idea that it
is Christ who will be the judge of history. Christ as judge means
that when the historical confronts the eternal it is judged by its
own ideal possibility, and not by the contrast between the finite
and the eternal character of God. The judgment is upon sin and
not finiteness. This idea is in logical accord with the whole
Biblical conception of life and history, according to which it is
not the partial and particular character of human existence
which is evil, but rather the self-love by which men disturb the
harmony of creation as it would exist if all creatures obeyed the
divine will.

The second facet in the symbol of the last judgment is its
emphasis upon the distinction between good and evil in history.
When history confronts God the differences between good and
evil are not swallowed up in a distinctionless eternity. All
historical realities are indeed ambiguous. Therefore no absolute
distinction between good and evil in them is possible. But this
does not obviate the necessity and possibility of a *final* judgment
upon good and evil. To be sure the righteous, standing before
the last judgment, do not believe themselves to be righteous,
and their uneasy conscience proves the final problem of history
to be that, before God, "no man living is justified." There is no
solution for this final problem short of the divine mercy and the
"forgiveness of sins. . . ."

The third facet in the symbol of the last judgment is to be
found in its locus at the "end" of history. There is no achievement or partial realization in history, no fulfillment of meaning
or achievement of virtue by which man can escape the final
judgment. The idea of a "last" judgment expresses Christianity's
refutation of all conceptions of history, according to which it is
its own redeemer and is able by its process of growth and

development, to emancipate man from the guilt and sin of his existence, and to free him from judgment.

Nothing expresses the insecurity and anxiety of human existence more profoundly than the fact that the fear of extinction and the fear of judgment are compounded in the fear of death. The fear of extinction is the fear of meaninglessness. When life is "cut off" before any obvious completion; when *finis* so capriciously frustrates the possibility of achieving *telos,* the very meaningfulness of life is called into question. But before faith can apprehend the divine mercy which completes our incompleteness and forgives our sins it must confront the divine judge. In that confrontation it is not death but sin as the "sting of death" which is recognized as the real peril. For the ending of our life would not threaten us if we had not falsely made ourselves the centre of life's meaning.

Literalistic conceptions of the allegedly everlasting fires of hell have frequently discredited the idea of a final judgment in the minds of modern Christians. But moral sentimentality in modern Christianity would have probably dissipated the significance of the idea of judgment, even if a literalistic orthodoxy had not seemed to justify the dissipation. It is unwise for Christians to claim any knowledge of either the furniture of heaven or the temperature of hell; or to be too certain about any details of the Kingdom of God in which history is consummated. But it is prudent to accept the testimony of the heart, which affirms the fear of judgment. The freedom of man, by which he both transcends and is creative in history, makes the fear of a judgment beyond all historical judgments inevitable. Many a court of opinion may dismiss us with a: "Well done, thou good and faithful servant"; but we will deceive ourselves if we believe such a judgment to be final. If men are fully aware, they will discern an accent of the fear of judgment in the fear of death. The fear of death arises merely from the ambiguity of finiteness and freedom which underlies all historical existence; but the fear of judgment is prompted by awareness of the mixture of sin and creativity which is the very substance of history.

3. *The Resurrection*

The idea of the resurrection of the body is a Biblical symbol in which modern minds take the greatest offense and which has long since been displaced in most modern versions of the Christian faith by the idea of the immortality of the soul. The latter idea is regarded as a more plausible expression of the hope of everlasting life. It is true of course that the idea of the resurrection transcends the limits of the conceivable; but it is not always appreciated that this is equally true of the idea of an immortal soul. The fact is that the unity of historical existence, despite its involvement in and transcendence over nature, makes it no more possible to conceive transcendent spirit, completely freed of the conditions of nature, than to conceive the conditions of nature transmuted into an eternal consummation. Either idea, as every other idea, which points to the consummation beyond history, is beyond logical conception. The hope of the resurrection nevertheless embodies the very genius of the Christian idea of the historical. On the one hand it implies that the condition of finiteness and freedom, which lies at the basis of historical existence, is a problem for which there is no solution by any human power. Only God can solve this problem. From the human perspective it can only be solved by faith. All structures of meaning and realms of coherence, which human reason constructs, face the chasm of meaninglessness when men discover that the tangents of meaning transcend the limits of existence. Only faith has an answer for this problem. The Christian answer is faith in the God who is revealed in Christ and from whose love neither life nor death can separate us.

In this answer of faith the meaningfulness of history is the more certainly affirmed because the consummation of history as a human possibility is denied. The resurrection is not a human possibility in the sense that the immortality of the soul is thought to be so. All the plausible and implausible proofs for the immortality of the soul are efforts on the part of the human mind to master and to control the consummation of life. They all try to prove in one way or another that an eternal element in the nature of man is worthy and capable of survival beyond death. But every mystic or rational technique which seeks to extricate the eternal element tends to deny the meaningfulness of the historical unity of body and soul; and with it the meaningfulness of the whole historical process with its infinite elaborations of that unity. The consummation of life in these terms does not mean the preservation of anything significant in either the individual or the collective life of man in history.

As against these conceptions of consummation in which man denies the significance of his life in history for the sake of affirming his ability to defy death by his own power, the Christian faith knows it to be impossible for man or for any of man's historical achievements to transcend the unity and tension between the natural and the eternal in human existence. Yet it affirms the eternal significance of this historical existence from the standpoint of faith in a God, who has the power to bring history to completion.

PART V

FRONTIERS

Can theology bear the religious, the antireligious, the secular?
In this orientation to the next group of readings, we reverse the
pattern of earlier sections and list some pertinent questions at
the outset: Must psychological understanding be a foe of theology or can the two be partners? Is it still the case that an
"increasingly 'pro-religious' atmosphere" suffuses American
society (*Will Herberg*) or has religion in fact disappeared "as a
lively factor in modern life" (*William Hamilton*)? Has religion
become a largely profane form of behavior? Have the anti-
religious drive and the allegiances of secularism turned into
effectively sacred causes? Do men today still need God or can
they fulfill themselves totally apart from reliance upon God?
What are the theologian's norms for evaluating the secular
world, secularization, and secularism? Does the validity of faith
depend upon its usefulness?

Recent theology has moved out along a number of frontiers.
We cannot examine all these but we can give expression to the
live confrontation theology is engaged in with the religious
world, the antireligious impulse, and secularist forces.

The essay by Will Herberg makes vivid the twentieth-century
encounter of theology with depth psychology. From the point of
view of Herberg's argument, the theologian whose faith-
standpoint is a biblical one may find himself on the side of
Sigmund Freud in opposition to religion—or at least to what is
here called "natural religion." On the other hand, Herberg
speaks of Freud's own form of idolatry in opposition to biblical
faith, his faith in science. And William Hamilton observes that
Freud shared something of the conviction of Nietzsche "that
God must be dethroned and killed to make way for the proper
evaluation and freedom of men."

Whether the sentiment that God has in fact been killed or has
died for some other reason comprises a theological judgment, or

merely implies a *coup de grace* for the entire theological enterprise, will turn upon how broadly or restrictedly we construe theology. Professor Cobb's definition reproduced earlier is of the broad variety: "any coherent statement about matters of ultimate concern that recognizes that the perspective by which it is governed is received from a community of faith." On this interpretation, the implicitly theological stance of a man who attests that god is dead is made manifest through inquiry respecting his own unavoidable, "ultimate concern," together perhaps with the identity of the community he serves. But if theology is taken to mean a reflecting upon God as real and living, obviously "God is dead" comprises an antitheological, or at least post-theological, assertion.

The existential question is directed to each one of us: Can we truthfully apply the words "death of God" to God himself or can we apply them only to the human beings (perhaps including ourselves) for whom God is "dead"? A college student recently wrote, "God's promises and threats do not interest or frighten me." Were we forced to conclude that the basic assumption of any theology of revelation, i.e., "God makes himself known," no longer had any meaning for us as contemporary men, the consequences of the "death-of-God" theology for theological endeavor would be clear. Theology would either come to an end or have to become nonrevelational (with the issue of whether there can be a nonrevelational theology as one of the accompanying dilemmas). But it has to be pointed out that the question, "Does God make himself known?" is in a decisive sense pretheological. In this question human beings are addressed as human beings. Thus do we stand once again in an existential place.

Professor Hamilton's exposition exemplifies one standpoint within the so-called death-of-God theology. The author does not go quite to the length of concluding that God has died (although he does make much of the "withdrawal" of God and our consequent "situation of being without God"). Other literature of the "radical theology" (as this recent movement is also called) avows the death of God as a historical, objective happening. It is a moot question whether the "radical theology" is more a consequence of thinking arising from within circles of faith, or whether it has been fathered by extrinsic influences. On the first alternative, some interpret the "radical theology" as a movement through, beyond, and in tension with the thought of Paul Tillich (cf. the Hamilton discussion). On this same alternative, the contribution of the martyred German theologian Dietrich Bonhoeffer becomes paramount, with his conviction that, paradoxically, God is regnant precisely when men are able to live and act in utter freedom from him. For the second alternative mentioned, *Langdon Gilkey's* appraisal is of considerable relevance, although his analysis of the impact of secularism has application to a great deal of today's theology, not just to the "radical theology." From the side of Gilkey's interpretation, the current theological mood, including the "death-of-God" position, is an outcome of historical-cultural pressures and not a matter of independent theological attainment. Gilkey is not prepared to compromise the reality of God and his revelation. *Harvey Cox,* acknowledging the facticity of "the secular city," also means to reassert the integrity of theology by envisioning "a new way of conceptualizing the Other" from out of the challenges and opportunities of urban civilization. In the article by *Sam Keen,* as well as in the work of Cox, theology is standing up for itself, trying earnestly to know "where it is to say Yes to the secular mind and where it is to say No." Keen epitomizes the whole existential option of theology: The question of God is the question of whether there can be hope.

Jacob Neusner shows forcefully many of the major ways in which secular reality is a matter both of contention and of solidarity between Jewish understanding and Christian understanding.

The younger generation of today tends to be action-oriented. From its point of view, the potential worth of theology is contingent upon a readiness and capacity to contribute to the solving of practical problems. Although essentially moral issues are the business of other volumes in this series, the fact remains that the theological vocation itself is seen neither steadily nor whole apart from its bearing upon the social world, upon morality. From the perspective of *Gustave Weigel,* such relevancy must be understood paradoxically: a genuinely "useful" faith has to be entirely unfettered by expedience. A parallel point may be offered in behalf of theology as such. Whatever else theology does or ought to do, it must ever judge us and our partialities. Its primary value comes from being itself. And whenever it becomes a way of living, hard journeys of mind and heart are the prerequisites and the constant companions.

16

BIBLICAL FAITH
AND NATURAL RELIGION*

Will Herberg

[A recent number] of the *American Journal of Psychiatry* carries a remarkable article by Jules H. Masserman, the distinguished teacher and writer on psychoanalysis. It is entitled, "Faith and Delusion in Psychotherapy: The Ur-Defenses of Man." Not only is this article intensely interesting on its own account, for Dr. Masserman could not be dull if he tried; it also raises, though indirectly, what seems to me to be the basic problem in our understanding of faith and religion. It is this problem that I want to discuss here in the light of Dr. Masserman's analysis.

I

Dr. Masserman begins with a sensational reversal of Freud on religion. Freud, it will be remembered, considered religion to be an illusion, and good rationalist that he was, he therefore felt it his duty to try to dissipate that illusion. Psychic disturbances he regarded as at bottom disturbances of the patient's sense of reality; the underlying aim of psychotherapy he held to be the restoration of that sense, with the consequent strengthening of

* Reprinted with permission from an article of the same title in *Theology Today*, XI, 4 (January 1955), 460–67.

the ego over against the id and the superego. Masserman, in his very opening paragraphs, breathtakingly invites the reader to turn Freud upside down. "Let us," he says, "examine the direct opposite of the usual concept that psychotherapy is based upon the dissipation of misconceptions and the recognition of some favored system of putative 'truths.' Is it possible, instead, that *psychotherapy actually consists in the re-establishment of certain delusions necessary to mankind?* Is it conceivable that these protean and all-embracing delusions are so essential in protecting us against harsh reality that existing without them would be as excruciatingly unbearable as existing without our skin?"

Consider "puny man," Masserman goes on; "what basic defenses can—nay, *must*—he evolve, else suffer from anxiety so deep and pervasive that life would be intolerable? . . . At least three basic processes," he believes, "are as essential to man's 'psychic' economy as, to quote a physiologic analogy, independence of motility, respiration, and nutrition are necessary to the maintenance of his 'bodily' integrity. These three psychologic maneuvers, in fact, constitute what may be called the Ur-defenses of man. Each of these three is contrary to the bitter evidence of our senses, and may therefore be called 'wishful,' 'fantastic,' or indeed 'delusional'—and yet each is an article of faith so universal as to approach all that man can know of truth—namely, what he believes by common consent."

II

What are these "curiously unrealistic, paradoxical but ubiquitous, Ur-defenses of man"? Masserman lists and discusses three of these, which he formulates with profound insight.

1. *"The delusion of invulnerability and immortality.* The first of these delusions is essentially simple: it denies danger and death categorically by affirming man's triumph over both."

2. *"The delusion of the omnipotent servant. . . .* The second Ur-defense . . . is the Ur-defense of the Mastery of the Omnipotent. This is designed to bolster and indemnify the delusion of nonvulnerability in a most subtle and satisfactory way" by leading man to believe that he has divine and all-

powerful servants at his command to do his bidding and protect him against the world.

3. *"Man's kindness to man.* This brings us to the last of man's Ur-defenses (a cynic might say his ultimate delusion), namely, that in time of need one can seek and actually obtain succor from one's fellowman. . . ."

I am doing Dr. Masserman an injustice with this bare listing. Each of these Ur-defenses he discusses and illustrates at length, drawing upon his great resources as a psychotherapist and observer of the ways of men. Each of these Ur-defenses, moreover, he relates to some phase of infantile experience. "Just as the Ur-defense of Omnipotence dates from the pre-conceptual period of so-called primary narcissism, and just as the Delusion of Magical Mystery dates from the blind service accorded us by our parents, so," he explains, "does the professed ideal of human trustworthiness date from a somewhat later period of childhood when we have learned to recognize our parents (and especially the mother) as human beings apparently actuated by self-sacrificing devotion to the satisfaction of our needs." For Freud, this reduction of beliefs to infantile experience would have been virtually equivalent to condemning them as irrational delusions unworthy of rational man; but not for Masserman. So far from condemning these "Ur-defenses men cherish and live by," Masserman even raises the question of whether it would not be well to "reconsider the appropriateness of the term 'delusion' when applied to ubiquitous concepts of invulnerability, power, and communion so consummately necessary to man's existence"; perhaps it would be better to speak of them as "wishful assumptions, needful prejudices, essential convictions, categorical beliefs, articles of faith, . . . axioms here miscalled delusions." In any case, they are "substitutive or compensatory beliefs," quite necessary to make human life at all livable. What, then, should be the attitude of therapy? "As to therapy," Dr. Masserman says, "my presentation has not 'proved' the thesis that treatment must in part be directed toward restoring and respecting man's cherished and essential delusions—but then, very few dissertations 'prove' much beyond the fact that the speaker can read his own writing. Nevertheless, we dare not disregard the evidence that delusions, in a deeply humanitarian sense, are indeed sacred, and that we tamper with them at our patient's—and our own—peril."

There we have it. What Freud regards with such distaste as irrational delusion, Masserman holds to be "essential convictions, . . . sacred . . . necessary to man's very existence." What Freud, in his rationalist zeal, is so intent upon dissipating, Masserman urges us to understand and cherish and warns us against tampering with. On a psychoanalytic basis, Masserman, the Freudian, reverses Freud and vindicates religion.

For there cannot be any doubt that Masserman's analysis constitutes a vindication of religion against the psychoanalytic rationalists. The fundamental religious beliefs, he reiterates, are articles of faith "so universal as to approach all that man can know of truth—namely, what he believes by common consent." In making this defense of religion against Freud and the rationalists, Masserman not only reflects the new "pro-religious" atmosphere of our time; he also falls in with certain neo-positivist "conventionalistic" tendencies in modern thought. His paper is, indeed, of great symptomatic significance, and I have no doubt it will be hailed by more than one "professional" champion of religion as providing very welcome, ultramodern scientific support for their position.

III

Upon the man of biblical faith, however, Dr. Masserman's findings will make a rather different impression. Dr. Masserman does, indeed, vindicate religion against Freudian anti-religion, but what kind of religion does he vindicate? That is the basic question, and it takes us to the heart of the matter.

Any one at all acquainted with the Bible and the structure of biblical faith will be struck by the strange fact that the very beliefs Dr. Masserman, with considerable justice, takes to be the "essentials" of religion because they are the Ur-defenses of man, biblical faith is especially concerned to *reject*. This may, at first sight, seem incredible, but serious second thought will show that such is indeed the case.

1. The first Ur-defense, says Dr. Masserman, is man's belief in his invulnerability and immortality: "it denies danger and death categorically by affirming man's triumph over both." But the Bible rejects this belief as categorically as man makes it: "As for man, his days are like grass; as a flower in the field so he flourisheth; for the wind passeth over it, and it is gone, and the place thereof knoweth it no more" (Ps. 103:15–16). "All flesh is grass, and all goodliness thereof is as the flower of the field; the grass withereth, the flower fadeth, when the breath of the Lord bloweth upon it: surely the people is grass. The grass withereth, the flower fadeth; but the word of our God stands forever" (Is. 40:6–8). If there is one thing the Bible makes clear, it is that man is *not* immortal, *not* invulnerable; he is of all creatures the most mortal, the most vulnerable. Whatever "eternal life" he may look forward to, or hope for, comes not as a consequence of his nature (the Bible knows nothing of the "immortality of the soul"), but as the promise and grace of God. Man's very claim to immortality and invulnerability is, in biblical faith, understood as a revealing aspect of the pretensions to self-sufficiency that are at the heart of sin.

2. The second Ur-defense, according to Dr. Masserman, is the conception of the "omnipotent servant," the belief that man has at his command an all-powerful divine servant or servants to help him deal with the world. Merely to state this belief is to indicate how abhorrent it is to biblical faith. Biblical faith insists that man is ever at the command of God, as his slave or "servant"; the very notion that man has God or the divine at *his* command must appear to biblical man as a blasphemous abomination, and indeed the Bible denounces it so consistently and continuously that it would be superfluous to introduce any documentation at this point. The "omnipotent servant" of Dr. Masserman's "articles of faith" is, in the Bible, sovereign Lord to *serve* whom is man's proper life.

3. Finally comes the third Ur-defense, "that in time of need one can seek and actually obtain succor from one's fellowman." What does the Bible say to this? It tells us first something about our "fellowman," that is, about ourselves: "The heart [of man] is deceitful above all things, and desperately wicked; who can

understand it?" (Jer. 17:9). It warns us repeatedly against placing any final reliance on men's goodwill ("Cursed is the man who trusts in man and makes flesh his arm," Jer. 17:5). And it presents us with the spectacle of Jesus, the very pattern of sacrificial love, brought to the cross with every man's hand against him, abandoned by all, even by his own disciples. The view of the Bible on this "third Ur-defense" would seem to be unequivocal.

No; the Bible denies most emphatically that we are immortal and invulnerable, that we have omnipotent divine servants at our command, that everybody really loves us. The Bible, in fact, teaches the opposite. But these beliefs, as Masserman points out, are at the foundation of religion.

IV

What then shall we say, that the Bible teaches anti-religion? Well, in a way it does.

What Dr. Masserman, with keen insight, describes as man's "essential convictions," "articles of faith," "Ur-defenses," are in fact the foundations of "natural" religion. Dr. Masserman is right in pointing to man's primordial religious need; he is right, too, in suggesting that this need is forever driving man beyond himself, beyond experience, beyond rationality, beyond life itself. Man is *homo religiosus,* "by nature" religious. He cannot live his life, or understand his existence, simply in its own terms. Perhaps that is the best indication of what it means to be human: to be a human being means to be forever searching for something "larger" beyond the self in which to ground the meaning and security of existence.

Biblical faith knows this very well; but it knows something more. It knows that because man is "sinful" man, "fallen" man, it is with *himself* that his search for God begins and ends. Sin means radical egocentricity: it means ousting God from the center of things and making the self—its interests, concerns, ideas, hopes, and aspirations—the center of existence. Sinful man, being *man,* needs God and searches for him; but because he is *sinful,* the god he finds is a god he constructs—if not with his hands, then with his heart and mind—to suit his purposes. And his purposes are precisely to make himself feel ultimately in control of things, to give himself security and a sense of invulnerability and power. This is man's "natural" religion, the religion to which he "naturally" tends. (I use the quotation marks to indicate that the "nature" that prompts man in this direction is not the nature with which man is endowed in the order of creation, but a "fallen" and "corrupt" nature, in a real sense, an *unnatural* nature.) It would not be too difficult to show that the "religions of the world" are, in their infinite variety, all variations of this theme. Dr. Masserman does better; he reduces this "natural" religion to its psychological essentials, and shows how "natural" it really is.

Precisely because this religion is "natural," elaborated by man to satisfy his "natural" need for security and significance, biblical faith denounces it as false and idolatrous. In the name of the living God, it scornfully rejects as delusive self-deceptions the "Ur-defenses" that man erects. Man is not immortal or invulnerable; he is "as the grass that withereth." Man does not have the divine at his command; God is utterly transcendent, supremely holy, and all human attempts to manipulate the divine are sacrilegious and destructive. It is folly to place ultimate reliance on mere flesh and blood; ultimate faith belongs to God and to God alone. In other words, "natural" religion is incorrigibly *self*-centered and *man*-centered, while biblical faith is from first to last *God*-centered.

V

The very search for final meaning and security in this world, which is what gives rise to "natural" religion, biblical faith rejects as vain and idolatrous. The prophetic books ring with this theme. Luther was certainly true to his biblical sources when he branded the feeling of *securitas,* the feeling of having all things nicely under control, as the greatest peril to the life of faith. Religion, at least the "natural" religion we have been discussing, aims to give us that feeling, and that is why we must agree with Reinhold Niebuhr that: "Religion qua religion is naturally idolatrous, accentuating rather than diminishing the self-worship of men and nations by assuring them an ultimate sanction for their dearest desires" (*Christianity and Crisis,* February 8, 1954).

"Religion qua religion" is concerned with bolstering man's self-esteem and security in the face of a hostile universe; biblical faith is concerned with shattering all human securities and bringing man, in "fear and trembling," face to face with God. Among the human securities that biblical faith is out to shatter is the very security religion is designed to bring. In this sense, it is quite true that biblical faith is "anti-religious"; it is indeed a faith whose very purpose it is to "end" all religion and bring man directly under the command, judgment, and redeeming grace of God.

True enough, the shattering word of judgment is not the last word of biblical faith; beyond judgment is the divine grace that brings the "peace that passeth understanding." But this "peace" is not the product of man's complacent belief in his own power and significance; it is not grounded in any "Ur-defenses" of the ego. It comes, if it comes at all, when all man-made securities, social, intellectual, moral, and spiritual, have been smashed, when all human pretensions and defenses have been abandoned. In short, it comes, if it comes at all, only after man has given up the comforts and consolations of "religion." Herbert W. Schneider somewhat scornfully reports the outburst of a "fundamentalist" preacher: "I tell you, brethren, God *hates* religion; he wants faith" (*Religion in Twentieth-Century America,* p. 147). But this preacher, whatever his views on evolution or Jonah's whale, was speaking the authentic biblical word.

Is Dr. Masserman wrong, then, when he asserts that the three Ur-defenses he describes are "essential convictions," something we cannot help but believe? No, he is right; we are all of us "natural" (that is, sinful) men and therefore we all tend "naturally" to "natural" religion. However much we may reject or repudiate it, we are always lapsing into it. We all constantly tend to idolatry; our minds, as Calvin puts it, are "idol-factories." God's grace, received in faith, gives us power to resist and overcome idolatry, but this is something that Dr. Masserman, as scientist, can hardly be expected to deal with. And because we all of us, however "faithful," remain sinners, in that sense, "natural" men—*simul justus et peccator*—Dr. Masserman's analysis remains relevant to our condition at all points.

VI

But the paradox is still there. Dr. Masserman's Freudian vindication of religion against Freud is something that the man of biblical faith must reject. Incredible as it may seem, Freud, with his *rejection* of religion, was closer to, or at least less distant from, the biblical position than Dr. Masserman with his *vindication* of it. For Freud denounced man's religious beliefs, what Dr. Masserman calls the Ur-defenses, as dangerous delusions, and here biblical faith agrees with him. Freud's own Ur-defense was his faith in science; this, too, biblical faith strips away as idolatrous and delusive. It is, therefore, even more radical in its "anti-religion" than Freud, but it cannot help but recognize that in Freud's iconoclasm there is an aspect of God's truth almost completely lost in the "pro-religionism" of our time.

The paradox is not limited to Freud and psychoanalysis. When Marx denounced religion as the "opium of the people," he was, unknowingly, repeating the words of Charles Kingsley, the militant evangelical Christian. And he was proclaiming a truth, or at least an aspect of the truth, the same truth that leads Reinhold Niebuhr to say: "Religion qua religion is naturally idolatrous. . . ." It is again a truth, or an aspect of the truth, that we are in danger of losing sight of in the increasingly "pro-religious" atmosphere of the day.

Marx and Freud spoke better than they knew. They employed the glimpse of truth they had for idolatrous purposes, thus perverting, even demonizing it. Nevertheless, there was a truth, or at least a glimpse of truth in what they said. Their atheistic intentions should not blind us to this fact. After all, does not God make even the wrath of men to praise him?

THE DEATH OF GOD THEOLOGY*

William Hamilton

THE DEATH OF GOD

I am not here referring to a belief in the non-existence of God. I am talking about a growing sense, in both non-Christians and Christians, that God has withdrawn, that he is absent, even that he is somehow dead. Elijah taunted the false prophets and suggested that their god may have gone on a journey, since he could not be made to respond to their prayers (I Kings 18:27). Now, many seem to be standing with the false prophets, wondering if the true God has not withdrawn himself from his people. This feeling ranges from a sturdy unbelieving confidence in God's demise to the troubled believer's cry that he is no longer in a place where we can call upon him. Arthur Koestler represents the confident mood:

God is dethroned; and although the incognisant masses are tardy in realising the event, they feel the icy draught caused by that vacancy. Man enters upon a spiritual ice age; the established churches can no longer provide more than Eskimo huts where their shivering flock huddles together.

The patronizing and confident tone of this announcement reminds us of both Feuerbach and Nietzsche. In the famous

---

* Reprinted with permission from *The New Essence of Christianity*, by William Hamilton (rev. ed.; New York: Association Press, 1966), pp. 55–68. Footnotes omitted.

passage in "The Gay Science" where the idea of the death of
God is put forward by Nietzsche, a madman is portrayed as
searching for God, calling out for him, and finally concluding
that he and all men have killed him. The man's hearers do not
understand his words, and he concludes that he has come with
his message too early. He goes on to wander about the city's
churches, calling out, "What are these churches now if they are
not the tombs and sepulchers of God?" Koestler's igloos and
Nietzsche's tombs are spiritually, if not architecturally, related.
But in spite of Nietzsche's statement that the madman had come
too soon, his declaration of God's death was heard and believed. And in the nineteenth century, as DeLubac writes, "man
is getting rid of God in order to regain possession of the human
greatness which, it seems to him, is being unwarrantably with-
held by another. In God he is overthrowing an obstacle in order
to gain his freedom." Freud shared something of this Nietz-
schean conviction that God must be dethroned and killed to
make way for the proper evaluation and freedom of man. And
of course, as against many forms of religion, even this strident
cry bears some truth.

But Koestler's confident assurance of God's dethronement
and death is not the only way modern man describes his sense
of God's absence or disappearance. When Dr. Tillich refers to
the death of God he usually means the abolition of the idea of
God as one piece of being alongside others, of God as a big
person. Death of God for him is thus the death of idols, or the
false gods. The novels of Albert Camus, on the other hand,
portray not only a world from which the false gods, and the
holy God of the theological revival, have departed, but a world
from which any and all gods have silently withdrawn. The world
of these novels is a world in which the word God simply refuses
to have any meaning. This is not treated as a good thing or a
terrible thing; it is just a fact that is ruefully assumed. It is the
God described by the best and most sophisticated theologians of
our time, who seems to many today to have withdrawn from his
world. When we feel this, we do not feel free or strong, but
weak, unprotected, and frightened.

We seem to be those who are trying to believe in a time of the death of God. Just what do we mean when we say this? We mean that the Augustinian-Reformed portrait of God itself is a picture of a God we find more and more elusive, less and less for us or with us. And so we wonder if God himself is not absent. When we speak of the death of God, we speak not only of the death of the idols or the falsely objectivized Being in the sky; we speak, as well, of the death in us of any power to affirm any of the traditional images of God. We mean that the world is not God and that it does not point to God. Since the supports men have always depended on to help them affirm God seem to be gone, little wonder that many take the next step and wonder whether God himself has gone. Little wonder that Lent is the only season when we are at home, and that that cry of dereliction from the cross is sometimes the only biblical word that can speak to us. If Jesus can wonder about being forsaken by God, are we to be blamed if we wonder?

Beyond the Death of God

Now, a believing Christian can face without distress any announcement about the disappearance of the idols from the religious world of men, but he cannot live as a Christian for long with the suspicion that God himself has withdrawn. How is it possible to turn this difficult corner, and to move from an acknowledgment of God's disappearance to a sense of some kind of reappearance and presence? This sense of the separation of God from the world, Ronald Gregor Smith writes,

does not lead to mere or sheer undialectical atheism. Any assertion of the absence of God and even further of his non-existence among the phenomena of the world is dialectically confronted by the equal assertion of his presence. I am sorry if this sounds like a mere verbal trick, but it cannot be helped.

There is something disarming about Gregor Smith's unwillingness to look carefully at the connections between the sense of disappearance of God and the problem of his reappearance. But his way of putting it does indeed sound like a verbal trick, and we must try to discover if there are not ways of moving from the one state to the other.

One of the favorite contemporary attempts to do this might be called the Augustinian doubt maneuver. Augustine noted that he overcame his temptation toward skepticism by observing that even skepticism implied some affirmation of truth, the truth at least of the skeptical position.

Everyone who knows that he is in doubt about something, knows a truth, and in regard to this that he knows he is certain. Therefore he is certain about a truth. Consequently everyone who doubts if there be a truth has in himself a true thing on which he does not doubt.

This may or may not be a convincing way to overcome radical skepticism. But it certainly cannot be used to mean that we can, by a kind of interior maneuver, affirm that we know the very thing we doubt. Augustine did not use it thus; we may doubt one truth, but that implies, he tells us, that we know another thing in our act of doubt, namely, that we are doubters. But some Christians have tried to claim that somehow doubt implies faith. God's existence, we are often told, is most profoundly proven in the very experience of doubting or denying him. Of course, passionate doubt has a resemblance to passionate faith. Both have a deep concern for the problem of truth; both real doubt and real faith deeply care. But it is not good enough to suggest that "There is no God" or "I cannot know that there is a God" really bears the same meaning as "Thou art my God." Let us continue to say that doubt is a necessary way for many of us to faith; that faith never overcomes doubt finally and completely; that lively faith can bear a good deal of doubt around the edges. But the depth of doubt is not the depth of faith; these are two places, not one, and a choice must finally be made between them. We cannot evade such a problem by a trick of redefinition.

This confusion of doubt and faith obscures the problem of moving from an affirmation about the disappearance of God to an affirmation of his presence. I wonder if the following, and quite beautiful, passage from Dr. Tillich, is not also obscure in its apparent identification of having with not-having.

To the man who longs for God and cannot find Him; to the man who wants to be acknowledged by God and cannot even believe that He is; to the man who is striving for a new and imperishable meaning of his life and cannot discover it—to this man Paul speaks. We are each such a man. Just in this situation, where the Spirit is far from our consciousness, where we are unable to pray or to experience any meaning in life, the Spirit is working quietly in the depth of our souls. In the moment when we feel separated from God, meaningless in our lives, and condemned to despair, we are not left alone. The Spirit, sighing and longing in us and with us, represents us. It manifests what we really are. In feeling this against feeling, in believing this against belief, in knowing this against knowledge, we like Paul, possess all.

Now this is less specious than the doubt-equals-faith position. And it points to a profound truth. Faith is never the claim to own or possess. God comes to us finally when we confess that we have nothing in our hands to bring. Our not-knowing alone leads to knowing; our not-having is the only way to possession. All this is true, and very close to the Protestant conviction that God's access is to sinners and not to saints. But it will not do. Such a word as Dr. Tillich's can do much. It can persuade the man who struggles for God that there is a sense in which he has been found. It can portray the Christian tradition attractively as one which knows, welcomes, and lives with the experience of struggle and not-knowing. But it will not serve to transform an experience of not-having into an experience of having. For all of our verbalizing, these remain two different experiences, and we are not finally helped by those who do not face openly the distinctions.

The curious thing about this matter of God's disappearance is that even in those moments when we are most keenly aware of God's absence we still, somehow, find it possible to pray for his return. Perhaps we ought to conclude that the special Christian burden of our time is the situation of being without God. There is, for some reason, no possession of God for us, but only a hope, only a waiting. This is perhaps part of the truth: to be a Christian today is to stand, somehow, as a man without God but with hope. We know too little to know him now; we only know enough to be able to say that he will come, in his own time, to the broken and contrite heart, if we continue to offer that to him. Faith is, for many of us, we might say, purely eschatological. It is a kind of truth that one day he will no longer be absent from us. Faith is a cry to the absent God; faith is hope.

An identification of faith with hope is possible, but a little more can be said. The absent one has a kind of presence; the one for whom the Christian man waits still makes an impact on us. W. H. Auden has described this presence very accurately.

> In our anguish we struggle
> To elude Him, to lie to Him, yet His love observes
> His appalling promise; His predilection
> As we wander and weep is with us to the end.
> Minding our meanings, our least matter dear to Him. . . .
> It is where we are wounded that is when He speaks
> Our creaturely cry, concluding His children
> In their mad unbelief to have mercy on them all
> As they wait unawares for His world to come.

In this there is waiting, but also something else. God is also the one whom we struggle to elude; as Augustine says, "Thou never departest from us, and yet only with difficulty do we return to thee." He speaks to us at the point where we are wounded. And even though our wound is our separation from him, the separation is not absolute. The reflections of Psalm 139 and Genesis 32:24–25 in this fragment from Auden remind us of part of our situation.

Thus, neither "death of God," "absence of God," nor "disappearance of God" is wholly adequate to describe the full meaning of our religious situation. Our experience of God is deeply dissatisfying to us, even when we are believers. In one sense God seems to have withdrawn from the world and its sufferings, and this leads us to accuse him of either irrelevance or cruelty. But in another sense, he is experienced as a pressure and a wounding from which we would love to be free. For many of us who call ourselves Christians, therefore, believing in the time of the "death of God" means that he is there when we do not want him, in ways we do not want him, and he is not there when we do want him.

The rediscovery of the divinity of God . . . seems defective on two counts. It gives us a portrait of God that does not seem able to receive honestly the threat posed by the problem of suffering, and it does not accurately enough describe the curious mixture of the disappearance and presence of God that is felt by many today. I am not sure just what ought to be our proper response to this curious mixture. There seems to be some ground for terror here, so that we can partly agree with Ingmar Bergmann when he said recently that "if God is not there, life is an outrageous terror." Yet in another sense we face the special texture of our unsatisfactory religious situation with calmness. Most of us are learning to accept these things: the disappearance of God from the world, the coming of age of the world, as it has been called, the disappearance of religion as a lively factor in modern life, the fact that there are men who can live both without God and without despair. We are coming to accept these calmly as events not without their advantages. Perhaps our calmness will disappear when we face the possibility that God will even more decisively withdraw—that he will withdraw from our selves as he has already withdrawn from the world, that not only has the world become sheer world but that self will become sheer self. For if there are men today who can do without God, it still seems to be true that we cannot do so. We are afraid of ourselves without him, even though what we know of him may be only a pressure and a wounding.

Finally, this portrait of the situation between man and God today, in the time (as we have called it) of the death of God, is not satisfactory if this is all we know. We have really described a bondage, not a freedom; a disturbance and very little else. If this were all there were to the Christian faith, it would not be hard to reject it. Is there, then, a deliverance from this absent-present disturber God? There is, and the deliverance will somehow be connected with another image of God—what we have already referred to as the impotent God—that emerges when we try to take our next step and say something about Jesus the Lord. But I have not stated, and I do not want to state, that we can know nothing of God apart from Jesus. We can and do know something, and it is just this unsatisfactory mixture of his presence and absence, his disturbance. As we move towards the center of the Christian faith, Jesus Christ, will we be able to overcome the instability of our belief in a time of the death of God or, even reckoning with Jesus, will something of this experience remain?

18

SECULARISM'S IMPACT
ON CONTEMPORARY THEOLOGY*

Langdon Gilkey

THE peculiar character of the current theological situation lies in the fact that it is dominated by the massive influence of secularism. Secularism is, so to speak, the cultural *Geist* within which all forms of thought, including the theological, must operate if they are to be relevant and creative. It functions in our period much as idealistic dualism functioned in the Hellenistic world, providing basic attitudes to reality, categories of thought and evaluations of meaning and goodness.

This is not to argue that all of the implications of secularism must or could be accepted by theology, any more than all the implications of idealistic dualism were accepted by the thinkers of the early Church. But there is no question that the creative forms of patristic thought, as well as the "heresies," were set within the fundamental structures of Hellenism. My own feeling is that our theological relation to secularism as the basic mood of our age is roughly analogous, and that our task is in this sense similar to theirs.

Secularism is not so much a philosophy as the pre-rational basis of all potent contemporary philosophies. Like all fundamental cultural moods or historical forms of consciousness, it

* Reprinted with permission from an article with the same title in *Christianity and Crisis*, XXV, 5 (April 5, 1965), 64–66.

exists on the level of what are called presuppositions and thus is expressed *in* the variant forms of a given culture's life rather than being one of these forms. It is, therefore, not easy to characterize briefly.

Four terms seem to me helpful in describing it: naturalism, temporalism, relativism and autonomy. These words express an attitude that finds reality in the temporal flux immediately around us, effectiveness solely in the physical and historical (or human) causes in that process, knowledge possible only of that passing flux from the position of one within it, and value only in the fulfillment of its moments. This attitude emphasizes the here and now, the tangible, the manipulatable, the sensible, the relative and the this-worldly.

This cultural or historical viewpoint, practically synonymous with the modern mind, has been expressed with progressive radicality in a wide variety of philosophies beginning roughly 200 years ago: empiricism, Kantian *criticism,* Hegelianism, evolutionism and process thought, pragmatic naturalism, and now existentialism and positivism. What is significant about the historical development of this *Geist* is that all the elements of what we might call "ultimacy," with which it began in the eighteenth and nineteenth centuries, have steadily vanished from it: the sense of an ultimate order or coherence in the passage of things, of a final purpose or direction in their movement, and of a fundamental goodness or meaning to the wholeness of being.

We are thus left with a kind of "raw" or radical secularity in which no ultimate order or meaning appears. This is expressed both by positivism and by secular existentialism, especially in the latter's literary forms. However different these two points of view may be, each in its own way reflects a concentration solely on immediate knowledge or value, and asserts either the meaninglessness of ultimate metaphysical or religious questions (positivism), or the complete absence or irrelevance of ultimate answers (existentialism). Man is no longer felt to be set within an ultimate order or context, from which he draws not only his being but the meanings, standards and values of his life; he is alone and alien in the flux of reality and quite autonomous with regard to meaning and value.

This is almost as vast a departure from the "secular" evolutionary philosophies of a century ago as it is from the classical Christian world-view. It is no accident that the phrase "God is dead" is taken as the symbol of present-day secularism. But since for this mood existence also "is the absurd," we should add that *all* the gods are dead—that is, all those structures of coherence, order and value in the wider environment of man's life. Darwin and Nietzsche, not Marx and Kierkegaard, are the real fathers of the present mood.

This developing modern mood has, of course, had increasing influence on the theology of the last 200 years. At first this was largely confined to (1) the acceptance of naturalistic causality and, by extension, the methods and results of science with regard to spatio-temporal facts; (2) the appropriation of the attitudes of historical inquiry, resulting in at least a qualified relativism with regard to both scriptural writings and doctrines; (3) the emphasis on religion as of value for *this* life and on ethics as having relevance only for one's concern for his neighbor's welfare. In the nineteenth century these and other elements of the modern mentality began to transform traditional theology completely.

Liberalism succeeded in relating itself to the earlier forms of this secular mood by using the remaining elements of ultimacy (an ultimate order of process, the progressive direction of change, etc.) as the ontological bases for its theological elaborations; but this broke down in the twentieth century with the general loss of faith in these immanent structures of ultimate meaning.

Neo-orthodoxy rejected these "secular" ways of talking of God and used the older non-secular biblical categories, while accepting the whole modern understanding of the spatio-temporal process now de-sacralized of all ultimacy. Out of this came an uneasy dualism, with a naturalistically interpreted world and a biblically understood God giving meaning and coherence thereto.

The developing problem of this God's historical activity—where the two diverse worlds were joined in his "mighty acts"—became more and more evident. One might say that, not unlike today's Roman Catholics, the neo-orthodox thought they could accept secularism "secularly," i.e., as exclusively an attitude toward ordinary history and nature, without compromise to the autonomous biblical superstructure that was set upon that secular base. The present crisis in theology illustrates the increasing difficulty of that strange marriage of heaven and earth, of *Heilsgeschichte* and *Geschichte*.

What is the form of this crisis? In theology the crisis has revealed itself in the virtual disappearance of discourse about God, surely a crisis in *that* discipline if there ever was one! This was first evident in the aforementioned difficulty of relating the biblical God to a naturalistically interpreted process. Then in Bultmannian theology, where the problem was made explicit, God was shoved further and further into the never-never land of sheer kerygmatic proclamation.

Theological understanding contented itself with an existential analysis of man and a hermeneutical analysis of a relativized Scripture and experienced "word-events"—though why such analyses should be called "theological" without the inclusion of God remains problematic at best. For if only the effects of divine activity in history, documents and experience can be spoken of—but not that activity itself—one is very near to sheer secularism.

It is not surprising that at this point a "religionless Christianity" should appear powerfully in our midst, a Christianity that seeks to understand itself in some terms other than man's dependence upon God, and to realize itself totally in the "secular," in the service to the neighbor in the world. The end result has been the appearance of the "God is dead" theologies, which openly proclaim the truth of the new secularity described above, reject for a variety of reasons all language about God, and in a thoroughly secular way concentrate on life and action in the modern world. The power of secularism is vividly revealed here, for in these most recent theologies secular presuppositions and attitudes have utterly infected those formerly inoculated against them.

Probably, however, the purely intellectual difficulties of neo-orthodoxy did not themselves lead to its sudden demise but were reflections of a more basic problem: the fundamental mood of secularism in all of us with which neo-orthodoxy was in the end unable to cope. Apparently what has happened has been that the trans-natural reality that neo-orthodoxy proclaimed—the transcendent God, his mighty acts and his Word of revelation—became more and more unreal and incredible to those who had learned to speak this language. Younger enthusiasts began to wonder if they were talking about anything they themselves knew about when they spoke of God, of encounter, of the eschatological event and of faith. Do these words point to anything, or are they just words, traditional symbols referring more to hopes than experienced realities?

Because of this experience of the unreality, or at least the elusiveness, of the divine, younger theologians began to listen anew to positivist accusations of "meaninglessness" and existentialist affirmations of the death of God. And since, it seems to me, this sense of elusiveness remains the predominant reality of the present religious situation, the questions of the reality of God and the possibility of language about him are our most pressing current theological problems, prior to all other theological issues.

I say this for two reasons. (1) The effort to interpret Christian theology without God is a failure. Such efforts have had vast significance in revealing the power of secularism inside as well as outside the Christian community. But they show themselves to be halfway houses to humanism and thus unable to maintain, without some category of deity, any peculiarly Christian elements.

(2) Other contemporary theological problems—for example, the question of the Christ of faith, the historical Jesus and their relation to the words of Scripture, or the issues centering around the Word of revelation, our reception of it and its relation to Scripture and to the modern mind (i.e., the currently popular

"hermeneutical problems")—are clearly secondary to the problem of God. While the Bible remains in *any* theological atmosphere a book of immense historical, literary and linguistic interest, it is of direct *theological* concern only if it is first presupposed that through it a divine word comes to man. Only if we know already that the Bible is the word of God can theology unfold its concepts without further prolegomena from its contents. And only then does the question of the meaning of its message for our day become the logically primary theological question.

At present, however, serious questions are being asked about the reality of God, and all the more about the reality of *any* revelation, let alone one through these documents. In such a situation these questions must be settled before we can treat the Bible as the source of truth and therefore of theological truth.

19

TO SPEAK IN A SECULAR FASHION OF GOD*

Harvey Cox

ON April 30, 1944, Dietrich Bonhoeffer wrote to one of his friends from his prison cell words that have both tempted and tormented theologians ever since. "We are proceeding toward a time," he wrote, "of no religion at all. . . . How do we speak of God without religion. . . . How do we speak in a secular fashion of God?"

No wonder Bonhoeffer's question bothers us. It reminds us of two incontrovertible facts. The first is that the biblical faith, unlike Buddhism, for example, must *speak* of God. It cannot withdraw into silence or cryptic aphorisms. A God to whom human words cannot point is not the God of the Bible. Bonhoeffer's question also reminds us, however, that the word *God* means almost nothing to modern secular man. His mental world and his way of using language is such that he can neither understand nor use the word *God* meaningfully. This reveals the impasse: if man cannot speak of God in the secular city, then all we have said about secularization as the work of God for man is nonsense and the whole thesis of this book is erroneous. It is clear that we must deal with this painful question of

* Reprinted with the permission of The Macmillan Company from *The Secular City*, by Harvey Cox, pp. 241-43, 257-68. Copyright © Harvey Cox 1965. Footnotes omitted.

Bonhoeffer satisfactorily or all that we have said so far becomes implausible.

Significantly, Bonhoeffer himself supplies a much-needed clue for where to start in seeking to answer his question. Many years before his imprisonment he wrote this paragraph in his commentary on the Second Commandment:

"God" is not for us a common concept by which we designate that which is the highest, holiest and mightiest thinkable, but "God" is a name. It is something entirely different when the heathen say "God" as when we, to whom God himself has spoken, say "God" . . . "God" is a name. . . . The word means absolutely nothing, the name "God" is everything.

Here Bonhoeffer drops an invaluable hint about how we should proceed. He reminds us that in the biblical tradition, we do not speak "about God" at all, either "in a secular fashion" or in any other. When we use the word *God* in the biblical sense, we are not speaking about but "naming," and that is an entirely different matter. To name is to point, to confess, to locate something in terms of our history. We can name something only by using the fund of memories and meanings we carry with us as individuals and as a species. This makes the act of naming, whether naming God or anything else, more than merely a theological or linguistic problem. Theologies and languages grow out of a sociocultural milieu. They spring from one or another epochal *manière d'être*. This makes the problem of "speaking in a secular fashion about God" in part at least a sociological problem.

But speaking about God in a secular fashion is not just a sociological problem. Since we live in a period when our view of the world is being politicized, in which . . . the political is replacing the metaphysical as the characteristic mode of grasping reality, "naming" today becomes in part also a political issue. It becomes a question of where, in the push and pull of human conflict, those currents can be detected which continue the liberating activity we witness in the Exodus and in Easter. Speaking of God in a secular fashion is also a political issue.

But the sociological and political considerations in no sense exhaust the depth of Bonhoeffer's riddle. Despite the efforts of some modern theologians to sidestep it, whether God exists or not *is* a desperately serious issue. All the palaver about the terms *existence* and *being* and all the sophisticated in-group bickering about nonobjectifying language cannot obscure the fact that there remains an indissoluble question after all the conceptualizations have been clarified. It is the question the Spanish philosopher Miguel Unamuno rightly felt overshadows all other questions man asks: Is man alone in the universe or not?

So Bonhoeffer's query has three parts. It is first of all a *sociological problem*. We say problem because it can be answered at that level with relatively little difficulty. It is also a *political issue*. An issue is a somewhat more demanding challenge. It requires us to take some risks and make some choices, to take sides. It necessitates our indicating where that same reality whom the Hebrews called Yahweh, whom the disciples saw in Jesus, is breaking in today. But finally, Bonhoeffer presents us with what is a *theological question*. He makes us answer for ourselves whether the God of the Bible is real or is just a rich and imaginative way man has fashioned to talk about himself. No amount of verbal clarification can set this disagreement aside. In the last analysis it is not a matter of clear thinking at all but a matter of personal decision. Luther was right: deciding on this question is a matter which, like dying, every man must do for himself. . . .

When all the preliminary work has been done and the ground has been cleared, the question Bonhoeffer poses is still a *theological* one. In the present theological climate it is especially important to remember this, since where theologians are not busily trying to dress God in tribal costume or enlist him in their existentialist histrionics, they may be just as avidly whittling down the fact that God does make a difference in the way men live. Their opportunity to do this arises from a new situation in theology. There have always been important similarities between biblical faith and atheism, as contrasted, for example, to belief in demons and spirits. But in our time this similarity has produced a rather novel heresy. It is a kind of atheism expressed in Christian theological terminology. This curious phenomenon is made possible by the fact that the biblical doctrine of the hiddenness of God comports so very well, at one level at least, with contemporary atheism or, better, "nontheism." The two can easily be confused unless real care is used. Thus the hidden God or *deus absconditus* of biblical theology may be mistaken for the no-god-at-all of nontheism. Though He is very different from Godot in Samuel Beckett's play, like Godot He has the similar habit of not appearing at the times and places men appoint. Because the two have often been jumbled, it is important that we distinguish them here.

Carl Michalson describes the biblical doctrine of the hiddenness of God in these terms:

> . . . it is God's way of life to be hidden. He is *ex officio* hidden. Hiddenness is intrinsic to his nature as God. . . . The doctrine of the hiddenness of God . . . is not a counsel of despair or a concession to human finitude, but a positive description of God himself which performs a merciful service. *It prevents man both from looking for God in the wrong place* and from esteeming God's role in reality with *less than ultimate seriousness.*

This biblical God's hiddenness stands at the very center of the doctrine of God. It is so commanding that Pascal was echoing its intention when he said, "Every religion which does not affirm that God is hidden is not true." It means that God discloses himself at those places and in those ways he chooses and not as man would want. And he always discloses himself as one who is at once different *from* man, unconditionally *for* man, and entirely *unavailable* for coercion and manipulation *by* man. It is his utter hiddenness which distinguishes God from the tribal deities man coaxes and expiates, and from the metaphysical deity man grandly includes in a rounded system of thought. Using God for the kingpin in an ontological system is not much different from wheedling Him into watering my corn. The hidden God of the Bible will not be utilized in either way.

But what part does Jesus of Nazareth play in this hiddenness of God? If Jesus were a theophany, an "appearance of God" in the customary religious sense, then in Jesus the hiddenness of God would be abrogated. But this is not the case. God does not "appear" in Jesus; He hides himself in the stable of human history. He hides himself in the sense that we have just mentioned, showing that He is not anything like what religions have wanted or expected from their gods. In Jesus God does not stop being hidden; rather He meets man as the unavailable "other." He does not "appear" but shows man that He acts, in His hiddenness, in human history.

No wonder the religious compulsion of man, whether in its mythological or in its metaphysical form, has never been too happy with Jesus. In Jesus, God refuses to fulfill either tribal expectations or philosophical quandaries. As Bonhoeffer says, in Jesus God is teaching man to get along without Him, to become mature, freed from infantile dependencies, fully human. Hence the act of God in Jesus offers slim pickings for those in hope of clues for the erection of some final system. God will not be used in this way. He will not perpetuate human adolescence, but insists on turning the world over to man as his responsibility.

The summons to accountability before God also precludes, however, the verbal byplay in which theologians sometimes try to convince contemporary nontheists that the differences among men today over the reality of God are merely verbal. They are not. Although to the neutral observer there may appear to be no difference between the god who absents himself, who refuses to bark at man's whistle, and the no-god-at-all; there is all the difference in the world. Given the fact that man in dialogue fashions the meanings by which history proceeds, that he is free to take responsibility for history, one utterly crucial question remains: Is this responsibility something which man himself has conjured, or is it *given* to him?

The biblical answer, of course, is that it is given to him. For the Bible, after mythological and metaphysical overlay has been scraped away, God is not simply a different way of talking about man. God is not man, and man can only be really *"response*-able" when he *responds*. One must be responsible *for* something *before* someone. Man, in order to be free and responsible, which means to be *man,* must answer to that which is not man. Professor Ronald Gregor Smith sums it up when he says that theology, in order to be theology, has to do with what men "are not themselves"; it concerns

what they do not and never can possess at all as part of their self-equipment or as material for their self-mastery, but with what comes to them at all times from beyond themselves.

Such contemporary theologians as Fuchs, Ebeling, and Braun, who are rightly concerned that God not be confused with an object among other objects, have performed an invaluable service to theology. They are justified in emphasizing that there can be no relationship to God which does not include a relationship to man. But it is also true that if God is not an object of man's knowledge or curiosity, He is also not to be identified with some particular quality in man or in human reciprocity, and He is not just a confused mode of speaking about relationships between men.

There is, of course, no high court before which those who affirm God's reality and hiddenness can press their case against those who suspect, as Kafka did, that there is No One There at all. But the difference is real. It is both pointless and patronizing to try to suggest to nontheists that they are really Christians who don't know any better, that the problem is just semantic or conceptual. Nontheists deserve to be taken seriously, not treated as children. In fact, only when we do take them seriously, as they understand themselves, can any real dialogue begin, and they do have much to offer us. Because the experience of the *deus absconditus* and that of the no-god-at-all are so similar, because we share the common discomposure of those who live in a dissonant and exhilarating time, we need the nontheists. But we need them as they are, not as we would like them to be.

The difference between men of biblical faith and serious nontheists is not that we do not encounter the same reality. The difference is that we give that reality a different *name,* and in naming it differently, we differ seriously in the way we respond.

Paul M. van Buren contends in his thoughtful book on the secular meaning of the Gospel that our principal difficulty today in using the language of traditional religion is not bad religion but bad language. He then goes on to a discussion of the logical structure of the language of faith, in the course of which he says that modern man has difficulties with any word which refers to what he calls the "transcendent." I think at this point van Buren is wrong. The problem is not bad language. Language merely reflects reality. It is pliable and flexible. It can change. The problem *is* bad religion, as van Buren should have seen if he really wanted to suggest a "secular meaning" of the Gospel, as the title of his book implies.

But I also believe that van Buren is wrong when he states that modern, secular man does not experience the transcendent. The transcendent means that which, as Gregor Smith says, ". . . man cannot possess at all," that which is not part of the self's equipment but comes from beyond the self. No doubt urban-secular man experiences the transcendent in a radically different *way* than did his tribal and town forebears. He may find it, as Bonhoeffer once said, "in the nearest Thou at hand," but he does meet it. It is his experience of the transcendent which makes man man. Writing on "Art and Theological Meaning" in a volume of essays on Christian esthetics, Amos Wilder says:

If we are to have any transcendence today, even Christian, it must be in and through the secular. . . . If we are to find Grace it is to be found in the world and not overhead. The sublime firmament of overhead reality that provided a spiritual home for the souls of men until the eighteenth century has collapsed.

Wilder believes correctly that in this "one-story world" the transcendent is still present. Because the "overhead" world is gone, artists and poets will be more important to us that ever in dealing "at first hand with life, beyond the fences of social or religious propriety."

But where else does the transcendent God meet us in the secular city? Whatever the name we give Him, however we finally respond to Him, where does He find us? Is it only through the artists?

We have already suggested that God comes to us today in events of social change, in what theologians have often called *history,* what we call *politics.* But events of social change need not mean upheavals and revolutions. The events of everyday life are also events of social change. The smallest unit of society is two, and the relationship between the two people never remains just the same. God meets us there, too. He meets us not just in the freedom revolution in America but also in a client, a customer, a patient, a co-worker.

But how? God is free and hidden. He cannot be expected to appear when we designate the place and time. This means that God is neither close nor far *as such,* but is able to be present in a situation without identifying with it, and He is always present to liberate man. This does not mean that He is there to be walked over. God frees us by supplying that framework of limitation within which alone freedom has any meaning. The freedom of man depends on the prior freedom of God, and man would be a prisoner of his own past if it were not for God who comes in that future-becoming-present where human freedom functions.

Thus we meet God at those places in life where we come up against that which is not pliable and disposable, at those hard edges where we are both stopped and challenged to move ahead. God meets us as the transcendent, at those aspects of our experience which can never be transmuted into extensions of ourselves. He meets us in the wholly other.

We have said that naming is remembering and hoping. It is a social act and is influenced by changes in social structure. In naming God, in attributing to Him a designation which relates Him to human experience, all cultures utilize symbols drawn from some aspect of social life. There are no other sources of symbols. They use political life and call God the "King"; or they utilize family relationships and call Him "Father"; or they use occupational designations and call Him the "shepherd." Thus changing family and political structures inevitably result in different symbolizations of God. To insist on calling God the "shepherd" in an industrial society may seem pious but it really marks the height of unbelief. It suggests that God will somehow slip out of existence if men alter the names they use for Him.

In the tribal society God was experienced as the One who exerted His rule over the evil spirits and lesser gods. Since tribal society is based on kinship ties, man's relationship to God was frequently symbolized with family titles. Because authority was predominantly horizontal, and tribal man's individuality was of a low order, some kind of mystical, often exotic, union with the deity was this era's characteristic relationship. It remains so even in higher religions growing out of kinship cultures such as that of India. Israelite religion had no place for this *absorptionist* type of mysticism. Family images were used, but only with considerable restraint in the Old Testament. In town culture, where a break was made with primordial kinship ties, the symbolization of the deity tended to be political. God became the chief, the ruler, the king. The most frequent relationship to God was that of the subject and the sovereign, the servant and the master.

In technopolitan culture, both horizontal kinship and vertical authority patterns are disappearing. What replaces them is a work team. A team of physicists at work on a research project or a team of land surveyors may appear to the casual observer to have the same relationship to each other as a group of tribal people mending nets. But the similarity is illusory. In the tribal setting, work groups are patterned by familial connections and locked in kinship prescriptions. The modern work team . . . is first of all task-oriented. No doubt people receive an enormous amount of personal satisfaction from the relationships they have in the team. But this arises as a by-product; it is not the purpose of the team. Team relationships at work tend to be of a different character from family relationships. Most importantly, though people may involve themselves in the team deeply while they are at work, they have other roles and relationships which are not drawn in.

The tribal relationship is of a *pre*-I-Thou type. The deficient individuation of tribal man prevents his experiencing God as fully "other." Not only does he find God in a horizontal way, but he is always a part of God and vice versa. Man *participates* in God. In a society marked by *vertical* authority, the period of town culture and individualism, man tends to experience God in the classic I-Thou encounter. God is seen as another who has authority *over* me. The relationship is one of *confrontation*. We have suggested earlier that a new type of interhuman relationship seems to be emerging in urban society, one that is just as human as I-Thou but is qualitatively different. It occurs often in the kind of work team described above, a relationship one has in addition to I-Thou experiences in the family and with intimate friends. But it is more significant and very different from the I-It relationship. Rather than participation or confrontation, it is a relationship of *alongsideness*.

In an earlier chapter we suggested designating this peculiarly urban phenomenon the I-You relationship. It describes very well the rewarding relationship one has with a fellow team member, with whom one has worked on a research project or painted a house. It derives from work that is done together by two persons for whom the work is the key to their mutuality. This is a newly evolving mode of human relationships. It is authentically human and more or less unprecedented in previous cultures, but the important thing about this emergent I-You relationship for our purposes is that it is bound to influence our symbolization of God in one way or another. It may be that in addition to the I-Thou relationship with God, and the mystical experience which is already exceedingly rare, contemporary man could meet God as a "you."

Is this so farfetched? Recent discussions of the concept of the covenant in the Old Testament suggest it means that Yahweh was willing to stoop so low as to work in tandem with man, to work on a team, no matter how poorly the human partner was working out. Whether or not this is true, it can certainly be said that in Jesus of Nazareth God did show that He was willing to take man's side of the unfulfilled covenant, to become the junior partner in the asymmetric relationship. It is not demeaning to suggest that the notions of teamwork and partnership need to be explored much more in our conceptualization of God. He who is "high and lifted up" suggests in the life of Jesus that he is willing to put himself in the position of working within a group, of washing his fellows' feet and of needing someone to carry his cross. What seems at first sight irreverence may be closer to the heart of the self-humbling truth of God than we imagine.

The idea of an I-You partnership between God and man is strongly hinted by the language of Galations 4 which we discussed earlier. In this passage man is viewed as a son and heir. The emphasis is on *son* as opposed to child, and on *heir* as having assumed responsibility. This implies that the strictly vertical relationship which informs a father's relationship to his minor boy is discarded for the adult partnership which obtains between a grown man and his father.

Perhaps in the secular city God calls man to meet Him first of all as a "you." This has far-reaching implications. It suggests that man is not to become fascinated with God himself. Like his relationship to his work partner, man's relationship to God derives from the work they do together. Rather than shutting out the world to delve into each other's depths the way adolescent lovers do, God and man find joy together in doing a common task. Of course this type of relationship will not satisfy the man who is driven by a compulsive interest in "finding" or "experiencing" God. Such people are always dissatisfied by the admittedly sparse revelation of Himself which God has made. It is not the kind of revelation which encourages delving. God wants man to be interested not in Him but in his fellow man.

There is a kind of religiousness abroad today which engages in endless quests for a succession of holy grails. This spirit, celebrated in Somerset Maugham's *The Razor's Edge,* has a powerful attraction for many people today, especially those who describe themselves as "interested in religion." But it runs directly counter to the grain of the Bible.

Of course there is some religious questing in the Bible. The Psalmist could say that his heart panted after God like the hart after the water, but God's answer was never uncertain: Yahweh was more interested in justice rolling down like mighty waters than in religious aspiration. Paul had little patience with the religious questers after the unknown God he ran across in Athens. "This unknown God," he said, "I declare unto you." In Jesus of Nazareth, the religious quest is ended for good and man is freed to serve and love his neighbor.

But how do we name the God who is not interested in our fasting and cultic adoration but asks for acts of mercy? It is too early to say for sure, but it may well be that our English word *God* will have to die, corroborating in some measure Nietzsche's apocalyptic judgment that "God is dead." By what name shall we call the One we met both in the life of Jesus and in our present history as the liberator and the hidden one?

Perhaps we should not be anxious about finding a name. Our present fit of tonguetied verbosity, of empty and ambiguous words, will work itself out in experience, the way it always has. "The story of the word 'God,' " says Cornelis van Peursen, "is that it has no given meaning, but acquires a meaning in history. . . ." Naming was the process by which Israel drew more and more reality into history by relating it to the One who had brought them up out of Egypt. First the origin of history, then its consummation were included in this process of "radiation" by which God was named as he was encountered in the world. God manifests himself to us in and through secular events. The meaning of the word *God* will be altered or a new name will emerge as we encounter that presence in events which draws them into the history of which we are a part, the history of God's liberation of man. Secular talk of God is pointing and naming. As van Peursen says,

. . . it is in a functional way that man comes into contact with the reality of God, that God acquires a meaning in history. . . . As the Church we have to respond to the world through our acts . . . transmitting the old message of a Name . . . which is taking on a new meaning in history, and especially in the functional history of our time.

We cannot simply conjure up a new name. Nor can we arbitrarily discard the old one. God does reveal His name in history, through the clash of historical forces and the faithful efforts of a people to discern His presence and respond to His call. A new name will come when God is ready. A new way of conceptualizing the Other will emerge in the tension between the history which has gone before us and the events which lie ahead. It will emerge as the issues of the urban civilization are drawn into that rehearsal of the past, reflection on the present, and responsibility for the future which *is* history.

This may mean that we shall have to stop talking about "God" for a while, take a moratorium on speech until the new name emerges. Maybe the name that does emerge will not be the three-letter word *God,* but this should not dismay us. Since naming is a human activity embedded in a particular socio-cultural milieu, there is no holy language as such, and the word *God* is not sacred. All languages are historical. They are born and die. Presumably God will continue to live eons after English and all other present languages have been totally forgotten. It is only word magic to believe that there is some integral connection between God and any particular linguistic vocable. . . .

The Exodus marked for the Jews a turning point of such elemental power that a new divine name was needed to replace the titles that had grown out of their previous experience. Our transition today from the age of Christendom to the new era of urban secularity will be no less shaking. Rather than clinging stubbornly to antiquated appellations or anxiously synthesizing new ones, perhaps, like Moses, we must simply take up the work of liberating the captives, confident that we will be granted a new name by events of the future.

20

HOPE IN A POSTHUMAN ERA*

Sam Keen

> *But what is the philosophy of this generation? Not God is dead, that period was passed long ago. Perhaps it should be stated death is God. This generation thinks—and this is its thought of thoughts— that nothing faithful, vulnerable, fragile can be durable or have any true power. Death waits for these things as a cement floor waits for a dropping light bulb.*
>
> —Herzog, BY SAUL BELLOW

WESTERN culture is undergoing a fundamental crisis in its understanding of what it means to be human. In the past, there have been periods of crisis and re-evaluation—the breakup of the Greek city-state, the emergence of Christianity, the Renaissance, the Reformation, the industrial revolution. All previous periods, however, have shared a consensus about human life which today is widely questioned and rejected.

This consensus has been twofold. First, there has been virtual agreement in the Western tradition that there are certain built-in limitations with which every man must reckon if he would lead an authentically human life—the necessity for labor, the in-

* Reprinted with permission from *The Christian Century*, LXXXIV, 4 (January 25, 1967), 106–9.

evitability of disease and tragedy, the brutal fact of death—and that in spite of these limitations man has experienced life as a gift because his world has been a meaning-full and value-full arena within which he might act responsibly. Second, previous ages assumed that man lives in a cosmos governed by a mind or minds more potent and enduring than his. Man has until now thought of himself as belonging not only to the relativities of history but also to an order or reality not subject to the law of destruction and tragedy that rules within history. Because he has understood himself as an "amphibious" creature, belonging to both the profane and the sacred, the earth and the heavens, traditional man has conceived of the authentically human life as one lived in full awareness of both the limitations and the transcendent destiny of man. To be human has involved combining the virtues of realism and hope.

In our time this traditional view of man is called into question at both points. The idea of human limitation has come under attack both practically and theoretically. In the first place it has become obvious that some of the limitations previous cultures regarded as basic to the human condition are giving way before the advance of science. Cybernation promises to eliminate labor for most people in some not too distant future. Disease after disease is being conquered, with the result that life expectancy is twice what it was in the Middle Ages. Recently it was hinted that even the frontier of death may not be impervious to scientific advancement. In the future those suffering from incurable diseases may be quick-frozen and later thawed when a cure has been found. While this possibility does not seem imminent, that it can be seriously discussed reveals something important about the twentieth-century mind: it is offended by the suggestion that there are any a priori limits to the human condition. Even death itself must not be considered a limit with which scientific man may not negotiate!

Awareness of death has been repressed in our culture, much as the Victorian era repressed awareness of sex, because we are unable to accept the idea of built-in human limitations. Saul Bellow is right in suggesting that the underlying philosophy of our generation is "death is God." But Dietrich Bonhoeffer is also correct in saying that death is no longer experienced as a border-situation by most people in our culture, because they have ceased to fear it. A repressed awareness may give rise to anxiety but not to fear.

THE NEW ANTHROPOLOGY

More and more, modern man is also rejecting the traditional notion that human life has only limited creative potentialities because the world into which man emerges already has meaning and value. In spite of the sense of expanding limits and the greater promise of modern life, contemporary man increasingly experiences life not as a gift but as a burden, and the world not as a place filled with value, to be wondered at, but as a morally neutral arena of blind physical laws. In this neutral world man must assume the responsibility for creating meaning. The clue to the mentality which is increasingly dominating Western culture is the fact that the process Feuerbach longed to see has taken place: the predicates traditionally assigned to God have now been reclaimed by man.

No one has articulated this new anthropology with more clarity and power than Jean-Paul Sartre. Man exists, according to Sartre, in a world that, objectively, is devoid of all meaning. It is therefore up to man to do what God was once thought to do—to create *ex nihilo,* to improvise value and meaning out of unlimited freedom. The current of meaning and value now flows only one way—from man to the world. Man is a giver, a creator of meaning, not a recipient.

The second area of the traditional consensus has fared no better. Modern man understands himself as belonging totally to the flux of history. Since he can believe only in what he can experience and think, and since his modes of thought are empirical, pragmatic and operational, he finds himself increasingly cut off from the possibility of relating in hope to any transcendent reality. The ancient, amphibious character of man is denied. Modern man lives a profane life, in a secular city, in a bungaloid world. We may expect him to be realistic, but the growing testimony is that the virtues of faith and hope are impossible for him.

It would not be too extravagant to say that the fundamental thesis of the new view of man which is coming to dominate the twentieth-century intellectual is that modern man has become posthuman. To be a "modern man" is to recognize that one is discontinuous with traditional man. It is to join in the refrain "Nothing like us ever was." Somehow, because we belong to the twentieth century, we are supposed to be freed from the limitations that governed past human beings and also to be incapable of believing in the reality of anything that transcends the testimony of sense and experience.

ACCEPTANCE OF THE SECULAR

The dominant tendency of modern theology is to adapt Christian faith to the presuppositions of the twentieth century mind. Bonhoeffer set the mood in suggesting that the "religious premise" of traditional man is no longer valid for the man who has "come of age"; the Christian must learn to live in the secular world. The death-of-God theologians have followed this lead in maintaining that there can be a Christian style of life which is not informed by the traditional Western understanding of the limitations and transcendent destiny of man. In the view of William Hamilton, for example, the Christian theologian of today is "a man without faith, without hope, with only the present and therefore only love to guide him" ("Thursday's Child," *Theology Today,* January 1964). When Paul van Buren accepts the principle of empirical verification and thus is forced to reduce the rich New Testament language about God and the eschatological destiny of man to the principle of "contagious freedom," he also compresses the Christian life into the present moment. Thomas J. J. Altizer achieves the same effect by limiting theology to an Incarnate Word which can be known only as we are open to the experience of the moment before us. In accepting the working assumptions of the secular mind, modern theology has more and more come to concentrate upon the present moment, has given itself over to the categories of

what Marcel has called "established experience," and consequently has been unable to articulate an adequate doctrine of
faith or hope.

My concern here is to question whether a religious style of
life can exist in the acid soil of the promethean view of man
which characterizes secular thought. I would maintain that there
are two movements which belong essentially as well as historically to any theistic style of life. I call these the abdication from
the pretensions of omnipotence and the positing of a ground for
hope. If these two movements are essential to a religious style
of life, Christian theology will have to be far clearer than it now
is about where it is to say Yes to the secular mind and where it
is to say No.

ABDICATION OF OMNIPOTENCE

The movement toward religious faith begins with the realization that the self is not God, is not absolute power, knowledge
or responsibility. A friend of mind described this experience by
saying, "I decided to hand in my resignation as manager of the
universe. I was surprised to find how quickly it was accepted."

Perhaps this comment seems a little silly, an insult to common sense; isn't it obvious to everyone who has ever lived,
experienced pain, observed his own failure or contemplated
death that no human being is omnipotent? Astonishingly enough
it is not! A growing body of opinion and evidence suggests that
most people harbor illusions of immortality and omnipotence.
Sartre argues convincingly that the whole project of human
consciousness is directed toward becoming God. Karen Horney
makes a similar point in psychological terms. She shows that the
key to neurosis lies in an effort to actualize an idealized,
godlike image of the self rather than devoting the energies to
realization of a realistic set of goals. The neurotic says to
himself, "Others might have to struggle for success, but it
should come easily to me; others may fall prey to disease but
not me. I am insulated from misfortune by my unique gifts, my
position, my potentialities." The neurotic's working assumption
is that he is an exception to every cosmic rule. We need only to

remind ourselves that the neurotic search for glory is an aspect of every personality.

This hidden pretension of omnipotence is nowhere more clearly seen than in the illusions of immortality we all harbor. Tolstoy in "The Death of Ivan Illych" graphically illustrates the destruction of such illusions and the shock which comes to a man when he discovers he is mortal.

Ivan Illych saw that he was dying, and he was in continual despair. In the depths of his heart he knew he was dying, but not only was he not accustomed to the thought, he simply did not and could not grasp it.

The syllogism he had learned from Kiezewetter's Logic: "Caius is a man, men are mortal, therefore Caius is mortal," had always seemed to him correct as applied to Caius, but certainly not as applied to himself. That Caius—man in the abstract—was mortal, was perfectly correct, but he was not Caius, not an abstract man, but a creature quite quite separate from all others. He had been little Vanya, with a mamma and a papa, with Mitya and Volodya, with the toys, a coachman and a nurse. . . . What did Caius know of the smell of that striped leather ball Vanya had been so fond of? Had Caius kissed his mother's hand like that, and did the silk of her dress rustle so for Caius? . . . "Caius really was mortal and it was right for him to die; but for me, little Vanya, Ivan Illych, with all my thoughts and emotions, it is altogether a different matter. It cannot be that I ought to die. That would be too terrible."

We are always ready to ignore our limitations—which, I suspect, accounts for American funeral practices, as well as for the slight revulsion we all feel in the presence of the poor, the crippled or the seriously ill. We do not want to be reminded of our mortality! But theology must constantly remind man of his mortality, for hope becomes a possibility only where there is a vivid awareness of the tragic limitations of human experience. Omnipotent beings have no need of hope, for they are not threatened by extremities.

I fear that Bonhoeffer has done modern theology a disservice in suggesting that death and the other boundary situations of human existence should not be central considerations of theology. One looks in vain among the radical theologians for any concerted effort to deal with the problems of death. Theology has escaped from the extremities and turned them over to pastoral psychology. And yet, much as we would like to forget, we cannot. The malevolent trinity of suffering, tragedy and death has yet to be dethroned. Lucidity demands that we deal with human life in light of its limitations.

DESIRABLE DISILLUSIONMENT

Let us consider the abdication of the hidden claims to onipotence from another perspective.

To give up such claims is to become disillusioned, in the best sense of the word. It requires a considerable amount of energy to harbor an illusion. When we abandon our claims to omnipotence we stop nourishing the illusion that the world is as we would like it to be. With great relief we are finally able to declare that "things are what they are." When Margaret Fuller wrote to Carlyle, "I have decided to accept the universe" (Carlyle is reputed to have replied, "By Gad, she'd better!"), she articulated a sentiment which may be linguistically odd but which is psychologically and religiously profound. To lose our illusions and accept the rules of the game of life is a prerequisite to human freedom and responsibility. As long as we harbor claims and illusions of omnipotence, we judge both our successes and failures, our responsibilities and limitations, by fantastic standards which we inevitably fall short of. But once we accept the limitations that constitute the human condition we become free to explore the possible.

To accept the rules of the game is not equivalent to mere resignation. Rather, it is to live in an attitude of wonder. Once we are able to confess that we are not the center of the world, we perceive things in an altogether new way. We are set free to admire rather than possess, to enjoy rather than exploit, to accept rather than grasp. In the attitude of wonder we experience life as a gift. G. K. Chesterton has expressed this beautifully. There are, he says in *Orthodoxy,* two convictions that grow out of the experience of wonder. "First, that this world is

a wild and startling place, which might have been quite different, but which is quite delightful; second, that before this
wilderness and delight one may well be modest and submit to
the queerest limitations of so queer a kindness." In wonder we
perceive that it is not the case, as Sartre contends, that we are
condemned to a neutral world in which human freedom must
create all meaning and value. Merleau-Ponty has more accurately stated that "we are condemned to meaning." When we
abandon our fantastic claims we find, as traditional man always
knew, that our power to create meaning is limited on the one
hand by the fragility of human life and on the other by the
givenness of the world into which we emerge.

POSITING A GROUND FOR HOPE

We come now to consider a second aspect of religious faith.

Seemingly, the world of the spirit loathes a power vacuum no
less than does the political world. When realism prevails and we
acknowledge that our infantile strivings to have dominion over
all things are doomed to failure, the question of God inevitably
arises. If I am not the source of a deathless and victorious
power, is there any such power? If I am not God, is there a
God? Is there any force, mind or person working at the heart of
things to accomplish what I desire but cannot achieve; to bring
order out of chaos, meaning out of contingency, triumph out of
tragedy? Or is human history "a tale told by an idiot"?

The question of God is not the question of the existence of
some remote infinite being. It is the question of the possibility of
hope. The affirmation of faith in God is the acknowledgment
that there is a deathless source of power and meaning that can
be trusted to nurture and preserve all created good. To deny
that there is a God is functionally equivalent to denying that
there is any ground for hope. It is therefore wholly consistent
for Sartre to say that human beings "must act without hope," or
for Camus to warn that hope was the last of the curses which
Pandora took from her box. If God is dead, then death is indeed
God, and perhaps the best motto for human life is what Dante

once wrote over the entrance to hell: "Abandon hope, all ye who enter."

The concept of hope has been so little examined in our time that it is frequently thought to mean the same thing as optimism or illusion or mere agnosticism about the future. There are, however, crucial differences. Optimism is based upon illusion—in the Freudian sense—in that it arises out of a drive for wish fulfillment which ignores contrary evidence. The optimist conspires to ignore the facts because they suggest an interpretation he does not want to make. Contrariwise, the believer's affirmation of a ground for hope is made in the knowledge that by all realistic calculations human history is ultimately tragic. It is in light of this certain knowledge that the believer sets himself to examine his experience to determine whether there is any basis for hoping that what is penultimately the case is not ultimately so.

AFFIRMING THE UNKNOWABLE

It is important to realize that the believer is clear that experience renders an ambiguous verdict. In both the inner world and the outer world it is as Ecclesiastes has told us: there is both building up and tearing down, creating and destroying. And if the life force seems ingenious in circumventing all that threatens life and growth, it is nevertheless true that finally death wins. Thus the question of hope becomes the question of the adequacy and the finality of the categories of human understanding.

Hope begins with the realization that human experience is finally inadequate to deal with all the possibilities that reality harbors. We might say that to hope is to take experience seriously but not to absolutize it. Gabriel Marcel says (in *Homo Viator*) that at the basis of hope is the realization that "the more the real is real the less does it lend itself to a calculation of possibilities on the basis of accepted experience."

This is not yet, however, the full meaning of hope. The humanist and the skeptic share with the believer an agnosticism about the adequacy of human categories of thought and experience to comprehend the limits of the real. Such agnosticism is merely epistemological humility. But we confuse the issue if we identify faith with mere agnosticism. Faith and hope arise out of agnosticism, but they go on to proclaim an affirmation about the unknowable.

There is a leap of faith which can be taken only as an act of courage in which a man says, "Although the categories of experience yield evidence that is at best ambiguous and is sometimes indicative of the finality of death and the triumph of evil, I *nevertheless* decide to trust that there is a deathless source of human life in which the meaning created within human history is conserved and brought to fulfillment." It is in this positing of the trustworthiness of the ground of life that we find the essential element of the religious consciousness.

Surely William Hamilton and the other radical theologians are wrong in suggesting the possibility of a form of Christian life in which faith and hope have been eliminated. Hamilton seeks to describe the Christian theologian and Camus's rebel with the same formula; echoing the previously quoted description of today's theologian, he says of the rebel: "Faith is abolished for the rebel; hope is quite absent. But love remains; 'rebellion cannot exist without a strange form of love' " ("The Christian, The Saint, and the Rebel," in *Forms of Extremity in the Modern Novel,* edited by Nathan A. Scott, Jr.).

Although I have the greatest admiration for the heroic spirit of Camus, I do not think we should confuse the style of life he recommends with any form of religious or Christian faith. *He* did not. Religious faith involves a movement in which the believer goes beyond the categories of present experience and posits a metaempirical ground for hope. This is precisely the movement Camus refused to make. He wished to live in the certainties and to live without appeal. To eliminate the movement beyond the certainties of the present moment of experience is not to make Christianity palatable to the empirical and secular mind of the twentieth century. It is to eliminate the religious option.

Religious faith, in any of its theistic varieties, involves essentially those virtues of realism and hope that it has involved historically. In many ways modern technology has changed the face of the earth and the texture of human life. We can perhaps realize a security and abundance of life which to traditional man would have seemed utopian and in this sense become posthistorical. Yet as we savor the bittersweet taste of life which is always accompanied by tragedy and as we face the mystery out of which life arises and into which it speeds, we remain *merely human,* indistinguishable from the man of the first or the thirty-first century. Perhaps in the face of this mystery we are able to be most fully human and free when we have the courage to be both lucid and hopeful.

21

JUDAISM IN THE SECULAR AGE*

Jacob Neusner

NO RELIGION may be adequately compared to another. Each has its particularities which render comparison a distortion. Judaism cannot be compared to Christianity, for example, as if each component of the one had its functional or structural equivalent in the other. Christians understand by "religion" a rather different phenomenon, for it seems to Jews, perhaps wrongly, that Christians lay far greater stress upon theology and matters of belief as normative and probative than does Judaism. A Christian is such by baptism or conversion, by being called out into a new and sacred vocation of faith. A Jew is never *not* a Jew according to Jewish law. He is *born* into the Jewish situation. There was never a time that he was a man but not a Jew. There can be no time when he will cease to be a Jew, for, as the Talmud says, though he sin, he remains "Israel." The Jewish ethnic group is never perceived by Jewish theology to be a secular entity, therefore, and therein lies the root of much misunderstanding. Christians speak of "secular Jews," by which they mean Jews divorced from the profession of Jewish faith and the practice of the *mitzvot*.† But Judaism does not, and cannot, regard such Jews as "secular," for they are all children

---

* Reprinted with permission from an article with the same title in *Journal of Ecumenical Studies*, III, 3 (Fall 1966), 519–29. Copyright © 1966 by Duquesne University. Footnotes omitted.

†[*Mitzvot* (sing., *mitzvah*) bears the double meaning of divine commandments and their fulfillment—ED.]

of Abraham, Isaac, and Jacob. Their forefathers stood at Sinai and bound them for all time by the terms of a contract to do and hear the word of God. That contract has never been abrogated, and though invididuals may forget it, its Maker can never forget them. A Jew who does not keep the covenant still has its imprint engraved in his flesh. His children do not require conversion if they choose to assume its responsibilities. The world, moreover, has understood the indelibility of the covenant, for it has persisted in regarding as Jews many who regard themselves as anything but Jewish; and it has murdered the seed of Abraham into the third generation.

These remarks by no means represent the universal judgment of the Jewish community, which has mostly lost a theological understanding of itself. The larger part of Jewry regards being Jewish—"Jewishness"—as mostly an ethnic affiliation, and prefers to understand that affiliation in a this-worldly and secular way. Judaism, that is, the corpus of Jewish Tradition from biblical and Talmudic times onward, has a very different view, one more familiar to educated Christians from their studies of religious history, but less familiar from contemporary observation. It should be clear that I understand Jewish existence within the norms of classical Jewish theology. We are a people called forth to constitute a kingdom of priests and a holy nation, to serve as God's suffering servant and to bear upon ourselves the burden of humanity. Our collective vocation began with the call to Abraham, Isaac, and Jacob, carried us to Sinai, and will at the end of days reach fulfillment. "Secular" Jews do not see things this way, but however they see themselves, this is, I believe, how Judaism sees *them*.

It is a fact, moreover, that Jews quite alien to the Torah retain a very vivid sense of being part of a historical, if not of a supernatural, community. They yearn to see their children marry other Jews, though this may represent no more, in the eyes of the world, than an ethnic loyalty. They insist that their children associate with other Jews, even though association may have what Christians will regard as a wholly secular setting. But Judaism cannot regard the Jewish group as a secular enterprise, as I said, for it advances a very different view of what it means to be a Jew. It lays great stress upon community, upon the chain of the generations, upon birth within the convenant. As Professor Monford Harris writes: "The secularized gentile is precisely that: a secularized gentile. But the secularized Jew is still a Jew. The Jew that sins is still a Jew, still a member of covenantal Israel, even when he denies that covenant." One cannot stress this fact too much: *there can be no Judaism without Jewishness,* that is, without ethnic identification. Judaism cannot be reduced to its "essence," whether that be construed as ethical, theological, or even behavioral. We know full well that there can be Jewishness without Judaism, and against this many of us struggle within the Jewish community. In our effort to keep the issues of Judaism to the fore, we may criticize the ethnic emphasis of the community as it is. But we struggle within that community precisely because it is what it is: all that is left of the remnant of Israel in this world. Its worldliness is a challenge. But the ethnic-Jews are right, and we are wrong, when they see as quite legitimately *Jewish* welfare activities of no particular Jewish relevance, and when they stress the value of association with other Jews for its own sake. They want thereby to preserve the group. Our regret is that they seem to have forgotten why. But the instinct is fully sound, and we critics must never forget it.

And who are these Jews, who cannot despite themselves achieve secularization? They are the bearers of an unbroken myth, a this-worldly group affirming the world and joining in its activities with religious fervor, yet regarding themselves, whether they be religious in the Christian sense or not, in terms the objective observer can regard only as preposterous, or religious. These Jews see themselves as a group, though their group should have ceased to hold them when the faith lost its hold upon them, and that is a paradox. They see themselves as bound to others, in other lands and other ages, whom they have never seen, and with whom they have practically nothing in common but common forefathers. This too is a paradox. They see their history as one history, though they are not everywhere involved in it. They reflect upon the apocalyptic events of the day as intimately and personally important to them. They died in Auschwitz. They arose again in the State of Israel. They respond passionately, no matter how remote they are from Judaism, to the appeal of the flesh, of Israel *after the flesh,* and see themselves in a way that no religious Jew can call secular, however secular they themselves would claim to be. This too is a paradox: They bear fears on account of the past, though that past is nothing to them except that it is the Jews'. They have nightmares that belong to other men but are not within their personal experience at all, except that they are Jews. They see themselves as brands plucked from the burning, though they never stood near the fire. The classical faith demands that each man see himself as redeemed at Sinai from bondage to Pharaoh. The modern Jew, secure in America or Canada or Australia or the State of Israel, persists within the pattern of the classical faith, but in a far more relevant form of it. He was saved from Auschwitz and rebuilt the land. The ties that bind other groups of immigrants within the open societies in the West have long since attenuated. Despite the decline of faith, the ties that bind the Jews are stronger than ever, into the third and fourth, and fifth generation and beyond. Nor can one ignore the mystery of Soviet Jewry, of whom we know so little and understand nothing. They persist. They ought not. All we know is that almost fifty years after the Bolshevik revolution, young people, raised in isolation from their Tradition and from the Jewish world, trained to despise religion and above all Judaism, profess to be Jews, though they need not, and accept the disabilities of Jewishness, though these are by no means slight. Before this fact of contemporary Jewish history we must stand in silence. We cannot understand it. No worldly or naturalist explanation suffices to explain it. In my view, it is not a secular phenomenon at all, though it can be explained in a worldly way to the satisfaction of the world.

This is the paradox of the secular age. The Jews have said for almost two centuries that they are a religious group, and have accepted, by and large, the Christian world's criteria for religion. They have told the world they are different by virtue of religion, though they claimed that religion for them means what it means to others. And yet the secular world sees Jews who are not different from itself, for they have no professed religion. By their own word, such Jews, and they are very many, should have ceased to exist. Yet they are here, and they are Jews, and "Jewishness" is important to them in terms that the Christian and secular worlds alike find not at all "religious."

A second paradox is that the Jews have allied themselves with secularizing forces from the very beginning. Claiming to be merely Germans, or French, or Canadians, or Americans of the Jewish faith, they have chosen for themselves a place among those who struggled for the secularization of culture, politics, art, and society. The reason is, alas, that they had no choice. The forces of religion, meaning Christianity wherever it was established, invariably allied themselves to those of reaction, in opposing the emancipation of the Jews. Rarely do we find an exception to the rule: the more he was a Christian, the more he hated Jews. It is therefore no paradox at all that Jews have favored the secularization of institutions and of men, for if they hoped for a decent life, it was only upon a secular foundation that emancipation was possible. Even today, moreover, Christians would still prefer to use the institutions of the common society to propagate their faith. The public schools are still supposed to celebrate the great events of Christian sacred history, and Jewish children must still confront, and deny, the Christian message once or twice a year.

Christian opposition to secularization is by no means a mere vestige of earlier days. It is rather, I think, a fear of the need to believe *despite* the world, a fear of faith itself. For many centuries it has been natural to be a Christian. The world was mostly Christian, and where it was not, it was the realm of the devil and the Jews. Christians could aspire, therefore, to the creation of a metaphysic and a natural theology which, from the bare artifacts of the world, would rise, in easy stages, to the heights of Calvary. Metaphysics, religious philosophy, natural theology—these are naturally Christian enterprises, for only a

Christian could conceive so benign and friendly a vision of the world that he might ask the world to strengthen, even to provide reasonable foundations within experienced reality for, his Gospel. It is no accident that Judaism has produced only a highly parochial metaphysic, very little natural theology, and a religious philosophy whose main task was to mediate between Judaism and the world. Judaism has had to stress revelation, and not a worldly apprehension of faith, because the world for two thousand and more years has offered little solace. Judaism has had to say *no* to many worlds, though it is not therefore a habitually negating tradition. It has had to say to pagans that God is not in nature; to mighty empires that the King of Kings alone is king; to Christians that redemption is not yet; to Bolshevism that Israel lives despite the "laws" of history. It has had to say no because of its first and single affirmation: We shall do and we shall hear. The result is that Judaism has looked, as I said, for very little help from the world. It has not presumed that the artifacts of creation would lead to Sinai; that a natural theology would explain why a Jew should keep the Sabbath or refrain from eating pork; that a communicable, non-mythological metaphysic would show Israel in a rational situation. In its early centuries, Christianity comprehended the Jewish situation. The apostle Paul offered not a reasonable faith, beginning with worldly realities and ending at the foot of the cross. He offered a scandal to the Jews and foolishness to the Greeks, and said it was faith, and faith alone, which was demanded of the Christian; and it was by virtue of that faith, for it was a very difficult thing, that the Christian would be saved. Scandal and foolishness are sociological realities. From the fourth century onward, to be a Jew was a scandal to the Christians and foolishness, later on, to Islam. It was faith despite the world, and not because of it, that Judaism required, and received. This is the kind of faith with which Christianity begins, and, I believe, which is demanded once again. The Christian today is called to choose between Christ and the world, for the world is no longer his. I do not say it is a better world on that account, but it *is* a different world. I do not think however Judaism has suffered for its recognition and acceptance of the situation of *Golah,* of exile not only from the earthly land, but also from the ways of the world. If Christianity is entering a time of exile, it need not fear greatly, if Christians are prepared to affirm their faith through faith, and not merely through a reasoned apprehension of reality, which is not *faith* at all. As Christianity enters the Jewish situation, it need not, therefore, fear for its future. *Golah* is not a situation to be chosen, but to be accepted at the hand of God as a test of faith and an opportunity for regeneration and purification. We do not choose to go into exile, any more than the Christians would choose to abandon the world. Having gone into exile, having lost the world, Jew and Christian alike may uncover new resources of conviction, new potentialities for sanctity, than they knew they had. We who witnessed the destruction of an ancient temple learned of new means of service to the creator, that God wants mercy and not sacrifice, in Hosea's terms— deeds of loving kindness in those of Rabban Yohanan ben Zakkai. It is the world, and not the temple, that became the arena for God's work. Having lost the world, or wisely given it up, Christians too may recall that "the whole earth is full of His holiness," and that every day and everywhere the world provides a splendid opportunity for witness.

Finally, the advent of secularization offers still another welcome challenge to both Judaism and Christianity. In the recent past, exponents of both traditions have accepted the world's criteria for the truth or value of religion, both Judaism and Christianity. In its grosser form, this acceptance has led to such arguments for religion as those that claim religion is good for one's mental health, or important as a foundation for ethical behavior, and valuable as a basis for a group's persistence, or a nation's. In all instances religion has been evaluated for its service to something else, to health, to decency, to group solidarity. In its more refined form, the worldly argument in behalf of religion has stressed man's need of religion in the face of the absurd; or his dependence upon religion as a source of cogent and unified world-views. We have been told that religion is an answer to human needs. We are supposed to conclude that we ought therefore to foster it. These arguments represent the final blasphemy, the affirmation of faith for worldly purposes. Though Cox does not necessarily suggest it, secularization represents an inquisitorial judgment: the world does not *need* religion. It can provide a sound basis for mental health, a reasonable, though tentative, foundation for ethical action, even —as the Jewish community seems to prove—an adequate basis for group life, without faith in any form. Man does not need religion to overcome the absurd, for he can accept the absurd with the same enthusiasm and life-affirming vitality that he accepts the other artifacts of reality. He can meet his needs elsewhere than at the holy altar.

We who affirm that God made the world need not claim in his behalf that he needs to have done so. We who hold that God acted freely and out of love need not deny that love and that freedom in the name of worldly rationality. Mankind does not need religion. The worldy uses of religion have far more acceptable, secular surrogates. Man does not need to believe in God to avoid insanity, or absurdity, or social disintegration. He does not need to accept revelation in terms that render revelation the result of worldly ratiocination. Mankind is challenged by the world's own power to accept or reject revelation, to affirm or deny God, upon judgment of the real issues. These issues are, Did God make the world? Does Providence govern history? Is Torah, meaning truth, from Heaven? The world cannot resolve them for us, and in the joyful acceptance of its perquisites, Jews and Christians alike are much enriched. They regain the opportunity to believe, as I said, and to assent with rejoicing to the imperative of Sinai, to accept in submission the yoke of heaven, to love God with all our heart. These have been the classical paradigms of Jewish existence. This world once more renders them vivid.

Judaism is both admirably equipped, and completely unprepared for secularization.

It is well equipped to confront an uncomprehending world, as I have said, because of the exigencies of its history. It is, moreover, able to face this world with something more constructive than ungenerous disdain. It has always regarded the world as the stage upon which the divine drama may be enacted. The world presents Judaism with its highest challenge, to achieve sanctity within the profane, to hallow the given. For this task, Judaism comes equipped with Torah and *mitzvot,* Torah which reveals God's will for the secular world, *mitzvot* which tells us how to carry out that will. Through *mitzvah,* we sanctify the secular, not in a metaphysical sense, nor through theologizing intractable givens. One sees the setting sun and lights a candle, the one a natural perception of the course of the earth upon its axis, the other a perfectly commonplace action. But he adds, "who has commanded us to light the Sabbath light," and the course of nature becomes transformed, and a commonplace action transforms it. We don a piece of cloth with fringes, and say, "who has commanded us concerning fringes." That cloth is no longer like any other. It serves as a means of worshipping our Creator. We build a frail hut of branches and flowers at the autumn season, an act of quite natural celebration of the harvest. But we say, "who has commanded us to sit in the Sukkah," and those branches become a sacred shelter. Our table becomes an altar, and the commonplace and profane action of eating food becomes the occasion to acknowledge the gifts of Him who gave it. We speak of our people's humble happenings, of their going forth from slavery to freedom, but doing so is rendered by the commandments into a sacred action, a moment of communion. We open our minds to the wonders of the world, and this too is Torah and requires a benediction. A man takes a wife, and we proclaim the blessings of Eden, the memories of besieged Jerusalem, and the hope for future redemption. Our Tradition leads us not away from the world, but rather into it, and demands that we sanctify the given, and see it as received, commanded from Heaven. All things inspired a sense of awe and call forth a benediction. Nothing is profane by nature, nor is anything intrinsically sacred but that we make it so. The heavens tell the glory of God. The world reveals his holiness. Through *mitzvot* we respond to what the heavens say; through

Torah we apprehend the revelations of the world. Judaism rejoices, therefore, at the invitation of the secular city. It has never truly known another world; and it therefore knows what its imperatives require.

Judaism has always, moreover, understood history, or social change, to be in some measure exemplifications of divine sovereignty. It has understood daily affairs to reveal more than commonplace truths. The destruction of a worldly city was understood from prophetic times onward to be a call for penitence and *teshuvah,* return to God. The sorrows of the age were seen as the occasion for renewed inwardness, prayer, repentance, and doing deeds of compassion, so that men might make themselves worthy of the compassion of God. It has at the same time recognized a tension between event and divine will. Judaism has never merely accepted history, any more than it accepted nature, but sought rather to elevate and sanctify the profane in both. History does not speak God's will in unequivocal terms, for history is to be interpreted, not merely accepted, by means of the Torah. We have seen in revelation a guide to understanding events, and have never uncritically accepted events as themselves being unexamined meaning. All things are seen under the aspect of Sinai, and all events must be measured by the event of revelation. We are not, therefore, at a loss to evaluate the changes of an inconstant world. We have, moreover, demanded that God, like ourselves, abide by the covenant. In times of stress, we have called him to account, as much as ourselves. To offer a most recent example:

The journal of Chaim Kaplan contains the following passage:

There is a rumor that in one of the congregations the prayer leader came and dressed himself in a *kittel* [shroud] and prepared to lead his poor and impoverished people in the *Neilah* [closing prayers for the Day of Atonement] service, when a boy from his congregation broke in with the news about the ghetto. At once the Jew dispensed with *Neilah*, took off his *kittel,* and went back to his seat. There was no point in praying when the 'Gates of Mercy' were locked. . . .

We have taken events so very seriously that we are prepared to call God to account, and even to remind him, as did Ezekiel, that his good name and ours are one and the same. What happens to us happens to him; the covenant measures the loyalty of both its signatories.

Judaism has offered a worldly understanding of man's part in the achievement of God's kingdom. Man is the partner in the building of the kingdom. He is needed to perfect the world under the sovereignty of God. Just as the commonplace may be profane or sacred, but the *mitzvot* consecrate, so too the world, society, may be sanctified. That sanctification is of a most practical sort. We are told to heal the sick, free the captives, loosen the bonds that enslave men. A starving world is an affront to God. All the technical skills of men possess the potentiality to achieve holiness, therefore, and all the vocations of men may serve to sanctify the world. The secular city, Professor Cox writes, requires the skill of men. The kingdom of God cannot do without men's abilities. The kingdom of God is meant to find a place in the history of this world, moreover, according to the eschatological theory of significant Jewish thinkers. The only difference between this world and the world to come, or the age to come, will be the end of subjugation to paganism, so said Samuel, the third-century Babylonian master. Israel is meant, furthermore, to live in this world, to bear witness to God in the streets of the city. For centuries, and most immediately in modern Judaism, Jews have seen themselves as bearers of the kingdom, as witnesses to the rule of God over the world. One need hardly stress, therefore, that Judaism is ready and eager for the worldly encounter.

That encounter, however, is by no means neutral. Judaism has seen itself under a very special vocation, as I said, to say *no* to the lesser claims to divinity entertained by this world. It has told the world that sanctity inheres in it, but denied that the world as it is is holy. It has offered the world the promise of redemption, but denied that redemption is just yet. It has borne unflagging testimony to the unredemption of mankind, and insisted upon a radical criticism of the status quo. These are the vocations, too, of the secular city, which denies ultimacy even to religion, all the more so to lesser structures. Judaism has insisted that the world is ever secular, both so that it may be sanctified and so that it may not lose the hope for ultimate redemption.

And yet Judaism is utterly unready for secularization in the current sense. Professor Cox writes that secularization is "the loosing of the world from religious and quasi-religious under-standings of itself, the dispelling of all closed world-views, the breaking of all supernatural myths and sacred symbols. . . ." Nothing in my understanding of Judaism suggests that Judaism can accept, or even comprehend, "the loosing of the world from religious . . . understandings of itself." If from my perspective there can be no "secular Jew," there can surely emerge no "secularized Judaism." Judaism begins with the affirmation of a supernatural apprehension of reality, however we may courage-ously try to formulate that apprehension in naturalistic or humanistic terms. It begins with the proclamation of the unity and sovereignty of God. It offers to the world the spectacle of a people bound to God's service and governed by his will. It tells the world that this people serves as the heart of humanity, the barometer of its health, and that its history becomes paradig-matic for the human condition. Judaism may cope with the world, may indeed affirm this age in the terms I have outlined; but it can never turn away from itself and its primary assent. Our prophets have offered the world the belief that at some times God may hide his face from man. This may be such an age. We can never confuse, however, our own difficulties in belief with ontological or anthropological Godlessness. Sinai has happened. We may not have seen his face, but we have the record that his glory passed before us. Not every age has an equal apprehension of the glory. A handmaiden saw at the Red Sea what was not given to the prophets to see. We know through Torah, and can never, therefore, claim ignorance, only frail forgetfulness. We may, as Rabbi Abraham J. Heschel says, be messengers who have forgotten our message. But we can never forget that we once had a message. We may comprehend the hiddenness of God; indeed, we are those who have most suffered in his absence. We can never confuse that comprehension of *our* condition with the illusion of *his*. We have lived for a long time within the gates of the secular city. Our Tradition has prepared us for, and our condition has taught us the imperatives of, its discipline. We have aspired to its liberties. But these imperatives we accept, these liberties we demand, *upon our own terms*. We are not secular within the secular city, but we are Jews, *yehudim,* upon whom the name of the Lord has been called. We cannot change our name, either to add to his discipline that of the world, or to win for ourselves the blessings of the world. In the city of this world, or in the world to come, we can only be ourselves, Jews. This is the final paradox of our current situation: we who have confronted the data of secularization long before our neighbors now rehearse our ancient response to these data. We who first told the world of its secularization need now remind it of its consecration.

22

THE PRESENT EMBARRASSMENT
OF THE CHURCH*

Gustave Weigel, S.J.

I

RELIGION can contribute to the welfare of the general community; it can help society. My only worry is whether it should.

It certainly cannot be the prime purpose of religion to make secular society more beneficent and the secular enterprise more satisfactory. That can indeed be the consequent of religion. But consequents are not the goals of deliberation; they are casual accretions to the proper goals of a planned effort.

Perhaps it would not be taken amiss if we were to say that man is not for society, but that society is for man. Given the needs of the human being, society is necessary for their satisfaction. This does not mean that society exists to grant man the objects of his every caprice and uncriticized impulse. Society is a reality no less than the individual, and if the individual needs society, he must respect its being. The needs of man show that he is more than an atomic individual; he is also of necessity a member of society, which is posited by the very fact that man exists. In consequence, man must adjust to the collectivity. It is

* Reprinted with the permission of The World Publishing Company from *Religion in America*, edited by John Cogley, pp. 224–43. Copyright © 1958 by The Fund for the Republic, Inc.

not the function of society to adjust to the isolated individual. But society must be human just as the individual is human.

Here is the nub of our problem. Neither the individual man nor secular society is an absolute. They are relative to each other. Just as we cannot expect society to accept every demand of the individual, so we cannot expect the individual to submit to whatsoever is commanded by society. The individual has rights which society cannot nullify and the commonwealth has rights which it cannot abdicate.

All historical malaise comes from the failure either of the individual to respect the rights of the collectivity or of the collectivity's tyrannical suppression of the rights of the individual. In our day we see it so concretely in the cold war which vexes the hearts of all the men of the world. Soviet Russia stands for community over the individual; the free society as championed by the United States stands for the individual over society. Both communities would anxiously object to this generalization. The Russians will insist that they are very much concerned with the individual and the Americans feel certain that they are preoccupied with the commonwealth. Both could bring much evidence to support their claims, and the evidence is convincing enough. Yet the original statement of the problem is valid, valid as a draftsman's linear drawing represents the solid object he is depicting.

In the wisdom man has achieved during the thousands of years he has lived on this little globe, conflicts, actual or possible, are settled by an appeal to a judge who is not identified with either of the conflicting parties. Here we have the solution of the social problem. We need an arbiter who will justly decide the rights of society and justly decide the rights of the individual. This judge can be neither society nor the individual.

But where can we find such a judge? That has always been the human problem. When the conflict is between the individual and society, society has in its favor the power of coercion and the individual has in his support the power of rebellion. The same situation exists when two communities are in conflict. In consequence the question of rights has usually been resolved by power.

Is the power of rebellion greater than the power of coercion? That is concretely the question which faces every generation in history. We are in a revolutionary moment. The rising of the East against the colonizing power of the western commonwealths shows very clearly that the power of rebellion is as great, if not greater than the power of coercion at the disposal of the western nations.

Now there is something irrational in this way of deciding rights. Power and right are on different planes of reality. Right can well be powerless and power can well be unrighteous. Neither can establish the other. The power of rebellion can counterbalance the power of coercion, but this leaves the whole question of right untouched.

These observations are by no means new. They have been recognized in every era of history. It is not surprising, then, to find that the sages of mankind have looked for something better and more rational to control the individual and society. It is amusing to find angry voices rail against the notion of original sin. Yet there is nothing more evident than original sin in the story of mankind. Man's impulse to the irrational is patent on every page of history, and the religious name for this impulse is original sin. The problem of human history is how to control original sin.

The older societies thought that they had a solution for the conflict of the individual with society. They put both the individual and society under God. God gave rights to each and God decided their disputes. God's action came through revelation and prophets made God's mind known. The prophet first manifested *torah,* the law.* Then the prophet spoke the judgment of God on those who violated *torah.* In a God-fearing people this process was most effective. King and people knew they were under God, and they accepted His word as decisive.

---

* [As Milton Steinberg indicates in an earlier selection, it is much more accurate to render this term as "guidance" or "teaching"—ED.]

But faith is a precarious thing. It can be lost, and when it goes, it is no longer possible to appeal to a revealing God. In this situation the wise men gave mankind another tribunal for the adjudication of conflict. Reason was impartial and uncommitted. Hence reason could control the affairs of man and society. If God is no longer present, then we turn to Natural Law, which is another way of speaking of the omnicompetence of reason.

However, the men who had rejected God saw that Reason with a capital R was another spelling for God, and out went the Natural Law as arbiter. If reason was written with a small r, then the question was: whose reason shall we follow?

That is where we are now and that is where we have been for many years. During this time of impasse, some optimistic voices simply proclaimed that the concrete conflict would be solved by power, for this is a beneficent drive in history which would insure that power in the long run would produce to the good for all, even though power is indifferent to right and wrong. There was no need to criticize power and bring it to judgment. Power is good, not perhaps in this or that case, but in the totality of its action. There was no reason over it and it was under no God. Hence reason and God were irrelevant factors in the discussion. Hence law itself was only the will of power, the will of the 51 percent. These had the power of coercion and that settled the matter.

In the century-old predicament we have reached a moment of disillusion. We can no longer accept this complacent submission to power. Power today is obviously fraught with the threat of destroying man, physically, culturally or both. It has to be judged and it has to be used in the light of judgment. Yet we are not prepared to recognize reason as an instrument of discovery. We still think it is only a device to implement the imperatives of arbitrary will. Hence there is no return to a belief in Natural Law, even though we hear isolated voices gingerly advocating it.

It is not surprising that in this situation the secular community is turning to the communities of faith to tame the monster of power roaring at the gates. The question we must ask however is whether in doing so the secular collectivity is not clutching at straws.

The secular community certainly does not want to be converted into a religious community. The insistence that civic society prescinds from religious commitment was never more visible than today. The political society feels quite magnanimous because it generously gives every citizen the right to be as religious or irreligious as he wishes. What then does the collectivity ask of its religious members? A favor in return for the favor of toleration granted. It is recognized that religion refuses to be intimidated by power. It has always stood up against it. The civic community is now asking that the men and women of religion harness this resistance to the chariot of the natural commonwealth. Religion, which before was tolerantly given the right to exist, is now invited to become an active dynamism in the common enterprise. Religion is now seen not merely as something to be tolerated but even as something to be used, and valuable because it can be used.

This innocent kindness of the natural civic society should not be a trap for religion. It easily can be. It is intoxicating to feel one's self esteemed after a long period of contempt. Good will and a spirit to please can stir the recipient of this new esteem. But the desire to please may be a subtle trend toward suicide. It is enlightening here to see what the Soviet government did during the last war. Every method to stimulate the defense of the land was used. As a result, the weakly masked persecution of religion was suspended. If the notion of Holy Russia helped Russians to fight the invader, then the notion of Holy Russia was encouraged. The priests who only a few years before were hampered and harassed, now received decorations for their defense of the fatherland. The government became kindly to religion. But there was no conversion, only accommodation.

Far be it from me to insinuate that the ideal relation of religion to secular society should be one of hostility. Reason itself suggests that there should be concord between a religious fellowship and the natural community in which it exists. Both collectivities should serve each other, though neither should be subservient to the other. However, what should be stressed is that religion deals with what concerns man ultimately, and therefore the ultimate allegiance must be religious. It may be a very bad religion, dedicated to an idol rather than to God, but it is a religion nonetheless. Any religion which does not divinize secular society will have an ultimate allegiance higher than its loyalty to the nation. Ancient Israel was a theocracy, but it did not adore the nation. Ancient Rome was not a theocracy but it did adore the state. In a free society, at least in principle, there is no preoccupation with what the people adore.

What then can a religion which does not adore the nation-state do for the civic community? It seems to me that it can fulfill its highest possibilities simply being true to itself. It must seek first the kingdom of God and its justice and all lesser goods will come as well. If there be any degree of validity in the religion, it will make for virtue. The more valid the religion the richer will be its manifestation of the virtues of unselfishness, sobriety, fulfillment of duty. These things are not just religious virtues but also positive contributions to the natural commonwealth, for the commonwealth cannot survive without them. It is precisely in this area that the civic community expects help from religion. The fruits of high religion are the love of man which results in help of the neighbor, self-control, industriousness, solidarity, patience and steadfastness. These fruits the political society wants. It does not care what they spring from. Often enough statesmen seem to think that religion has some kind of trick whereby these qualities can be produced, and they ask the churches for the trade-secret. One thinks of Simon Magus who when he saw the wonders caused by the imposition of hands by the apostles Peter and John, tried to buy the power. The trouble was that it was not for sale and no money could buy it. There was a power in Peter and John which they did not possess but which possessed them.

The higher religions are not merely seminaries of virtue. The virtue itself comes from a faith and the faith is the human reaction to divine revelation. According to St. Paul, faith comes from hearing. The revelation must be communicated to men, and those who communicate participate in the prophetic mission. The prophet speaks in the name of God. To this message faith can be given. We expect, then, that a valid religion will be prophetic. It will give witness to the divine message to which it clings in faith. In the secular community this witness is given. Faith is not a talent to be buried in the ground. Divine revelation is orientation and healing for those who believe, and the community which takes God at His word will be a sound society. As I understand Christian revelation, no natural community will ever surrender itself to God in faith. To believe, an inner grace is given, and grace is given to the elect. This is a hard doctrine, but it seems to be confirmed by the history of the world ever since the coming of revelation.

Even in the hypothesis that not all will believe, it yet remains true that the believer in love and enthusiasm will give witness to the faith that is in him. He will inevitably speak the good news to all his fellows to whom he is attracted in love by the very faith he possesses. Whether the neighbor accepts the witness does not particularly concern the prophet. He must speak even though no one will listen.

This prophetic function of religion is embarrassing to the secular community. It is disturbing; it is a source of division; it is a distraction from the concentration on the purely secular. Here is the paradox of the demand society makes. It wants the fruits of faith, but it does not want the prophetic root of those fruits. The prophet not only shows the way to salvation; he utters judgment on the action of the world. This is resented by the unbeliever and the resentment can become bitter and cruel. According to the accounts of history the fate of the prophets was an unenviable one.

If a man is truly religious, he must be ready and resigned to hostility from the unbelievers. But he must not foment such hostility. The word of God is never repellent even when it condemns. It calls not to anger but to repentance. But given the selfishness of men, the prophet must not be surprised when instead of receiving a welcome, he receives abuse. Still he must give witness. He is a prophet by the mere fact that he has active faith.

Here we have the temptation which faces religion in our time. As I have already stated, religion serves the secular commonwealth by just being itself. It does not have to run the government; it cannot be one of the enlisted forces of defense. It lives in secular society but its life has a source and direction not to be derived from or even restricted by the commonwealth.

Secular society today is trying to make a deal with the churches. It is saying: Give us your unswerving support in the pursuit of the objectives we have before us; in return we will cover you with honor. This does not sound like the tempter's words when he showed Christ all the glories of the world and offered them to Him in return for adoration. Yet it may be the same thing.

I know that secularists will be irritated by such an observation. They are making their offer in all good faith and as far as they are aware, there is nothing diabolical about it. They point out that their objectives are noble ones, not unworthy of religion. They may well be right, but there is nevertheless a temptation at hand. The churches are being asked for unswerving loyalty and enthusiastic allegiance. Yet the church can give such allegiance only conditionally, never absolutely. If society is pursuing a virtuous goal, the church will spontaneously pursue the same goal. If society pursues a sinful objective, the church must refuse cooperation. And it will be the church which will make the decision as to the goodness of the goal. The church which must first seek the kingdom of God and its justice, cannot do otherwise and remain the church. This is the high command, the categorical imperative.

II

So far our meditation might suggest to the unwary that the church must remain coldly aloof from the interests of the secular community. Actually this has not been the burden of my thought. The only thesis so far proposed is that it is not the purpose of the church to save the republic nor is it the function of the church to be a ministry of defense for government. As was said twice before, the church will aid the secular community by just being itself. It makes little difference if the church be numerous or meager. In either case it will be a light on the mountain and a leaven in the mass.

Hence the only complaint the political society can make is that the church is not herself in a given time and place. Actually something of this kind appeared recently in an article in *The Nation.* I refer to C. Wright Mills' "A Pagan Sermon to the Christian Clergy." I believe that Mr. Mills does not quite understand the nature of Christianity, but in his favor I must say that the line of thought he followed was that churches were not doing what was proper for them to do according to their own structures. He was not asking the churches to become instruments of the state; he bitterly complained that they did not do what by their own profession and tradition they should be doing. Concretely he found that the churches were not making their members aware of the monstrous immorality involved in modern public policy which relies at least in part on the threat that one nation can direct against another through atomic power. Mills believes that the churches are slavishly accommodating their message to the accepted prejudices of our environment. They are not trying to lead; they only follow.

In a sense I do not think that it is the role of the church to lead secular society. The church is here to give effective witness to the will of God. If anyone follows this message, it will be God's doing. If no one follows, it does not mean that the church failed in its mission. I think that Mills' latent error is that he supposes that the church should strive to be a secular good. This is never the church's obligation.

However, there is a valid ground in the exasperated criticism Mills made. An accommodating church is not being herself. Prophetic protest is an essential element of the church's preaching, and this protest must not be launched only against the little foibles of the individual but likewise against the gigantic immorality of public policy.

When the church is truly herself, the gospel will be preached and Christian action stimulated and organized in such a way as to be relevant to modern man. Old institutions can easily become bogged down by ancient habits originally formed to meet passing problems. The church is timeless; for that very reason she must be timely. No past moment is privileged that only in its terms can the gospel be heralded. The concerns of contemporary man must be the medium which the church uses to express the divine revelation. Antiquarianism has its charms but it is not to be a hobble on the divine word. If we cannot tolerate the notion of secular society making demands on the church, even less can we tolerate the notion of the church cutting herself off from the stream of human life in which she must perform her task.

Hence we do need religious activity in the problematic of our time. Religious thinkers in the light of revelation should give answers to the questions raised in our moment of history; they may not excuse themselves on the pretext that these questions are secular. The questions demand a religious answer, and that answer will be witness. Nor is it enough that the church deal with the issues in the genteel atmosphere of an ivory tower. The witness must come out into the street. Thought and action should be related. Action with no root in thought is sheer turmoil. Thought with no overflow into action is an esthetic narcosis. We need not only St. Thomas Aquinas making his glorious distinctions but also St. Francis wandering down the country roads singing the love of God and man for the refreshment of those who hear him. We need not only those who retire into caves on the mountain but also those who embroil themselves in crusades.

The church must make some kind of accommodation to the world. It is the accommodation of relevance. The church is in the world and nowhere else. There she lives and there she must work. The task of accommodation is always a hazardous job. Human beings can accommodate so much that they will cease to be what they were and become something thoroughly different. In her effort to accommodate, the church may become a mirror of the secular society to which it must prophesy. The faith of the church teaches her that God Himself will not allow her to undergo this total sea change; rather He will save her but for this end He usually uses chastisement.

Whether the church is to undergo chastisement or not we cannot say. Yet her task is clear enough. Instead of telling secular society what it must do to save itself, it might be better for men of the church to tell the children of the church what they must do to live. It may well be the most effective contribution which the church can make to free society.

Perhaps three things stand out for religious men to do. Material abundance offers a great opportunity for ease, luxury and decadence. In such a situation virtue is weakened and materialism tends to stifle faith. In such a moment, and in this land the moment is now, austerity must be preached. Nor is it enough to preach austerity by word alone. St. Francis not only preached poverty, he lived it as well. In order to be truly themselves the churches must voluntarily follow the example of ancient Nineveh excited by the threats of Jonah. Religious reform movements always included a return to simplicity of life where industriousness was the rule of being and sobriety the mark of faith. A consequent of such action is a morally stronger community made leaner by its fasting and more efficient in its effort to be creative under the command of God. Duty stands out more clearly than pleasure and when it does, the community can do almost anything. The call to austerity falls on deaf ears if it be directed to the secular community at large. The church must direct the cry to her own, and she can give motives higher than the well-being of the commonwealth. Here the church must act as church and in being the church she will aid the republic.

The second need of the church in our time is the deeper awareness of the reality of God in whom we live and move and have our being. In the hustle and bustle of today, it is hard for a man to think. We are rushing about in all directions with little attention to why we are moving at all. The world is becoming so visible that the invisible God is more hidden than ever. The man of faith today is a man of little faith. He seems to need prayer less because social organization gives him all he needs. But a self-sufficient humanity is man inflated with hybris, and hybris is the sin which the deity cannot tolerate in man.

Again it is not a question of speaking to the natural community, for in speaking to it, you must use the very media which bring about the sense of self-sufficiency. The church must speak to her own and get them to look away from the world with all its glamor and fascination, and turn to God. The church must preach retreat, though it need not be the retreat to the desert. It need only be a retreat to the heart where man can find the *Seelenfunklein* where God dwells. In God's presence man sees his own size and the presence of God gives man power to do and to suffer as he cannot do and suffer without God in view. The churches must preach prayer, must turn the mind of men to God. This will not take men out of the world, but it will show men God in the world, and they will act to please Him. It is well and good that we have monks and contemplatives, but something of the work they are engaged in must be shared by those who are not in monasteries and retreats.

The third thing we need is a truer and more effective love for all men, including those who are our enemies. Do good to them that hate you, is a religious message. Only through the force of faith is it possible. It is hardly necessary here to be dithyrambic about the beauties of love of one for the other. That song has been often sung. Yet the exhilaration given to life by a brother aiding brother, by a consoler sharing the pain and suffering of his neighbor, needs to be pointed out. This is what the church must do in a society where welfare is a secular project, achieved by machine-like organizations moving on the plane of science rather than love. The church must bring out the ancient truth that every man is his brother's keeper and that it is not enough to refer him to a social agency.

Much of the good done in our society is done without love. Charity today means just the opposite of the word we use to cover the activity inspired by love. It often means condescending and heartless giving in order to be free of the sight of misery. Aid given in that spirit produces hatred, for the recipient is not so much helped as humiliated. Once more it is useless to speak to the civil society about the matter. It has its charity-machines which in machine-like fashion turn out their alms and assistance. There is little else that secular society can do, and it is wonderful that it does as much as it does. But men and women of faith who know that God is in all men and that God is loving and to be loved, will go to their neighbor in an entirely different spirit than the organizations of public welfare. It is the church working on those within the church which can effectively produce genuine charity.

III

Perhaps my remarks have not been practical from the viewpoint of the secularist. He will be disappointed when he hears that the best contribution the church can make to the plight of free society is to preach austerity, God-awareness and love, to the members of the church. I am sorry if he is disappointed, but as I see it, the church can do nothing else. She cannot construct programs of atomic-power control. She cannot propose public policy which will bring peace. These things are the proper and exclusive function of the secular community. The church cannot take them over, nor is she equipped by her own nature to deal with problems which are purely secular.

Yet there is something very practical in these reflections. It is not the practicality of gadgets and devices. It is the practicality of the real. To act follows on being. If being is stressed and enhanced, action will be its spontaneous offshoot. We must keep the concept of being foremost in our attention. We have been too much afflicted by worrying exclusively about action. The "practical" is often highly impractical.

The whole burden of my effusion has been that the church can help the free society only in one way. She helps by being herself genuinely and integrally. She cannot be state counselor, guide or governmental ministry. But if the church is herself, then the secular society will be aided.

Pointing this general truth to the problems of the moment in which we live, I have suggested that the church stress in its members three virtues which are proper to faith: austerity, God-consciousness and brotherly love. If the church does this, she is what she should be. The overflow of these virtues will strengthen, vivify and aid the free society.

I am dubious about other programs like those which would harness the churches to the effort of society. They seem to be based on a misunderstanding and degeneration of religion and in spite of their seeming high practicality are most impractical. They will neither help the church nor help our free society.

PART VI

BEYOND THEOLOGY

23

WAITING*

Paul Tillich

BOTH the Old and the New Testaments describe our existence
in relation to God as one of waiting. In the psalmist [Ps.
130:5–7] there is an anxious waiting; in the apostle [Rom.
8:24–25] there is a patient waiting. Waiting means *not* having
and having at the same time. For we have *not* what we wait for;
or, as the apostle says, if we hope for what we do *not* see, we
then wait for it. The condition of man's relation to God is first
of all one of *not* having, *not* seeing, *not* knowing, and *not*
grasping. A religion in which that is forgotten, no matter how
ecstatic or active or reasonable, replaces God by its own
creation of an image of God. Our religious life is characterized
more by that kind of creation than anything else. I think of the
theologian who does not wait for God, because he possesses
Him, enclosed within a doctrine. I think of the Biblical student
who does not wait for God, because he possesses Him, enclosed
in a book. I think of the churchman who does not wait for God,
because he possesses Him, enclosed in an institution. I think of
the believer who does not wait for God, because he possesses
Him, enclosed within his own experience. It is not easy to
endure this not having God, this waiting for God. It is not easy
to preach Sunday after Sunday without convincing ourselves

* Excerpt from *The Shaking of the Foundations*, by Paul Tillich, pp.
149–52 (Copyright © 1948 Charles Scribner's Sons) is reprinted with the
permission of Charles Scribner's Sons.

and others that we *have* God and can dispose of Him. It is not easy to proclaim God to children and pagans, to sceptics and secularists, and at the same time to make clear to them that we ourselves do not possess God, that we too wait for Him. I am convinced that much of the rebellion against Christianity is due to the overt or veiled claim of the Christians to possess God, and therefore, also, to the loss of this element of waiting, so decisive for the prophets and the apostles. Let us not be deluded into thinking that, because they speak of waiting, they waited merely for the end, the judgment and fulfillment of all things, and not for God Who was to bring that end. They did not possess God; they waited for Him. For how can God be possessed? Is God a thing that can be grasped and known among other things? Is God less than a human person? We always have to wait for a human being. Even in the most intimate communion among human beings, there is an element of *not* having and *not* knowing, and of waiting. Therefore, since God is infinitely hidden, free, and incalculable, we must wait for Him in the most absolute and radical way. He is God for us just in so far as we do *not* possess Him. The psalmist says that his whole being waits for the Lord, indicating that waiting for God is not merely a part of our relation to God, but rather the condition of that relation as a whole. We have God through *not* having Him.

But, although waiting is *not* having, it is also having. The fact that we wait for something shows that in some way we already possess it. Waiting anticipates that which is not yet real. If we wait in hope and patience, the power of that for which we wait is already effective within us. He who waits in an ultimate sense is not far from that for which he waits. He who waits in absolute seriousness is already grasped by that for which he waits. He who waits in patience has already received the power of that for which he waits. He who waits passionately is already an active power himself, the greatest power of transformation in personal and historical life. We are stronger when we wait than when we possess. When we possess God, we reduce Him to that small thing we knew and grasped of Him; and we make it an idol. Only in idol worship can one believe in the possession of God. There is much of this idolatry among Christians.

But if we know that we do not know Him, and if we wait for Him to make Himself known to us, we then really know something of Him, we then are grasped and known and possessed by Him. It is *then* that we are believers in our unbelief, and that we are accepted by Him in spite of our separation from Him.

Let us not forget, however, that waiting is a tremendous tension. It precludes all complacency about having nothing, indifference or cynical contempt towards those who have something, and indulgence in doubt and despair. Let us not make our pride in possessing nothing a new possession. That is one of the great temptations of our time, for there are few things left which we can claim as possessions. And we surrender to the same temptation when we boast, in our attempt to possess God, that we do not possess Him. The divine answer to such an attempt is utter emptiness. Waiting is not despair. It is the acceptance of our not having, in the power of that which we already have.

Our time is a time of waiting; waiting is its special destiny. And every time is a time of waiting, waiting for the breaking in of eternity. All time runs forward. All time, both in history and in personal life, is expectation. Time itself is waiting, waiting not for another time, but for that which is eternal.